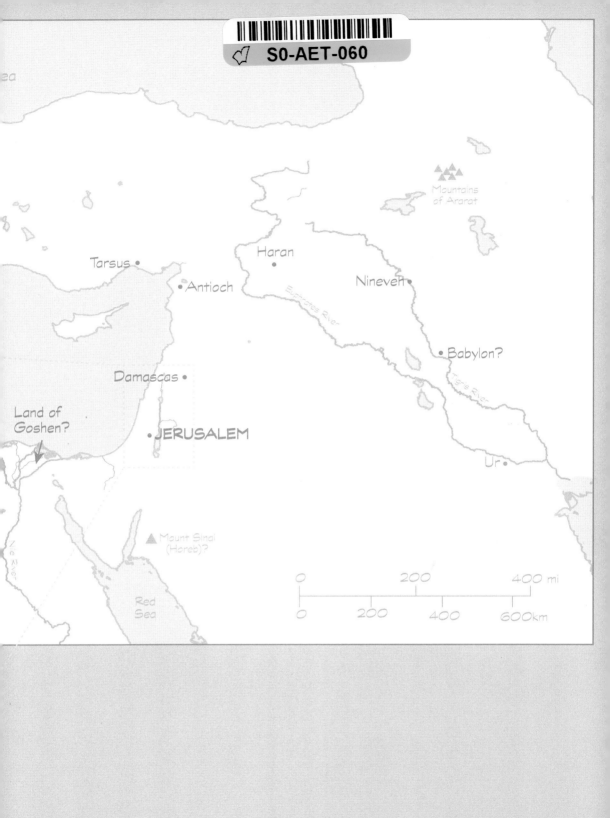

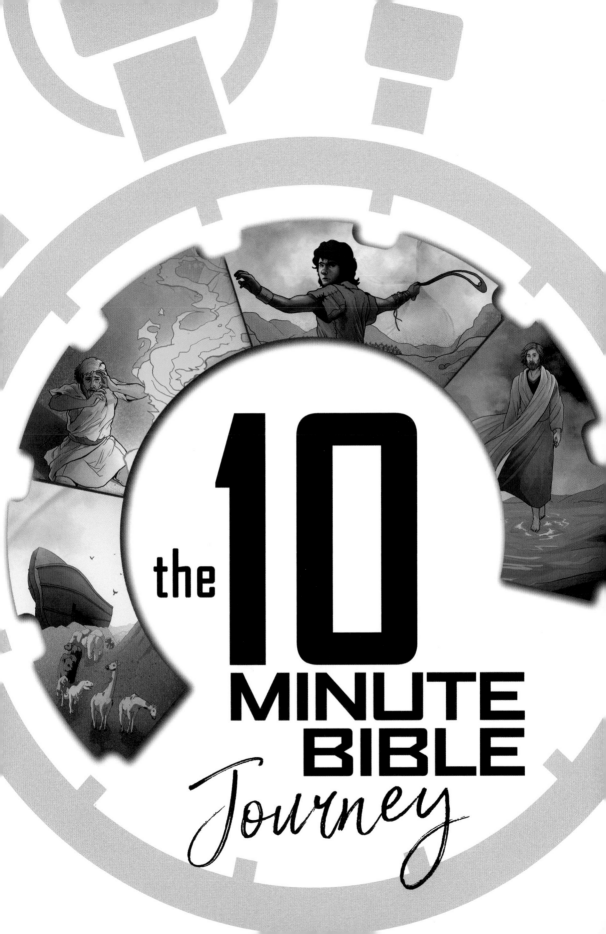

First printing: August 2017
Second printing: October 2017

New Leaf Press, P.O. Box 726, Green Forest, AR 72638

New Leaf Press is a division of the New Leaf Publishing Group, Inc.

ISBN: 978-0-89221-755-7
ISBN: 978-1-61458-613-5 (digital)
Digital edition features hundreds more references and endnotes than the print edition.

Library of Congress Number: 2017909198
Illustrations by Robert Forest & Lucas Silveira

Cover and Interior Design by Diana Bogardus

Unless otherwise noted, Scripture quotations are from the New King James Version of the Bible.

Please consider requesting that a copy of this volume be purchased by your local library system.

Printed in the United States of America

Please visit our website for other great titles:
www.newleafpress.com

For information regarding author interviews,
please contact the publicity department at (870) 438-5288.

New Leaf Press
A Division of New Leaf Publishing Group
www.newleafpress.com

"To pen a book that is a concise yet profoundly mean-
ingful summary of the most strategic events in the Bible
is an ambitious goal, but one that Dale Mason has met
well! Mason has crafted an overview that gives the reader
an exciting new perspective and the essential context on
events they may have read about many times. *The 10 Minute
Bible Journey* is as well-suited as a personal devotional, as
it is for group Bible Study and one-on-one discipleship. I
highly recommend this book for men and women of all ages!
A great, non-threatening way to jump to the next level in your
understanding of God's Word and the gospel of our Savior, Jesus Christ!"

—Cathy Allen, COO, Love Worth Finding Ministries

"Love it! The writing style is extremely engaging and the presentation of biblical
history is phenomenally seamless. The events selected to articulate the panoramic
biblical historical perspective are extremely well chosen."

—Bryan Osborne, apologetics speaker/chronological teaching specialist

"Dale Mason, in *The 10 Minute Bible Journey,* gives us the proverbial box top to
the Bible puzzle. In concise and easily digestible portions, he leads us through
the timeline of the Bible and shows the 30,000 foot view that puts everything into
perspective. People constantly ask me for a book they can use to lead their family
through the Bible in a systematic way...now I have the perfect resource to
recommend to them! This is a useful tool for parents, students, church leaders,
and anyone doing discipleship ministry. ...Nothing is more important in this
world than knowing God as He has revealed Himself through His Word; and
The 10 Minute Bible Journey will help you to accomplish that in an interesting,
creative and powerful way."

— Israel Wayne, author & conference speaker

"*The 10 Minute Bible Journey* gives readers an easy to understand overview of the
story of the world. I've been waiting for a book like this!"

— Tim Wildmon, President, American Family Association

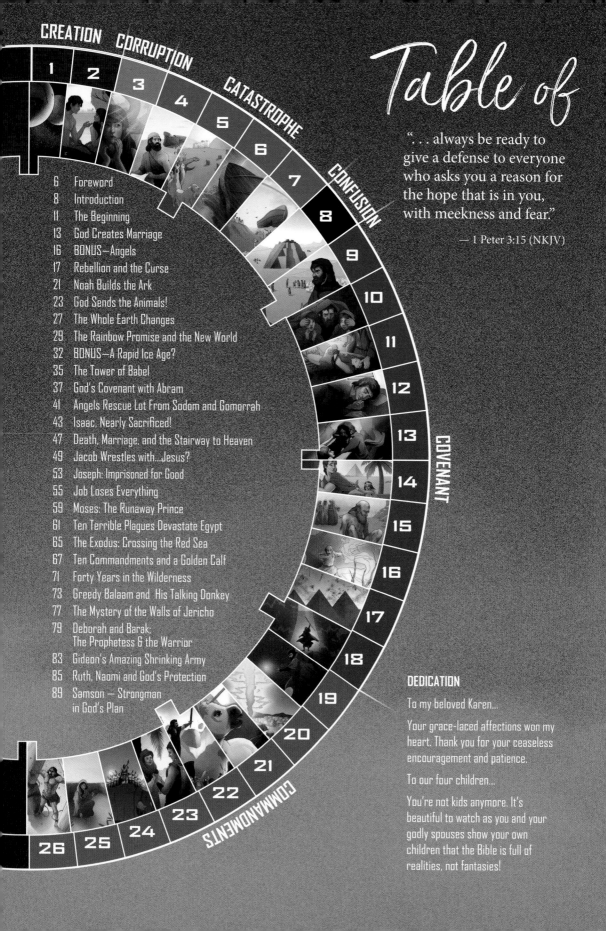

Table of

"... always be ready to give a defense to everyone who asks you a reason for the hope that is in you, with meekness and fear."

— 1 Peter 3:15 (NKJV)

CREATION

CORRUPTION

CATASTROPHE

CONFUSION

COVENANT

COMMANDMENTS

DEDICATION

To my beloved Karen...

Your grace-laced affections won my heart. Thank you for your ceaseless encouragement and patience.

To our four children...

You're not kids anymore. It's beautiful to watch as you and your godly spouses show your own children that the Bible is full of realities, not fantasies!

Contents

> "Biblical literacy is a
> precursor to biblical
> transformation."
>
> *Why Johnny Can't Read the Bible*
> Christianity Today Magazine

CROWN

CAPTIVITY

CHRIST

CROSS

CHRISTIAN ERA

CONSUMMATION

I met Dale and his wife Karen in the early '80s when I visited the USA from Australia to speak in various American churches on the topic of the relevance of the Book of Genesis. Dale was working in a Christian ministry called Films For Christ, which was known for distributing a movie entitled *The World That Perished*. This evangelistic film dealt with the account of Noah's Flood. We used the movie in Australia to reach thousands of people with the truth of God's Word and the gospel.

In 1986, my wife and I came to America for six months to work with Films For Christ. During this time, Dale and I spent many months on the road traveling across the USA together. Dale had organized scores of speaking events for me as part of a multi-city "book and film" tour. I conducted about 100 engagements: speaking in churches, doing interviews at TV and radio stations, and other outreaches. During these six months, we distributed thousands of books that we hauled to each event in a large trailer! After this successful 1986 speaking tour, my wife, our children, and I returned to Australia. But we all came back to the USA in 1987, where I would work for about seven years with the Institute for Creation Research.

Instead of returning to Australia in late 1993, our family, along with two other families, moved to Northern Kentucky to begin the Answers in Genesis ministry and eventually build the Creation Museum. As the ministry began to grow, and in God's providence, I met up with Dale again. In 2004, AiG had some special needs and I approached Dale about working with us. He agreed, and Dale has been with the ministry ever since and we continue to enjoy a strong friendship.

Several years ago, when Dale reached one of those "big decade" birthday markers, he shared a concern with me. He had been unable to find a book with a solid overview of the entire Bible that was written at an easy-to-read level that included faith-confirming apologetics. Well, I challenged Dale to write it himself! So, he did! And what a unique publication it is, filling a niche that had been missing for a long time.

I encourage dads, moms, grandparents, and teens to use this book as a special devotional. It's certainly different to any other devotional out there. It will give you an overview of the whole Bible and equip you with answers to help defend your faith.

You will love the way Dale has made the major accounts in the Bible flow from one event to the next. It's nearly seamless and in a way that the whole Bible makes so much more sense. With Dale's book, it is now so much easier to see how Jesus is prophesied in Genesis chapter 3 and is active behind the scenes throughout the entire Old Testament. It makes the New Testament come to life in a powerful way.

This book is also like no other because Dale has used his knowledge of apologetics that he has picked up at AiG, our Creation Museum, and the Ark Encounter. He has integrated that faith-confirming teaching into a survey that covers nearly all the most important events and heroes and heroines of the Scriptures. And with the illustrations and the one-of-a-kind timeline at the back, this book is one of the very best ways that adults and teens can get a great overview of the whole Bible quickly.

At our ministry of Answers in Genesis, we have a Sunday school program called the Answers Bible Curriculum. I see Dale's book as a tremendous complement to ABC as it gives teachers and parents a fast yet thorough summary of what they will be teaching over 3-4 years of the ABC curriculum. In as little as one weekend, or over 52 days of daily devotional times, an adult or teen will understand the big cornerstone events of the Bible. Along the way, they will get to know fun and little-known facts about many of the most-referenced characters of the Bible.

Enjoy and be blessed by this wonderful book.

—Ken Ham
President/CEO
Answers in Genesis

The 10 Minute Bible Journey is intended to be a fast-paced, apologetics-infused summary of the Bible. It reveals the amazing essentials of Christianity and tells why Jesus Christ is the only way to heaven. As I've told "seekers" and "believers" alike, getting to spend eternity with Jesus in the glories of heaven rather than separated from Him in the punishment of hell is not based on how good we are, what church we attend, or whether we've been baptized. Though important, those things do not determine our salvation. They are not the bottom line.

Friend, what we do with Jesus Christ is the bottom line when it comes to where we will spend eternity when our mortal life is through. Jesus said so Himself in various ways but probably most emphatically when He told His disciples, "I am the way the truth, and the life. No one comes to the Father [goes to Heaven] except through me" (John 14:6).

Where are you with Jesus? God spoke through the Apostle Paul when he said that no one is good enough to deserve heaven (Romans 3:23). So, why should Jesus allow you or me to spend eternity with Him? Have you prayed and asked Him to forgive you for your sins? Have you received Jesus as your Savior? Do you truly believe the book of His life? He said that those who are His followers seek to know what He said. Then they do it (John 14:22-24). The amazing true story and words of Jesus are recorded in the Bible, which opens our eyes to know Him better.

Like the Bible itself, *The 10 Minute Bible Journey* begins with "in the beginning" and points to the future return of Jesus. The Bible's journey is from rebellion to restoration, Genesis to Revelation, creation to heaven. It warns about the wide path to destruction, and it highlights the narrow gate to salvation (Matthew 7:14)!

In case the Bible is fairly new to you, here are some really important basic facts.

- The Holy Bible is the error-free collection of 66 smaller books. There is no other book like it.

- Over a period of at least 1,600 years, about 40 different authors from many walks of life wrote down the inspired text given by God's Holy Spirit.

- The first portion, the Old Testament, covers the first two-thirds of history. It runs from God's creation of the universe and mankind, to the years just prior to the birth of the promised Messiah.

- The final portion, the New Testament, covers the birth, ministry, death, and all-important Resurrection of Jesus, plus the rapid spread of Christianity in the first century A.D. It tells about the future Second Coming of Christ, how to be forgiven and spend eternity in heaven, and that those who are not forgiven will spend eternity in the very real place called hell.

However, this book is about the Bible; it is not the Bible itself. It is a carefully researched summary of the most strategic and faith-confirming accounts from the Bible's first book, Genesis, to its last book, Revelation. It includes faith-facts known as "apologetics" that confirm from science and other proof tests that the Bible is true.

The chapters in *The 10 Minute Bible Journey* are in the order that the events actually occurred. In our present era — when in most churches only the last portion of God's Word is taught — this "chronological" approach helps us to quickly understand the big picture of the Bible and the seamless storyline of Jesus. It helps us to easily place each event in relation to the others. It provides an overview, much like the picture on the box top of a jumbled jigsaw puzzle serves as a guide as to how the multitude of pieces actually fit together.

The Bible, as originally written down, is historically accurate. Therefore, in *The 10 Minute Bible Journey* approximate dates are included at the beginning of each account. These dates are based first and foremost on the Bible itself, and most are documented in the respected work of scholar and theologian James Ussher. His meticulous chronology of history is derived primarily from the dates of births, deaths, kingly rule, and other points in time. Though ridiculed by skeptics, especially those committed to belief in the idea of evolution, Ussher's chronology holds enormous value even today.

Whether you know the Bible well, or you long to see how all its amazing key events fit together, you will appreciate our Creator's plan for the restoration of creation and the salvation of mankind better than ever.

It is my prayer that you will be drawn passionately into God's Word, and an even deeper relationship with His son, Jesus.

Welcome to God's story — the true history and future of mankind!

—Dale Mason

Only God could create
everything from nothing:
light, the earth, the sun,
the moon, and the stars!

–1–

THE BEGINNING

Days 1-5,
c. 4004 B.C.

The first page of the Bible reveals the answer to the biggest question of all time.

How did everything come to be?

Some people believe in a "big bang" where a pinpoint of energy mysteriously appeared and exploded billions of years ago, somehow resulting in our exceedingly complex universe.

Some even believe the idea that space-aliens somehow evolved and seeded life on earth.

However, we have a book that is the eyewitness testimony of the only One who was there. That book, the Bible, reveals that creation is the direct result of the Creator God.

Genesis is the very first part of the Bible. It is 50 amazing chapters of flawless history. In Genesis, God tells us how the world came to be, how marriage and the family are to be structured, the origin of pain and death, why we wear clothes, the beginning of beauty and pleasure, and much more. The fascinating early pages of the Bible even make known the foundations of biology, zoology, anthropology, astronomy, and geology.

After revealing that the Creator made everything out of nothing by His Word,[1] the Bible summarizes what happened on each day of the creation week.

On day 1, God created time, space, the earth, and light. He separated light from darkness, and He made evening and morning. The words that God used to describe how long He took are very specific. Each of the days in the first chapter of Genesis is a normal, 24-hour period. God could have taken millions of years, but He did not.[2] He emphasizes repeatedly that He created in six consecutive, ordinary days. And science confirms that the Bible is true.

On day 2, God separated the water by an expanse called heavens; He placed some water below the expanse and some above it. Then there was another evening and morning.

On day 3, He gathered the waters under the expanse into one place and made dry land appear — one big continent, and one big ocean with spring-fed rivers flowing into it. The angels shouted for joy when God laid the foundations of the earth. He made plants and trees with seeds to reproduce after their kinds,[3] and He saw that it was good. Then there was evening and morning.

On day 4, three days after He created light, God made ongoing sources of light: the sun and stars. Plus he made the moon, which reflects the sun's light for us at night. Because of the sun, earth has heat, photosynthesis, the water cycle, and more. The sun is a fireball, equal to thousands of hydrogen bombs exploding continuously. The Creator's immense power is staggering. Scientists now estimate that trillions of billions of stars fill the universe — numbers far beyond comprehension.

On day 5, He created winged creatures and every kind of fish, including those the Bible describes as huge monsters of the sea.[4] In addition to exotic and exquisitely colored animals, there were swimming reptiles and water mammals like whales. These would have included sea turtles and beasts like the *shastasaurus,* which grew to nearly 70 feet long. Besides the small and beautiful birds, there were flying mammals such as bats, plus enormous flying reptiles like the pterosaurs, whose wings spread as wide as an airplane. Because all animals were originally vegetarian,[5]

they lived in harmony and did not eat each other. God blessed them to be fruitful and fill the water and the sky with creatures after their kinds.

The perfection and intricate design of all creation filled both God and His angels with joy. But the best was yet to come. In only a few hours, He was about to fashion His most special creation of all!

PRIMARY PASSAGES:

Gen. 1:1–23; John 1; Heb. 11:3; Col. 1:16, Job 38:4–7

KEY VERSE:

"For by Him all things were created that are in heaven and that are on earth, visible and invisible, whether thrones or dominions or principalities or powers. All things were created through Him and for Him."
—Col. 1:16

WRAP UP:

"Heavenly Father, thank You for revealing that You created everything in just six days, not billions of years. As I think of the infinite universe and earth's microscopic details, it leaves me in awe of Your power. Lord, it is so good to know that You made a perfect world. Please soften my heart and give me a clear mind. I want to know Your Word, the Bible, and I want to honor You, the Creator!"

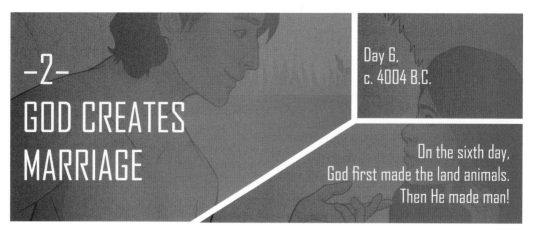

-2-
GOD CREATES MARRIAGE

Day 6,
c. 4004 B.C.

On the sixth day,
God first made the land animals.
Then He made man!

It was probably early in the morning when God made the earth bring forth land animals on day 6. He formed the original kinds of antelope, horses, elephants, rhinoceroses, turtles, giraffes, apes, cattle, cats, dogs, and many others — including dozens of different kinds of dinosaurs![1]

Next, God again took dust of the ground and formed the first man, Adam, and breathed life into him.

Adam and all of creation were perfect. There was no corruption, no disease, no death. Genesis reveals that God planted a special garden in Eden and placed Adam there to work it and watch over it.[2] Work was actually part of the original, perfect creation!

God then told Adam he could eat any plant that yielded seed and the fruit from all the trees in the garden, except one. He was not to eat from the Tree of the Knowledge of Good and Evil. If he did, he would begin to die.[3]

After God created Adam, He declared that it was not good for man to be alone. However, before making him a companion, God brought many of the animals to him to name. Thankfully,

Adam only had to name the birds, the livestock, and the beasts of the field. He did not have to name the fish or the hundreds of thousands of modern sea creatures. He did not name what now amounts to over a million species of insects, beetles, spiders, and other animals.[4] In all, Adam probably had to name fewer than 1,000 kinds of creatures. He could have done that in only a few hours.[5]

Adam undoubtedly realized that although there were many kinds of creatures, none was right for him. Also, each already had a mate, yet he did not.[6] Then in another miracle of creation, rich in symbolism about marriage, Genesis chapter 2 documents that God caused a deep sleep to come over Adam and then took a rib from His side and fashioned it into the first woman, Eve.

When God presented Eve to Adam, he was delighted![7] She was perfect in every way, and although they were both naked, they were unashamed.

In her perfection, Eve was exceptionally beautiful. It is important to realize that beginning at the beginning, in the Garden of Eden, the Creator intended marriage for one man to one woman. Eve undoubtedly excited something in the amazed young Adam, who saw her beauty and that she was uniquely suited for him.

Through the first marriage, God also established the basis for the family and its place in the world. He told Adam and Eve to be fruitful and produce many children,[8] and to exercise dominion over creation by caring for it and ruling over the creatures and environment.

Man is not an animal, nor is he an angel — both of which God made during the first six days. Rather, mankind is the most special creation of all because both male and female were created in the image of God. Although all humans and some animals have what the Bible calls *nephesh* — which is apparently both breath and blood—only humans are made in the image of God Himself.

At the end of day 6, God considered all He had made — the heavens, the earth, the angels, the animals, and Adam and Eve — and He pronounced everything "very good." There was no sin, suffering, or death. No shedding of blood. No disease. No thorns or thistles.[9] Everything everywhere was perfect!

Then, on the seventh day, He rested and blessed it. God gave man the pattern of working for six days and resting for one, as He did.[10]

PRIMARY PASSAGES:

Gen. 1:24–31; Gen. 2; Ezk. 28:12–15; Mark 10:6; Ex. 20:11

KEY VERSE:

But from the beginning of the creation, God 'made them male and female.' —Mark 10:6

WRAP UP:

"Wow! Father, You made the animals, and then you made Adam and Eve. We didn't evolve from stardust in some kind of primordial goo. You created us special on the sixth day of creation, in Your image. Then in the perfection of the Garden, You gave the amazing act of marriage and told the first husband and wife to produce many children! Please help me to honor marriage and family in the way you invented them, Lord. Please help me to be a good caretaker of the earth and the animals. I want to please You, Father."

When the first man Adam met his wife Eve, he was delighted! And everything everywhere was perfect.

BONUS
— Angels

A war arose in heaven soon after God pronounced all creation "very good." However, because the account of this event is spread throughout the Bible, with only the aftermath being addressed in Genesis, it is easily overlooked. In what must have been a fierce battle, God's army of loyal angels, led by Michael, their commander,[1] struggled against Satan (the great dragon) and the many angels that rebelled with him. Revelation — the last book of the Bible — seems to indicate that a third of all angels fought against God's authority and were cast down to earth.[2] The prophet Ezekiel also refers to Satan being cast down. Defeated in heaven, Satan continued his rebellion on earth, where man had been given dominion. In the Garden of Eden, Satan spoke through a serpent in order to entice mankind to follow him rather than God.

Many assume that the heavenly battle of the angels occurred long before man's creation, but it is clear that the fall of Satan and his minions had to occur after God declared that everything He had created was "very good," at the end of day 6. Otherwise creation would not have been seen by God as being without blemish.

Likewise, the fall of Satan and the angels we now call demons took place prior to when Satan — in pursuit of God's glory — entered the serpent and used it to beguile Eve into eating from the Tree of the Knowledge of Good and Evil.

While the Bible does not focus on the timeframe, it seems logical to assume that the period between day 6 and the Fall of Adam and Eve was very short, possibly only days or weeks, since Eve had not yet conceived the couple's first child.[3] Their bodies were operating perfectly, so it is likely that the window of time prior to sin was a few months at most.

–3–
REBELLION AND THE CURSE

It wasn't long before man's sin ruined the perfection of creation.

The earth was breathtaking. Its perfection would stand in awe-inspiring contrast to the terribly fallen world of today. Peace, tranquility, and joy were all that Adam and Eve knew. Evil, disease, and death had not yet gripped the world.

The Bible doesn't say exactly how long it was before Satan spoke through the serpent, but it may have been only days or weeks before Adam's disobedience brought the horrible impact of his sin on all creation. It is clear, however, that God decreed the Curse prior to when Eve conceived the first child.

Genesis chapter 3 documents that through the serpent Satan deceived Eve. She sinned by eating fruit from the forbidden Tree of the Knowledge of Good and Evil, which God had placed at the center of the Garden. Then she gave some to her husband, Adam. He was not deceived,[1] but *chose* to rebel against God.

Through Adam, sin entered the world.[2] The man and his wife realized they were naked, and quickly sewed fig leaves together to cover themselves. Later that day, God came walking in the Garden and called to Adam. However, he and Eve were hiding among the plants, so God confronted them.

Adam first blamed his wife, who gave the fruit to him. Then he blamed God, who gave the woman to him. Eve blamed the serpent, who deceived her.

Satan's strategy to get man to follow him rather than God was not *completely* successful, but enough that everything changed. Before Adam sinned, there was no death in the world. Now, perfection was shattered. Suffering and dying had begun. Yet God was not taken by surprise. In response to man's rebellion, He launched His plan for the eventual restoration of the perfection that will one day come through Jesus. He cursed the serpent, promising that one day he would receive a fatal blow from the offspring of the woman.[3]

Soon after God killed animals and made coats of skin to clothe the couple. Adam was driven out of the Garden, and neither he nor Eve would ever return.[4] Then, God placed cherubim and a moving, flaming sword at the entrance, guards to block the way to the Tree of Life and as a reminder that it was here that sin, suffering, and death began. How sad they must have been!

Now outside the Garden, Adam labored against weeds and thorns, and the ground no longer yielded food easily. Eve was blessed with pregnancy, but the fear and pain during childbirth were undoubtedly intense, especially due to all the unknowns of the first child's birth. Surely, the delivery of Cain was both awesome and bittersweet.[5]

Later, Abel and other sons and daughters were born. They married and had families of their own. Marriage between siblings and close relatives was fine until about 2,500 years later at the time of Moses, when God forbade close intermarriage, perhaps because the gene pool had become too corrupted.[6]

One day both Cain and Abel presented offerings to God. Abel brought fat portions from the firstborn of his flock, and Cain brought some of the fruit of his fields. God was pleased with Abel and his offering, but He was not pleased with Cain and his offering.

The grief of Adam and Eve was surely extreme when Cain — filled with jealousy that God accepted Abel's offering but not his — struck and coldheartedly killed his brother Abel. The first couple's first son committed the world's first murder. It would be hard to overstate the crushing heartache that must have gripped Adam and Eve, especially since it was their own disobedience years before that brought sin and its many miseries into the once-perfect world.

It may be that no parents have longed more intensely than Adam and Eve for the restoration that Jesus the Redeemer would one day bring to our terribly broken world.[7]

PRIMARY PASSAGES:

Gen. 3-4, Rom. 5:18-20, Rev. 12:4-10, Isa. 14:12-15

KEY VERSE:

"…sin lies at the door. And its desire is for you, but you should rule over it." —Gen. 4:7

WRAP UP:

"Eve believed Satan's lie, and then Adam decided to disobey You, Lord, by eating from the Tree of the Knowledge of Good and Evil. But thank You for not allowing them to keep eating from the Tree of Life. If they had not been kicked out of the Garden, they would have lived forever in the broken world with all of its sin and suffering, with no hope of everything being restored one day! Please help me to understand the big picture as I read to discover the key things that happened between the day Adam sinned, and the morning so many years later when Jesus rose from the dead!"

Suddenly perfection was broken. Suffering and dying began with the Curse after Adam and Eve sinned.

Noah led his family in building the Ark. Many pre-Flood people were very intelligent and skillful.

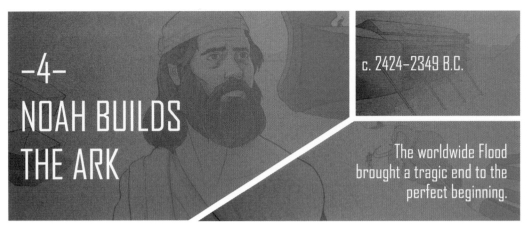

–4–
NOAH BUILDS THE ARK

c. 2424–2349 B.C.

The worldwide Flood brought a tragic end to the perfect beginning.

Family histories in Genesis reveal that the worldwide catastrophe known as Noah's Flood was unleashed less than 2,000 years after creation. Although it is clear that there were many people living by that time,[1] all humanity except one family followed the rebellion of Adam's sin against God. Death, suffering, and hate filled the earth, and by the time of the Flood, the thoughts of men were evil, continually.

God loves righteousness, but He hates evil. He was not surprised when Adam sinned, or decades later when Cain killed his brother Abel. The Creator was ready for what would happen, and now it was time for a massive step in His plan for man's salvation and creation's restoration.[2]

Beginning when Noah was 500, this "preacher of righteousness" and his wife were blessed with three sons. The first, Japheth, was born 100 years before the Flood. Shem was born two years later, then Ham.[3]

As Noah and his wife trained their sons to obey and praise the Creator, the boys matured into manhood. God tells us in the Bible that Noah followed God's

ways, so it is reasonable to assume that he loved his wife and trained his children in righteousness. Japheth, Shem, and Ham must have respected their parents and followed their instructions with care.

Genesis chapters 6 through 9 document that God told Noah to build a massive ship, called an ark, and instructed him to build it 300 cubits by 50 cubits by 30 cubits, with three levels. That's roughly 510 feet long by 85 feet wide by 51 feet high.[4] God told Noah to build it out of a specific type of wood and to coat it inside and out with pitch, which was probably based on the sap of trees in order to waterproof and preserve the wood extra well. It is likely that God gave Noah many other details, too.[5]

Because the world was exceedingly wicked, Noah and his family were surrounded by God-haters. Surely he was scoffed as a crazy man. But he stood firm and obeyed anyway.

Considering both the immense sinfulness of his culture and the magnitude of the task before him, Noah's obedience is perhaps the greatest example of persistent faith in all of Scripture.

It took many years to complete the huge Ark. We don't know how many were spent warning people, or harvesting timber, or actually building. But from the day when God declared that He would destroy man from the face of the earth until the Flood started, 120 years passed.

Noah's oldest son, Japheth was 100 when the Flood came.[6] Still young among the men of that time, Noah's three hard-working sons were undoubtedly strong. Although researchers are confident that Noah and his family could have built the Ark on their own, it is quite possible that Noah employed and continued to warn laborers and unbelieving relatives as well.[7]

We know from Genesis chapter 4 that even before the Flood, skilled tradesmen were making things out of metal. They were smart! In addition, the use of strong animals and labor-saving inventions such as pulleys, cranes, and wagons for the heavy lumber, are probable. After all, the mental and physical abilities of the people of Noah's day were much closer to the original perfection of Adam and Eve than to the sin-corrupted minds and bodies of humans today.

Moreover, because people lived considerably longer before the Flood,[8] they were able to experience, recall, and put to use far more than we can now. It is likely that we vastly underestimate the abilities and inventions of Noah and the countless other pre-Flood people!

PRIMARY PASSAGES:

Gen. 6–9

KEY VERSE:

"Then the Lord saw that the wickedness of man was great in the earth, and that every intent of the thoughts of his heart was only evil continually. And the Lord was sorry that He had made man on the earth, and He was grieved in His heart. So the Lord said, 'I will destroy man whom I have created from the face of the earth, both man and beast, creeping thing and birds of the air, for I am sorry that I have made them.' But Noah found grace in the eyes of the Lord." —Gen. 6:5–8

WRAP UP:

"Our Father, thank You for telling Noah to build the ark. He was such a great example of faith and dedication! With all the sin and evil that filled the world in his time, even worse than today, it must have been incredibly easy to be drawn into sin, and not to stay faithful to You in the six hundred years he lived before the Flood. Please help me to have faith that overcomes the pressures of this world, like Noah's."

–5–
GOD SENDS THE ANIMALS!

The Ark was finished, with hundreds of tons of food stowed inside. But what about the animals?

Once the Ark's massive hull was complete, it may have taken several more years to finish the cavernous interior. To help keep the animals safe and more easily managed on the violent ocean, Noah and his family constructed rooms,[1] and probably stalls, cages, coops, and aviaries, plus their own living quarters.

A few animals required large spaces, but the average size of a creature was about as big as a sheep. Since God created animals to eat plants — and we know from the fossil record that the earth before the Flood had a lush abundance — those He sent[2] to the Ark probably did not prey upon one another. In addition, because God only selected representatives of each *kind*, not of each species, there was plenty of room on the Ark for all of them, and for the food and other supplies.[3]

Many reptiles and some mammals grow throughout their lives, so God may have directed to the Ark the youngest of those that were able to reproduce. The Bible says that God sent pairs of every kind of bird and at least two of every land dwelling, air-breathing animal,[4] which obviously would have included a pair of each of the dinosaur kinds since dinosaurs were land animals.[5]

Noah surely used many of the pre-Flood world's amazing innovations as well, such as clever ways to capture, store, and distribute water. He also had to build waste disposal systems, ways to maximize light, and ways to flow fresh air throughout the huge ship.

In preparation, it was necessary to purchase or plant, harvest, and store huge stocks of grains, hay, and other foods. Noah's family likely dried berries, crushed grapes for jams and wine, and pressed olives and other fruits and vegetables for oils. They must have also taken many different spices, sweeteners like honey and syrups, and seeds to re-establish agriculture. They brought bedding, clothing, tools, and written records, including the history of Adam plus much more.[6]

Then, when everything was ready, seven days before the Flood began God did something that surely amazed any mocking onlookers. From near and far, by God's supernatural call, male and female of every kind of air-breathing land animal and bird arrived.[7] The procession plodded, crawled, scurried, hopped, flew, and perhaps slithered through the door, possibly for days.

In striking parallel to how God calls men and women to receive the gift of salvation in Jesus Christ[8], God chose each specific animal to escape the impending judgment. There was no coaxing, capturing, or gender checking needed. God called them and they responded from all over the earth's only original continent, and they entered the Ark of salvation.

The procession may have caused shocked scoffers to stand in astonishment, and wonder if the Flood that Noah had been warning about was about to take place!

The Bible tells us in Genesis 6, that after the animals entered the Ark, Noah's family kept them alive.[9] With simple innovations that would make caretaking easier, such as ways to keep them fed and cages free of waste for extended periods, the family of eight could certainly have tended all the animals.[10]

Scientists who have studied how many different kinds of land animals and birds there were before the Flood, agree that the creatures would require only

about one-third of the Ark. This would leave sufficient room for food, supplies, and possibly, to prove to others that there was room for them as well, if they had repented.

The worldwide Flood was about to start! Yet even with clear warnings that judgment was imminent, the people did not repent.

Sadly, that is how it will be before Jesus suddenly returns, like a thief in the night![11]

PRIMARY PASSAGES:
Gen. 6:1–7:16

KEY VERSE:

"Of clean animals, of animals that are unclean, of birds, and of everything that creeps on the earth, two by two they went into the ark to Noah, male and female, as God had commanded Noah." —Gen. 7:8–9

WRAP UP:

"Father, thank You for rescuing Noah's family and all the animals that You sent to the Ark. The whole world was against You, but You decided to start over with just righteous Noah and his family and that huge treasure chest of animals! Lord, please guide me to live for You as Noah did. Please help me to obey You and share about Your mighty works to my friends and loved ones."

The arrival of so many different animals surely worried any onlookers. Even so, no one repented of their sinfulness.

Soon, water would cover everything, everywhere. But God saved Noah, his family, and the animals He sent to the massive wooden Ark.

-6-
THE WHOLE
EARTH CHANGES

When the door closed,
everything changed.

Noah and his three sons labored together for decades, and by God's grace, they and their wives overcame great challenges in building the Ark. Now the ship was finished and loaded.

All four couples waited inside.

Imagine the array of thoughts and emotions that probably struck Noah's family when, with no human assistance, the Ark's thick door swung closed.

Outside, men and women may have stood in abrupt silence. Perhaps it was while some were laughing at the bizarre vessel and its eccentric builder that the great door unexpectedly sealed itself shut.

Scoffers are everywhere, and some in Noah's day may even have been close relatives; parents or siblings of Noah's daughters-in-law, the kindred of his wife, or of Noah himself. Thankfully, God closed the door. Noah did not have to decide when the unbelievers would be locked out forever.

Genesis tells us that Noah walked with God. In the Ark after the door closed, he may have been praying with his family as the earth began to quake. Perhaps lightning bolts filled the darkening sky

as blasts of thunder announced the impending deluge.

On that day, earth essentially exploded as all the fountains of the great deep burst forth.[1] One geophysics study suggests that superheated water and magma from underneath earth's crust would have caused parts of the ocean to violently flash-boil and blast supersonic jets of steam thousands of feet into the air, then fall in pounding, wind-driven gales.[2] We do not know if Noah's family could hear screams of terror, but the worldwide judgment on man's wickedness had begun.

Soon the timbers that steadied the Ark for decades began to fall away. Rising water enveloped the globe and released earth's hold on the solitary wooden sanctuary. Animal sounds echoed throughout the ship and mixed with the words of the eight men and women on board. The creatures rested in safety while Noah's family cared for them and for one another.

Meanwhile, everyone outside the Ark died and was wiped from the face of the earth.[3] Clouds, rain, and volcanic ash darkened the sun. There were 40 days and nights of torrential downpour. As the worldwide cataclysm continued, life went on inside the Ark. But research reveals that far beneath the shoreless ocean, enormous ruptures in earth's crust ran for thousands of miles. Billions of animals and plants were entombed in sediments that hardened into the rock layers we see all over the world.[4]

Water continued to flood into the depths, and the sea continued to rise. Earthquakes and fiery, magma-spewing volcanic eruptions ripped apart the original supercontinent, eventually splitting it into several smaller ones.[5] Finally, on the 150th day, water covered everything, everywhere.[6] The fountains of the great deep stopped and the ocean began to withdraw. It had been five months, and the Ark now came to rest on one of the mountains of Ararat.

Nothing today is as it was before Noah's Flood. Now, jigsaw puzzle shapes of distant coastlines remind us of the astounding judgment that transformed our planet. Pre-Flood cities, structures, and river channels are no more. Everything, even the place where the Garden of Eden had been, was wiped away[7] by the violent waves of erosion and rapid movements of the continents. Only God's Word adequately explains our planet's past.

Now grounded amid receding waters upon the mountains of Ararat, the vital work of Noah's family continued, and mid-way through the journey's seventh month, mountaintops became visible.[8]

In the middle of the journey's tenth month, Noah removed the covering of the Ark.[9] He waited, as the earth dried and vegetation spread.

In total, it was more than a year before God told Noah's family and the creatures to leave the Ark the Creator used to save them from the Flood. However, God's timing and provision were perfect. The animals could now survive outside and begin to fill the stark, vacant world that stretched out before them.

PRIMARY PASSAGES:
Gen. 7:10–8:17; 2 Pet. 3:5–7; Ps. 104:8

KEY VERSE:
"…the world that then existed perished, being flooded with water."
—2 Pet. 3:6

WRAP UP:
"Lord, it is hard to comprehend that as days became weeks, and weeks became months, and as the Ark moved in the storms, the ground far beneath the ocean's surface broke apart and the continents moved. Thank You for bringing the Ark to rest atop one of the mountains of Ararat, and for keeping Noah's family safe as more months passed and You sent wind to dry the land. They must have been so happy to watch from the Ark as grasses and flowers soon sprouted and spread. Thank You for the new start that You gave man after the Flood!"

-7-
THE RAINBOW PROMISE AND THE NEW WORLD

c. 2348-2242 B.C.

The century following the Flood was filled with extreme and rapid change.

More than seven months after the Ark ran aground on the mountains of Ararat,[1] God told Noah to release the animals. Ample vegetation and an uninhabited new world waited. At last, the creatures followed each other out of the massive wooden vessel, one kind after another.

The Bible does not say how steep the mountain was at the place where the Ark came to rest, but clearly even the less nimble land animals — such as the rhinoceros kind, the giraffe kind, elephants, and the various kinds of dinosaurs — were able to make their way down.

Once outside, Noah led his family in praise of God. He built an altar and sacrificed burnt offerings from each kind of the clean animals and birds, which God sent in groups of seven.

The Lord had unleashed His dreadful wrath on man's sin through the world-wide Flood, but Scripture says that He was pleased with Noah's offerings. God blessed Noah and his sons, and told them to be fruitful, increase in number, and fill the earth.[2]

God revealed that fear and dread of man would now come upon all the animals of land, sea, and air. Mankind was originally vegetarian but after the Flood, God gave permission to eat meat, as well.[3] Perhaps the animals received this new fear of man to help evade his tendency to overkill and improperly manage the creatures, since man would now be raising and hunting them for food.

God also told Noah's family that, because humans are made in God's image, no one is to murder, lest he be punished by being killed himself. It was here, in Genesis 9, that God established the death penalty; "Whoever sheds the blood of man, by man shall his blood be shed; for in the image of God has God made man."[4] This was nearly 850 years before God gave Moses the Ten Commandments.

Then the Creator promised that He would never again destroy all flesh with a flood. The beautiful rainbow in the clouds would be a sign of this promise.[5] After all that they had experienced, the spectacular, multicolored arch was surely an amazing sight to Noah and his family, and a sweet assurance of God's care for all people yet to be born.

In the decades after the Flood, lush forests grew around the world in temperate, well-watered environments.[6] As Noah's children explored the new lands, some features reminded them of pre-Flood terrain. Old-world names — such as Euphrates and Tigris for two of the rivers — were even used.

In the decades and first few centuries after the Flood, volcanoes continued to erupt, mountains continued to rise, and meteorites continued to blaze through the atmosphere and impact our planet's surface, but with rapidly decreasing frequency.[7] The combination of warm oceans and cool summers was the key to massive snow and ice buildup, starting at the North and South Poles.[8] The rapid, post-Flood Ice Age was about to begin.

Earth's transformation was immense, ongoing, and undoubtedly fearsome at times. We still feel residual affects today with ongoing volcanic eruptions, earthquakes, and wild weather.

By the point when Noah's grandsons were born, he had harvested a vineyard. All three of his sons probably lived nearby, since all were present on the day when Noah became intoxicated on too much of his wine and fell asleep unclothed in his tent. When Ham apparently ridiculed Noah to Shem and Japheth, Noah became so enraged that he spoke a curse upon Ham's youngest son, Canaan.

This damaged relationship between Noah and Ham may have played a part in the Babel rebellion that was soon to come.

PRIMARY PASSAGES:

Gen. 8:18–9:28, 10:32, 11:1–9

KEY VERSE:

"The rainbow shall be in the cloud, and I will look on it to remember the everlasting covenant between God and every living creature of all flesh that is on the earth.' And God said to Noah, 'This is the sign of the covenant which I have established between Me and all flesh that is on the earth." —Gen. 9:16–17

WRAP UP:

"Thank You for rainbows, God! Thank You for the beautiful promise that You will never again judge sin by a worldwide flood. What an amazing sign You gave, and it reminds us that You used a colossal Ark to save Noah's family and preserve mankind from the waters of the Flood. Thank You for eternal salvation, which can only come to us by Jesus, the true Savior!"

The rainbow is a reminder of God's promise that He will never again destroy all flesh with a flood.

Animals repopulated the planet quickly after the flood cataclysm. At the start, there were bountiful resources, wide-open spaces and very little predation, so the multiplication of species exploded in every direction.[1]

Certain fossils and other evidences help researchers understand how the creatures spread rapidly across the globe.[2] And by God's marvelous design of genetics, many thousands of new species — which are merely variations within the kinds — flourished in some of the most remote and inhospitable climates and habitats.

In countless instances, a new species within a created kind[3] that was well suited for a particular environment survived and multiplied, while species that were ill-equipped moved on or died out.[4] This pattern continues today.

The Bible documents in Genesis 8:4 that Noah's Ark came to rest somewhere in "the mountains of Ararat." We do not know whether the mountain on which the Ark landed was unstable and volcanic, but we do know that the one modern mountain known as "Mount Ararat" is a volcano; it may have risen during and/or after the Flood, we do not know. However, it is improbable that Noah's family originally settled in the cold, stark mountain range where the Ark came to rest (possibly somewhere in the eastern region of modern-day Turkey). Genesis chapter 11 tells us that they migrated from Noah's farm to the Plain of Shinar. Many believe that this plain was in modern-day Iraq, where the Bible states that the people congregated before God forced their dispersion at the Tower of Babel.[5]

Snow soon fell in copious volumes on the newly exposed northern and southern lands. The severe and incessant snowstorms, combined with cooler summers caused by sunshine-reducing volcanic ash and meteor impact dust, would have resulted in thick ice sheets and glaciers. These covered huge portions of the Northern and Southern Hemispheres, including areas such as the upper Midwest of the United States and substantial portions of Europe — all within only a few hundred years after the Flood.[6]

Various evidences indicate that eruptions and earthquakes diminished as the movement of the earth's tectonic plates slowed from meters-per-minute at the height of the Flood, to the present rate of only centimeters-per-year.

It is clear that the world's immense ice sheets and glaciers reached their maximum thickness and breadth very quickly.

One set of researchers based their findings on Ussher's chronology—which places the Flood at about 2350 B.C.—and the understanding that the city of Ur was a coastal seaport when Abram was born there in about 2000 B.C.. The Persian Gulf was full or nearly full at that time because most of the earth's huge glaciers had melted and released their stored water into the oceans. The research suggests that ice and massive glaciers accumulated within three centuries after the Flood, then melted and released their stored water to cover most intercontinental land bridges and many low-lying coastal areas during the next 100 years or so.[7]

Other researchers, using glacial and weather data, also support a recent and brief ice age but suggest the duration was 200–300 years longer.[8]

Both groups agree that the climate was erratic and there were extreme changes in weather during this period, known as the "rapid ice age," and that it was triggered by the global Flood of about 4,300 years ago.[9]

The Ice Age on the Timeline: Note the blue background behind a portion of the included fold-out timeline. The immense changes that reshaped the earth during the year-long Flood led to the intense but short-lived period commonly called the Ice Age. Seeing the Ice Age in light of the people who lived and migrated throughout the earth during that time brings a deeper understanding of God's judgment in earth's history and to the natural global warming that began only a few hundred years after the cataclysmic event experienced by Noah's family. The Earth has been warming since the Ice Age, about 4,000 years ago.

God created new languages to break up the one big group at the Tower of Babel. The people finally spread across the earth.

–8–
THE TOWER OF BABEL

c. 2242 B.C.

Sometimes, God has to move us out of our comfort zone.

More than one hundred years had passed since Noah left the Ark and much had happened!

The fossil record reveals that there were many earthquakes and volcanic eruptions as the movement of the continents slowed in the decades after the Flood.[1] Even so, forests and abundant vegetation spread across the warm and well-watered areas near the equator. Immense ice sheets and glaciers began to form near the poles. Animals continued to spread across the earth. And four generations of Noah's family may have totaled thousands of men, women, and children.

Noah was now over 700 years old. His three sons were all about 200. Each had the opportunity — the spiritual responsibility as husbands and fathers — to ensure that their children and grandchildren knew and could pass down the truth about creation, how sin and death started, and the promised coming Redeemer who will crush Satan and be the once-and-for-all ultimate sacrifice.[2]

However, in the four generations since the Flood, something began to go drastically wrong. The people did not spread out and instead settled in a region called Shinar, probably in modern-day Iraq.

One can easily imagine how this rebellion against God's command to fill the earth may have come about.

Beginning with Adam and Eve, everyone apparently spoke the same language. This made it easy for ancient people to build on the substantial knowledge and experiences of others, which helped them to achieve so much so quickly.

Much of the pre-Flood knowledge — such as Cain's experience as a city-builder, and Tubal-cain's skill with brass and iron — was passed from Noah and his sons to their descendants.[3] However, when those entrusted with great knowledge do not seek to honor the Creator and adjust their lives to live according to His plan, God is not pleased. This was the case just four generations after the Flood, when Noah and his sons were still living.

During the time of Noah's great-great-great grandson Peleg, the people were constructing a city with a very distinctive tower. Genesis 11 says that they wanted to make a name for themselves by building a structure to help them reach to the heavens, perhaps under the guise of being a place to sacrifice to God. It was likely a towering pyramid-like ziggurat.[4]

Before Babel was finished,[5] God confused the people with new languages. Scholars say that around 90 different root-languages originated in this middle-eastern region, and that the 7,500 languages and dialects of today all came from those.[6] Since God normally works through families, such as Noah's, it is likely that each immediate family spoke the same language. There may have been multiple families per language.

No longer able to communicate with those who suddenly spoke differently, and unable to finish the city, the different groups spread out and moved to other parts of the world. Now separated by language, the people expanded their domains and eventually established nations and empires. They took their knowledge of tower-building with them, as evidenced by the many ziggurats, pyramids, and tower mounds in countries near and far.

It was at this time that the human gene pool was split apart and physical characteristics in the various groups became distinctive. A wide variety of facial bone structures, skin tones from very dark to very light, different textures and colors of hair, eye shape, and other features started to be dominant in various language groups and the regions where those groups settled.

Today we mistakenly call groups with distinctive features races. However, the Bible is clear that we are all of one blood, and only one race exists — the human race.[7]

PRIMARY PASSAGES:

Gen. 11

KEY VERSE:

"Therefore its name is called Babel, because there the Lord confused the language of all the earth; and from there the Lord scattered them abroad over the face of all the earth."
—Gen. 11:9

WRAP UP:

"Lord, when I think of men on the Tower of Babel working and talking side by side, I think of how dependent they were on each other for safety. One moment they were talking and the next they were stunned because they were hearing gibberish! Fear would have grown quickly, and so would distrust. The people would have broken into groups based on who they could understand. That was a gentle way of forcing them to move out and begin filling the earth, as You commanded a century earlier! Thank You for your grace and patience then, and now, dear Lord."

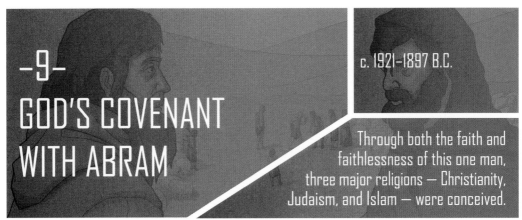

–9–
GOD'S COVENANT WITH ABRAM

Through both the faith and faithlessness of this one man, three major religions — Christianity, Judaism, and Islam — were conceived.

When first introduced in Scripture, Abram is 75 years old and lives in Haran. He moved here from Ur, a busy city on the Euphrates River near the southern coast of modern-day Iraq. It has been nearly 370 years[1] since the worldwide Flood, and about 260 years since the dispersion at the Tower of Babel.

It is possible that millions of people now lived throughout the earth. Abram is the tenth generation after Noah, who died only two years before Abram's birth. Noah's son Shem is still living.

We know very little about Abram's life prior to age 75, but the Bible does state that years earlier his father Terah set out from Ur with Abram, Abram's wife Sarai, and his nephew Lot. Terah's destination was Canaan (later called Israel) but when he reached the city of Haran — about two hundred miles northeast of Canaan — he settled there instead. In Haran, idolatry was rampant and Abram's father worshiped false gods.[2] But by His grace, God called Abram and pursued him, for God's glory!

Abram was very ordinary. He had stresses with work and family,[3] was sometimes a less-than-ideal husband,[4] and struggled to stay consistent in his walk with the Lord.[5] Nevertheless, the Creator loves to show His grace and power through ordinary people, and He had big plans for Abram!

Part of God's plan had been that Abram marry his half-sister Sarai, which was fine at the time. By God's design, Adam and Eve's original gene pool was perfect. Brothers and sisters and cousins married, and their children were free of genetic deformities. It was not until the time of Moses about 400 years after Abram, that God prohibited marriage between close relatives.[6]

After Abram's father died, God told him to leave the comforts of Haran, take Sarai and his nephew Lot, plus his possessions and servants, and go to Canaan. God promised 75-year-old Abram that all the people of the earth would be blessed through his descendants, though Sarai had not yet borne any children.

Years later, after God had greatly blessed both Abram and Lot with large herds and households, the two men agreed that one of them should move, because the land could not support their many animals and there was strife between their herdsmen. Abram allowed Lot to choose. Lot selected the better land,[7] and to live in the sin-filled city of Sodom.[8]

Although Abram's life is an amazing example of great faith and obedience, it is also a sad reminder that all who love God are fallen, imperfect people who often exhibit faithlessness. In Abram's case, the most striking examples are that on two separate occasions when he feared for his life, he told his wife — who was also his half-sister — not to tell that she was his wife. Only that she was his sister. When she was about 65[9] and later when nearly 90,[10] Sarai was so desirable that both a pharaoh and a king took her to become their wife. Yet, God protected and returned her to her husband.

Genesis chapter 17 states that when Abram was 99 and Sarai 90, God confirmed his covenant of a quarter century earlier and promised anew to make Abram the father of many nations. For Abram's part, he and all the males in his clan had to be circumcised.[11] Then God changed Abram's name to *Abraham,* and Sarai to *Sarah.* He swore to give Abraham the son of promise by his wife Sarah, who laughed because both were beyond childbearing years.[12] But it is in impossibility that God's power is seen!

First, however, a severe judgment would descend.

PRIMARY PASSAGES:

Gen. 11–18; Josh. 24:2

KEY VERSE:

"Now the Lord said to Abram. . . . I will bless those who bless you, And I will curse him who curses you; And in you all the families of the earth shall be blessed."

—Gen. 12:1, 3

WRAP UP:

"Dear God, sometimes You choose the weak to do big things. I'm glad. I love the way that You show Your power. Thank You for miraculously giving the elderly Abraham and his barren wife, Sarah, a son through the union of their marriage covenant! Thank You for showing me that You have kept Your promises! I need to follow the plan You've given us in the Bible and not try to get things my own way. Please remind me often that YOUR way is perfect. Please help me to live YOUR way, Lord."

God blessed Abram and Lot with so many animals and possessions that they could no longer live near one another.

Lot and his daughters were rescued by angels and escaped to a mountain cave high above the smoldering cities.

–10–
ANGELS RESCUE LOT FROM SODOM AND GOMORRAH

c. 1897 B.C.

Lot chose to raise his family in a city where wickedness was rampant. They paid a high price for that decision.

On a hot afternoon, not long after Abraham had healed from his circumcision,[1] the Lord and two angels in the form of men appeared at Abraham's tent. He was living in a wooded area close to Israel's modern-day Hebron. They told Abraham of a terrible judgment that was about to take place.

Because of the appalling sins of the people in Sodom and Gomorrah and that region, God was about to annihilate both cities and the neighboring towns. However, Abraham's nephew Lot and family lived in Sodom, so Abraham tried desperately to convince the Lord to reconsider. The Lord finally promised not to judge Sodom and Gomorrah if just ten righteous people could be found there. The two angels arrived at Sodom that evening.

Lot, now old,[2] was sitting at the city gate. It was here that elders sometimes met regarding civic matters. Lot recognized that the two visitors were not ordinary travelers and immediately went to meet them, bowing to the ground. He strongly urged them to come to his home rather than spend the night in the city square, undoubtedly concerned for their safety. At first they turned down his invitation but Lot insisted, and for good reason.

The events of that night and the next morning are detailed in Genesis and read like a horrible nightmare. When the angels arrived at Lot's home, he served them dinner. But before they could go to bed a mob of men from all parts of the city surrounded his house and demanded that he bring the two visitors outside so they could molest them. Lot implored that such wickedness not happen, and then in what must have been a desperate decision intended to protect God's messengers, Lot offered the depraved horde his two virgin daughters instead — whom they rejected.

Growing even angrier because Lot refused to turn over the visitors, the mob surged forward to break down the door. At the last moment, the two angels reached out, pulled Lot back into the house, and struck the raging Sodomites with blindness.

The angels ordered Lot to gather his family immediately so they could unleash God's judgment. With the men of the city now blinded, Lot was able to go out and warn his daughters' fiancés.

He told them what God was about to do, but they did not take him seriously.

At dawn, the angels pressed Lot to hurry lest he and his wife and daughters be caught in the judgment themselves. Lot hesitated, so the angels took them by the hands and led them quickly out of the city. The angels gave them permission to flee to the small town of Zoar, but warned them not to look back longingly.[3]

As Lot and his family arrived at Zoar, God began to rain brimstone and fire on Sodom and Gomorrah. However, his wife looked back. She disobeyed God's command and became a pillar of salt. For Lot and his daughters, though, their desperate rush to escape was honored.

The Bible tells us that every man, woman, and child in the valley was killed in God's righteous judgment.[4] Every house and all the vegetation burned up, leaving only ash.[5] From outside his tent many miles away, Abraham could see dark smoke rising from the valley where Sodom and Gomorrah had been.

The Bible's last words about Lot reveal that he was afraid to live in another city, so he took his two daughters — whose husbands-to-be had been killed in the destruction — and lived with them in a cave in the hills above Zoar.[6]

PRIMARY PASSAGES:

Gen. 18:16–19:30; 2 Pet. 2:6–8

KEY VERSE:

"Then the Lord rained brimstone and fire on Sodom and Gomorrah, from the Lord out of the heavens. So he overthrew those cities, all the plain, all the inhabitants of the cities, and what grew on the ground." —Gen. 19:24–25

WRAP UP:

"Lot chose to raise his family in a very dark place, even though he had other options. Father, You were willing not to destroy Sodom if there were just ten righteous people there. That should have been easy. Between Lot's family and his daughters' fiancés there were six people. But apparently, they had given in to the culture. Even Lot's own wife longed for Sodom more than she wanted to obey You. Lord, reveal my blind spots. Please show me how to help my family love and honor You above everything this world has to offer."

–11–
ISAAC, NEARLY SACRIFICED!

c. 1871 B.C.

Learning to trust!

When the Lord called Abram to move to the region we know as Israel, He promised that, like the stars of heaven, Abram's descendants would be too numerous to count. Yet ten years later, when Abram was 85 and his wife Sarai about 76, she was still barren. Aware that it was no longer possible for her to have babies naturally, Sarai suggested that her husband father a child by her servant, Hagar.[1]

Soon a boy was born, and they named him Ishmael. However, he was the result of man's faithlessness, not God's promise, and problems were to come.

Through Abram, we are reminded that God designed marriage and its blessings for one man and one woman; no other combination.[2] The son of God's promise would come through Abram's covenant wife Sarai, not the extramarital relationship with Hagar, regardless of how well intentioned it had been.

Fourteen years later, after Abram was circumcised and renamed Abraham, Sarah miraculously bore Isaac, the son of promise![3]

But Hagar despised her mistress and the teenaged Ishmael began to mock his young half-brother, Isaac. "You must send Ishmael and his mother away," said Sarah. But Abraham was distressed because the youth was his son.[4]

The Lord, however, told Abraham to do what Sarah asked and assured him that a great nation would come from Ishmael, also.

Though it must have grieved him deeply, Abraham obeyed. The Creator provided for Ishmael and his mother, and eventually all the Arab people of today descended from Ishmael.

Years passed and the toddler Isaac grew into a strong youth, and his father loved him greatly.[5] God again spoke to Abraham, but this time demanded the inconceivable.

Early the next morning Abraham arose and set out to make a burnt offering to God. He loaded his donkey and took two servants . . . and Isaac. On the journey's third day, Abraham told his servants to wait with the donkey while he and Isaac continued up a mountain.

Isaac asked, "Where is the lamb for the burnt offering?" Abraham assured his son, "God will provide the lamb."

It is hard to imagine how intensely

Abraham's heart must have ached, or how hard it was to finally tell Isaac what soon became obvious — he was the sacrifice God required![6]

It had been years since Abraham sent Ishmael away, possibly more than two decades. Now, God instructed him to kill Isaac, the only son of promise. Abraham's faith had become great, and though he did not understand God's ways, he knew the Creator could raise his son back to life.

The trust shown by Isaac was great as well. Just as Christ would carry a wooden cross on His back many years later, Isaac carried on his back the wood for the sacrifice. He was surely strong enough to escape from his elderly father. Instead, Isaac submitted. Abraham bound him, then placed him on the wood of the altar.

At the last possible moment, as Abraham was about to slay the youth with a knife, God called out from Heaven, *"Abraham! Stop! Do not sacrifice Isaac, for now I see that you do not love your son more than me."*[7]

Then Abraham looked up and saw a ram caught by its horns in the brush. Yes, God provided the sacrifice! It was faith in God's power over death that made Abraham willing to offer his beloved son. But God blessed that faith and provided a substitute.

Likewise, God lovingly sent His only begotten Son, Jesus. And Jesus allowed Himself to be killed, the substitute sacrifice for all who receive Him as Savior![8]

PRIMARY PASSAGES:
Gen. 18:9–15, Gen. 20–22

KEY VERSE:

"By faith Abraham, when he was tested, offered up Isaac, and he who had received the promises offered up his only begotten son, of whom it was said, 'In Isaac your seed shall be called,' concluding that God was able to raise him up, even from the dead." —Heb. 11:17–19

WRAP UP:

"Heavenly Father, Abraham showed incredible faith! He was willing to offer Isaac on that altar. He was willing to arrange the stones and the wood and get the fire ready. But he didn't stop there. He tied Isaac, the only son who could fulfill Your promise, and he laid him across the kindling. He had to be willing to obey You, no matter what! He had faith that You could bring his son back to life again, so he raised his sharp knife. . . . Lord, help me to see what my 'Isaac' is. What do I love more than You?"

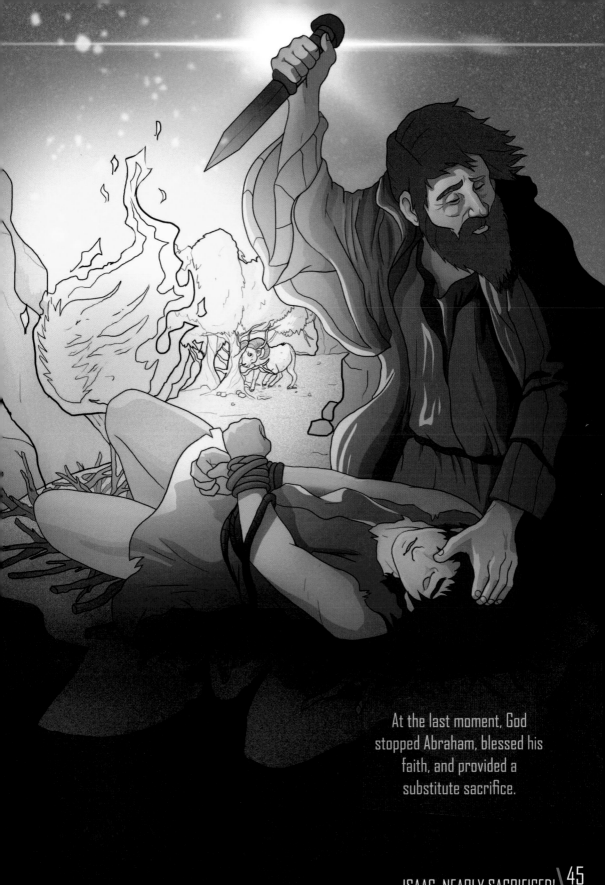

At the last moment, God stopped Abraham, blessed his faith, and provided a substitute sacrifice.

Exhausted and on the run, Jacob was awestruck by the dream of angels going up and down between heaven and earth.

−12−
DEATH, MARRIAGE, AND THE STAIRWAY TO HEAVEN

c. 1859–1759 B.C.

Sarah, Rebekah, and Jacob

More than a decade after God tested Abraham's faith by telling him to sacrifice his son, Isaac, Abraham's wife Sarah breathed her last. Sarah, the mother of Isaac, was God's chosen matriarch of the future Israelite people, and Abraham purchased a cave near Hebron as a tomb to bury her.

After about three years when Isaac was 40,[1] Abraham sent his most-trusted servant, Eliezer, to find a bride for Isaac among Abraham's relatives.[2] It may have been weeks before his ten-camel caravan arrived at the well outside Haran.[3] As the sun drew near to the western horizon, the godly servant prayed for specific confirmation about Isaac's wife-to-be. The description in Genesis 24 is a striking reminder that the Creator orchestrated this crucial moment in molding a chosen people.

God answered Eliezer's prayer down to its finest detail when the beautiful maiden Rebekah arrived. She showed great kindness to him and his caravan. Later that evening her father and brother gave permission for the marriage, and many valuable gifts from Abraham were bestowed. The next morning, Rebekah agreed to depart immediately.

Trusting God, she said goodbye to loved ones she might never see again and set out to meet her unknown groom in an unfamiliar land.

Some days later in a field in Canaan where Isaac was praying at evening, Rebekah dismounted her camel, and the couple finally met.[4] Obviously pleased by Eliezer's amazing report of the Lord's leading, Isaac and Rebekah soon married, and she gladdened his heart.[5]

However, God did not give children quickly. Finally, after 20 years of waiting, and Isaac's earnest prayer for his wife, Rebekah bore twins! The first was red and very hairy so they named him Esau. The second grabbed his brother's heel, so they named him Jacob.[6]

When they became adults, Esau loved hunting, while Jacob apparently helped oversee the family's herds. One day when Jacob was making stew, Esau came in. Tired and famished, he wanted to eat immediately. Jacob respected that God had given Abraham and Isaac an amazing inheritance and knew that Esau did not value it. So he offered his hungry brother a quick meal in exchange for his birthright.[7] Incredibly,

Esau agreed. He simply ate and left.[8]

When the twins were about 77[9] and their wealthy father had gone blind, Isaac was about to bestow the blessing of family leadership on Esau — who was ungodly, sexually immoral, and had sold his birthright to Jacob![10] However, God had revealed to Rebekah that the older would serve the younger,[11] so when she commanded Jacob to help deceive her husband in order to receive the birthright blessing, she felt justified. Rebekah prepared goat meat to taste like wild game, which Isaac was awaiting from Esau. Then she had Jacob wear Esau's clothes and placed goatskin on his smooth neck and hands. Jacob repeatedly lied to his blind father Isaac, who gave Jacob the blessing.[12]

Within minutes, Esau learned of the deception and wailed bitterly. He threatened to kill his brother, so Rebekah convinced Isaac to send Jacob north to find a wife among her nieces, away from pagan Canaanite women like Esau's wives, who brought them much heartache.[13]

Jacob fled Beersheba for Haran. Possibly that very night he dreamed of a ladder that connected earth and heaven. Angels went up and down.[14] Like us, Jacob was a sinner but God had chosen him, promised to protect him, and to give him and his descendants the land where he was sleeping. Genesis says that when he awoke he was awestruck, so he took the stone that had been his pillow, set it to mark the spot, and called the place Bethel. Then he started again to Haran.

Many years later, Jesus revealed that He is the ladder, the only true way to heaven.[15]

PRIMARY PASSAGES:

Gen. chapters 23–28, Gen. 35:28–29

KEY VERSE:

"So he came to a certain place and stayed there all night. . . . Then he dreamed, and behold, a ladder was set up on the earth, and its top reached to heaven; and there the angels of God were ascending and descending on it. And behold, the Lord stood above it and said . . . 'the land on which you lie I will give to you and your descendants. Also your descendants shall be as the dust of the earth; you shall spread abroad to the west and the east, to the north and the south; and in you and in your seed all the families of the earth shall be blessed.'"
—Gen. 28:11–14

WRAP UP:

"You bring good from bad, Lord. You even use broken, deceptive sinners to accomplish Your plan. Thank You so very much that in spite of Isaac's favoritism toward his immoral son Esau the hunter, and Rebekah's scheming and deception with her favorite son Jacob the shepherd, You made sure that Your sovereign will was accomplished. Your plan is never overwhelmed by man's feeble deceptions. Thank You, Lord, for Your love-filled grace!"

-13-
JACOB WRESTLES WITH ...JESUS?

c. 1739 B.C.

The origin of Israel

Encouraged by God's promise of protection in his dream of the stairway to heaven, Jacob continued his journey to modern-day Turkey. The trip was long and probably lonely.

When he finally arrived at the well outside Haran, Jacob met a beautiful shepherdess, his cousin Rachel. Obviously smitten, Jacob soon offered to work for her pagan father Laban for seven years in order to marry her. Genesis 29 says the years seemed like only days because of his love, but when at last their wedding day arrived, Jacob fell victim to an appalling deception.

Somehow, the anxious groom did not discover until the morning after the wedding that his bride was not Rachel, but her older sister, Leah![1] Perhaps she was veiled and the sisters were about the same size, or perhaps Jacob became drunk at the celebration. Regardless, Laban had switched brides without telling him, and Rachel's marriage bed was corrupted by her own sister.[2]

Though furious, Jacob may have remembered his own deception of his father Isaac. Still, his heart was for Rachel, so he agreed to serve *another* seven years. He married Rachel, whom

he loved, after fulfilling his weeklong wedding obligations with Leah, whom he did not love.

After the 14-years were complete, Jacob stayed six years more, building up his own herds.

Now 97, he led a complicated, often dysfunctional multi-marriage household and was the father of 11 sons and 1 daughter — the oldest child being about 12. God told him it was now time to return to Canaan.[3]

Jacob and his family and all his servants left secretly, while Laban was shearing sheep three days away. When Laban learned that his prosperous son-in-law had departed, he set out after him.[4] But God warned Laban not to try to stop Jacob. After strong arguments and accusations between the men, they entered a covenant not to harm one another, and Laban returned to Haran.

As Jacob began again on his trek with his clan, God sent angels to meet him.[5] This must have assured Jacob of God's protective presence as he faced what lay ahead.

When Jacob's twin brother Esau learned that Jacob was returning to Canaan, he headed north with 400 men. The Bible does not state why — perhaps Esau intended to kill Jacob or simply to display his power — but Jacob became extremely fearful and prayed for God's protection. Maybe he asked God to send the angels he had just seen, to guard his family.

Jacob selected over 500 animals as gifts for Esau and separated them into five herds. He sent them ahead and told servants exactly what to say to Esau as each herd passed by.

Later that night, Jacob organized his family and the rest of his livestock and helped them cross the Jabbok River at a shallow point. Having sent everyone ahead and fearful of his estranged brother, he returned alone to his camp. In the darkness, a man[6] appeared and wrestled against Jacob until dawn. Finally, the man wrenched Jacob's hip out of place and renamed him Israel, which means "he fights with God." It appears that the "man" Jacob wrestled was the pre-incarnate Jesus Christ.[7]

With the dawning of a new day, a new era in the life of Jacob began. Although he had organized his caravan into a long procession, he now rode to the front rather than hide behind, and God kept His promise of protection.

The elderly brothers reconciled, Esau returned south to his home in Seir, and Jacob built a house and corrals at Succoth east of the Jordan River. However, it would be nearly a decade before Jacob finished his journey to Hebron.

In the meantime, great sadnesses would befall.

PRIMARY PASSAGES:
Gen. 29–33

KEY VERSE:

"And He said, 'Your name shall no longer be called Jacob, but Israel; for you have struggled with God and with men, and have prevailed.'"
—Gen. 32:28

WRAP UP:

"This is such a good reminder that, where there is trust, relationships deepen. That is why our relationship with You can grow so deep. Lord, You are completely trustworthy! But trust is so easy to lose — like when Jacob thought he could trust Laban, but Laban deceptively snuck the wrong daughter into the honeymoon tent. The relationship with his son-in-law was never fully healed. Lord God, please guide me and help me to be more like You so that my family and friends can confidently trust me and see You through me."

Now alone at his camp, the fearful Jacob wrestled with an adversary who put his hip out of place, and renamed him Israel!

-14-
JOSEPH: IMPRISONED FOR GOOD

c. 1745-1635 B.C.

What man meant for evil, God meant for good!

After a tense, tearful reunion with his twin brother Esau, Jacob and his family slowly shepherded their animals to Succoth near the Jordan River. There they built corrals for the livestock, and a house.

Jacob's youngest son Joseph was about 6 and his oldest about 12. It is easy to envision his 11 boys helping and playing in the pastures,[1] together with their sister Dinah who was also about 6.

Eventually, Jacob moved further west into Canaan and purchased property. Years passed, and the children grew. Dinah had matured into a maiden of 14 or so when the prince of the area violated her purity.[2] Grieved and enraged, two of her brothers ruthlessly killed every man in his city.

Jacob was angered by their viciousness and feared revenge. God told him to go and worship at Bethel, the place where he dreamed of the stairway to heaven about 30 years earlier. He did, and eventually settled in Hebron. On the way, however, Jacob's beloved wife Rachel suddenly died while giving birth to Benjamin, and Jacob mourned.[3]

As years passed, Joseph proved himself as the most trustworthy of all Jacob's sons. He was given a colorful coat that signified his status, and his brothers were jealous. In addition, Joseph told them of dreams that seemed to say they would one day bow to him. They despised him, and things went terribly wrong when Jacob sent 17-year-old Joseph to check on his brothers while they were caring for the herds many miles away.[4]

As he arrived, his angry brothers threw Joseph into a pit and then sold him to traveling merchants. They dipped his ornate coat in blood to fool their father into believing a ferocious beast had killed him. Their deception worked, and Jacob was inconsolable in his grief.

Meanwhile, Joseph was taken to Egypt and sold to Potiphar, Pharaoh's captain of the guard.

Nevertheless, God had a purpose for Joseph's enslavement and blessed his labors, so he was placed in charge of all that Potiphar owned. The Bible describes how Potiphar's wife repeatedly tried to seduce the well-built young man. "How could I do such a wicked thing and sin against God?" Joseph told her and refused even to be with her.

Then one day when no one was around, she caught Joseph by his cloak and longingly said, "Come to bed with me!" He ran outside, fleeing the intense temptation and leaving his cloak in her hand.[5]

Though he did the right thing, Joseph was falsely accused and imprisoned.[6] But God blessed his honesty and hard work, and the warden put Joseph in charge of the other prisoners. Yet he yearned to be free. Finally, when he was 30, God gave Joseph the interpretations to two dreams that greatly troubled Pharaoh. Because of the coming famine that God revealed only to Joseph, Pharaoh put him in charge of all Egypt, and he organized a massive food storage and distribution program.

After seven years of exceptional abundance, the terrible famine began. Soon there was no grain growing anywhere except Egypt, so Joseph's brothers came south to purchase from Egypt's overflowing storehouses. However, when they arrived they were confronted by the dreaded ruler Zaphnath-Paaneah[7] whom they did not know, greatly feared, and immediately bowed down to.

The account of the incredible reunion of Joseph, his brothers, and his father that is detailed in the final chapters of Genesis bursts with intrigue. Who could have imagined that when his brothers sold him into slavery, he would one day rise to amazing power? Moreover, that they would unknowingly bow to Joseph — the exalted Zaphnath-Paaneah — to beg for food?

What his jealous brothers meant for evil, his promise-keeping God meant for good.

PRIMARY PASSAGES:

Gen. 34–45

KEY VERSE:

"Joseph said to them, 'Do not be afraid, for am I in the place of God? But as for you, you meant evil against me; but God meant it for good, in order to bring it about as it is this day, to save many people alive. Now therefore, do not be afraid; I will provide for you and your little ones.' And he comforted them and spoke kindly to them."

—Gen. 50:19–21

WRAP UP:

"Father, Your Word says that our prowling adversary, the devil, constantly aims evil against us. He wants to devour us. And sometimes we are accused and even punished for things we are not guilty of, like Joseph was. The devil wants us to forget that we constantly sin and deserve judgment. He wants us to be bitter and consumed with self-pity when circumstances seem unfair. But no one, not even the devil, can separate us from Your love, which is based in Jesus. Please help me to remember that what others intend for evil, You intend for good!"

–15–
JOB LOSES EVERYTHING

c. 1635 B.C.

Why do bad things happen to good people?

The account of Job provides an amazing window into the heavenly realm, and shows that "being good" does not ensure an easy life for God-followers.[1] It also reveals surprising details about some of the most awesome and misunderstood animals ever to inhabit earth!

As the book opens, sons of God, angels, are presenting themselves to God. So is Satan, the devil. God identifies Job as a blameless and upright man who fears Him and shuns evil. There is no one else like him on earth at the time.[2] Satan defiantly says, *It's easy to be upright when things are going well, but that Job will curse God when hard things happen.*

The devil receives permission to attack, and is ruthless. On a single day, Job's massive herds and flocks are decimated, all ten of his children die, and nearly all of his servants are slain. When he hears the crushing news, Job drops to the ground and worships! *"Jehovah gave, Jehovah has taken away. Blessed be the name of Jehovah."*

Next, Satan afflicts Job with painful, oozing sores over his entire body. His wife tells him to, *"Curse God and die."* Instead, he worships.

When three friends arrive to comfort him, Job is barely recognizable. Shocked, they sit silently in the dirt beside him for a week. Finally, Job wishes aloud he had never been born. A long, contentious exchange begins.

Night after night, month after month, Job suffers from boils, festering scabs with worms, terrifying dreams, and visions.[3] He used to be respected like a king.[4] Now, even children mock and torment him.[5]

He cries out to God, but receives no answer. All of Job's friends believe that the Lord rewards the upright and disciplines only the unrighteous. They believe Job has hidden sin. He still praises, yet he yearns to plead his case directly to God.[6]

Job is bone-thin, foul smelling, fearful, and in relentless pain.[7]

Finally, with commanding authority, God sets the record straight. Job's friends have completely misjudged both Job and God. Regardless of how things may look from the narrow perspective of humans, God is always in control!

The Lord declares that He created and sustains everything, including the magnificent universe, the deep-frozen waters, the sudden lightning, and the water-laden clouds.[8] He is not accountable to man.

Remarkably, almost a third of God's thunderous reply[9] focuses on two monstrous creatures, one of land and one of sea.[10] The land-dwelling beast is Behemoth, and the sea creature is Leviathan. Both were apparently living at the time of Job.[11]

In Job 40, God describes Behemoth as massive with huge strong legs and a tail that moved like a cedar tree. The beast could be found lounging in marshlands as well as on dry land.[12] Modern researchers liken the description to one of the extremely large sauropod dinosaurs, such as *Diplodocus* and *Dreadnoughtus*.[13]

God then describes a long, twisting, fire-breathing creature called Leviathan, which ruled the sea and had exceptionally solid body armor.[14] God emphasized His power and authority by pointing to His immense, multifaceted creation.

We live in a fallen world filled with pain and suffering that started in Eden, when Adam sinned. Since then, all have sinned, and God owes us nothing.[15] Yet the Creator promised to send a Redeemer, and Job was anxious for his arrival.[16] Until then we are to trust God, as Job did, even during painful suffering.

Life is not about us. It is about trusting, respecting, and worshiping the Creator and Savior, Jesus Christ.

In the end, God told Job to pray for his errant friends, then restored him and doubled his wealth. He even gave Job 10 more children, and 140 more years.[17] Job stayed true to God, and finished well!

PRIMARY PASSAGES:

Job (the entire book)

KEY VERSE:

"Who has first given to me, that I should repay him? Whatever is under the whole heaven is mine."
—Job 41:11 (ESV)

WRAP UP:

"Lord, it seems that You gave us this record of Satan's attacks on righteous Job to show that You are always in control. Always! I can almost feel Your thundering voice when You reminded Job and his friends that You created everything, including the countless stars, and animals that were so massive we still call them "monster" size just based on their immense fossils. You send the lightning, and You determine the paths of the clouds. Father, please help me to be more like Job. I want to trust and praise You, even in the hardest days of life."

Job worshiped God after losing almost everything precious to him; even after months of constant pain.

In the frightening miracle of the burning bush, God told Moses to get ready to bring the Israelites out of Egypt!

-16-
MOSES: THE RUNAWAY PRINCE

c. 1571–1491 B.C.

From birth to the burning bush

Three generations after the terrible famine that forced Jacob-Israel's family of 70 to move to Egypt, his descendants had greatly multiplied. They were called Israelites by God, and Hebrews by the Egyptians. A new Pharaoh feared their great number, so he enslaved them and worked them ruthlessly, yet they increased and spread out even more.[1]

Finally, Pharaoh commanded that all newborn Hebrew sons be thrown into the river. But one of the women who had a boy hid him. After three months when she could not hide him any longer, she waterproofed a basket and placed him in it, among the reeds at the bank of the Nile.[2]

When Pharaoh's daughter came to the river, she discovered the baby. He was crying, and she had compassion on him. To save him she paid his Hebrew mother to nurse him. After a time, Pharaoh's daughter named him Moses and brought him up as her son. Adopted[3] into the royal family, he was educated in the knowledge of the Egyptians.

Decades later, when he was 40, Moses went out to watch his own people, the Israelites, at their hard labor. Though

adopted into a family of immense power and wealth that provided him with more than his birth parents ever could, he was drawn to his blood relatives.[4] When he saw an Egyptian unjustly beating an Israelite, Moses defended the Israelite by killing the Egyptian and burying him in the sand.[5]

When Pharaoh heard what Moses had done, he was furious and set out to kill him. But Moses escaped east to the land of Midian. There, at a well, the runaway prince met seven shepherdesses — sisters. He defended them against other shepherds, then watered their flocks.

Moses married one of the sisters, Zipporah, and they had two sons.[6] They raised their family there and Moses shepherded the flocks of his father-in-law, Jethro.

Four more decades passed, and Moses was now 80. Perhaps he looked forward to an easier life as his sons took more responsibility in caring for the flocks. Regardless, God's plan for Moses was altogether unexpected, and it included a completely different kind of shepherding![7]

Exodus 3 documents that, one day as he

was tending the flock in the desert near Mount Horeb, The Lord God spoke to Moses from within a bush that burned but was not consumed.

It had been 430 years since God promised Moses' great-great grandfather Abram that He would make of him a great nation.[8] And for the last two centuries, the number of Abram's descendants had exploded even as they struggled as slaves in Egypt.

Now, in the frightening miracle of the burning bush, the Lord God told Moses to get ready to bring the Israelites out of Egypt. He would lead them to the Promised Land of Canaan — a land filled with abundant resources.

First, however, God would harden Pharaoh's heart. Though Moses would perform amazing miracles, Pharaoh would refuse to let the Israelites go and terrible plagues would befall.[9]

Moses made excuses, hoping to avoid the frightening task. Nevertheless, God taught him exactly what to say, gave him power to do miracles, and sent his older brother Aaron to go with him and speak for him.

Finally, Moses submitted to the Lord. The outlaw prince and his wife and sons began the trek from the comforts of their desert refuge to God's impending judgments on Egypt.

Forty years earlier the adopted Israelite gave up his royal status in the family of Pharaoh when he defended a fellow Hebrew. Now he would pave the way for the future birth of Jesus in Israel.

An unexpected and unwanted journey had begun!

PRIMARY PASSAGES:

Exod. 1–4; Acts 7:17–35; Heb.11:23–27; Num. 12:3

KEY VERSE:

"By faith Moses, when he had grown up, refused to be called the son of Pharaoh's daughter, choosing rather to endure ill-treatment with the people of God than to enjoy the passing pleasures of sin, considering the reproach of Christ greater riches than the treasures of Egypt; for he was looking to the reward."
—Heb. 11:24–26 (NASB)

WRAP UP:

"Creator God, when You spoke from the burning bush, Moses made excuses to get out of the job You called him to rather than obeying You quickly. I'm slow to obey, and I don't give You all the credit that You're due. Please forgive me, change me, and use me, Lord, as You did Moses! When You assign me an unwanted task, please change my attitude and remind me that You are always in control."

TEN TERRIBLE PLAGUES DEVASTATE EGYPT

c. 1491 B.C.

The runaway prince confronts Pharaoh.

Though Moses set out from Midian with his wife and sons at his side, he eventually sent them back to his father-in-law, Jethro, possibly for their safety.[1] Continuing on, the former prince could not know how historic his obedience and faith during the coming weeks would prove to be.

When Moses arrived in Egypt, the nation known for its massive pyramids and other man-made marvels was the greatest superpower on earth. Yet within only about a month, Egypt would resemble a nuclear wasteland.[2] Every field would be ravaged, its lakes and streams poisoned and undrinkable, livestock dead and bloated, all crops burnt or withered, every tree laid bare, and shallow mass graves throughout the land. Every family would be devastated.[3]

After meeting with Israelite elders to prove God sent him, 80-year-old Moses and his 83-year-old brother Aaron repeatedly confronted Pharaoh. They did exactly as God instructed.

But Pharaoh became extremely angry when Moses claimed that the Lord demanded that he release the Israelite slaves. "Who is The Lord? . . . I do not know the Lord, and I will not let Israel go!"[4] In addition, God hardened Pharaoh's heart so that no matter how devastating each plague against the Egyptians was, none broke his will. None, that is, until the terrible final plague.

In the first plague, at God's instruction Moses told Aaron to raise his staff and strike the Nile River, which the Egyptians worshiped. All the water, even in the lakes and wooden buckets, became blood. The fish died and the stench was overwhelming. To drink, the Egyptians had to dig.

Seven days later, the second plague brought countless frogs, which covered the ground everywhere. The slimy, croaking creatures even went up into the palace and the houses, kitchens, and bedrooms. Still Pharaoh would not let the people go.

Third, Aaron struck the dirt with his staff and lice crawled forth on man and beast.

In the fourth plague, dense swarms of flies were in Pharaoh's palace and everywhere in Egypt except Goshen, where the Israelites lived.

Fifth, God sent a severe disease upon the Egyptians' cattle, camels, donkeys, oxen, sheep, and horses. All the countless livestock that were in the fields died.

To unleash God's sixth miraculous plague, Moses threw ashes into the air. Boils and sores burst forth on all the Egyptians. Still, Pharaoh refused to let the people go. So God's seventh plague came — horrifying hail with thunder, rain, and fire. The Book of Exodus says that Egypt was ruined[5] because heavy hail beat down everything in the fields, even stripping every tree.

Next, like scavengers from the sky a strong wind delivered locusts, the eighth plague. An exceedingly dense swarm descended and covered the whole land. Within hours, they completely devoured anything green that remained.[6]

The ninth miraculous plague was darkness so black that it could be felt. No Egyptian could see anyone else or leave his home for three days, yet God's people had light where they lived.

Finally, the terrible tenth plague brought death to all the firstborn males and remaining cattle in Egypt. Even the son of Pharaoh died that night. The Lord passed over the homes of all the Israelites who sacrificed a lamb and put its blood on their doorframe, but the heart-wrenching cries of inconsolable Egyptian families filled the nation.[7] This was the first Passover.

About 1,500 years later, the blood of another lamb dripped from wooden beams as Jesus Christ, the sinless and only begotten Son of God, gave His life on Calvary's Cross. His blood paid man's sin-debt and made eternal reconciliation with the Creator possible.[8]

PRIMARY PASSAGES:

Exod. 4:18–12:36

KEY VERSE:

"I am the Lord your God, who brought you out of the land of Egypt, out of the house of bondage. You shall have no other gods before Me." Exod. 20:2–3

WRAP UP:

"Lord, the Passover deaths came like lightning at midnight throughout Egypt. Like the nine plagues that came before, they left the empire in shambles and its citizens in emotional ruin. The death of Pharaoh's own son finally broke his will and he agreed to let the Hebrew slaves go! If he had submitted sooner his country could have continued to thrive. Disobeying You only leads to destruction and heartache. Please remind me of that whenever I begin acting like Pharaoh. Please change my heart before its hardness brings ruin to my life and hurts my family."

Within weeks God's
ten terrible plagues were
complete, and Egypt resembled
a nuclear wasteland.

When Moses stretched out his hand and lifted the rod, the Red Sea parted and incredible glistening walls of water rose high on each side!

-18-
THE EXODUS: CROSSING THE RED SEA

c. 1491 B.C.

Pharaoh's pursuit and God's glory

On the night that the tenth plague brought death to every Egyptian household, there was loud wailing throughout the nation, and Pharaoh finally relented. The survivors urged the Israelites to hurry and leave the country.

Exodus reveals that the myriad descendants of Jacob-Israel — who toiled as slaves for hundreds of years — were suddenly freed and given gold, silver, and clothing. They were excited and departed quickly, lest Pharaoh again change his mind. They even packed their bread dough without yeast, because there was no time for it to rise.

The mass of humans, wagons, and animals carried what possessions they had been able to gather.[1] They moved out with boldness, and within days entered the wilderness near the Red Sea.[2]

The angel of God and a pillar of cloud led the multitude by day, while the angel and a column of fire led them at night. God's presence was obvious, yet Pharaoh again changed his mind. He set out with his army, including hundreds upon hundreds of his best chariots and officers. A week or two[3] after leaving Goshen, the Israelites were encamped by the sea, and Pharaoh's soldiers could be seen closing in. The people were terrified and said to Moses, "Is it because there are no graves in Egypt that you have taken us away to die in the wilderness?" But God told Moses to assure them that He would do the fighting. All that the Israelites had to do was to be still. Then Moses said, "The Egyptians you see today you will never see again."[4]

That night the angel of God and the pillar moved from in front of the former slaves to behind them. Its fire was light for the fearful Israelite families, and its back was a shroud of darkness in front of the boastful pursuers.[5]

As the chariots advanced with the best of Egypt's officers and charioteers, the hooves of powerful, snorting horses pounded the ground. But God held them back and with a strong wind made the deep water spread apart. It congealed into two walls and the sea's floor became dry.[6] What an amazing sight the sudden creation of this miraculous path must have been! Though the Bible does not reveal the exact crossing point of their phenomenal nighttime escape through the Red Sea, it was likely miles from shore to shore, with incredible glistening walls of water rising as much as one hundred feet or more on each side!

In Exodus 14, the Bible reveals that as the sun's rays broke over the eastern horizon, the arrogant Pharaoh and his bloodthirsty charioteers and horsemen rushed into the sea basin between the walls of water.[7] However, when they reached its midst, God broke the wheels of the chariots and told Moses to raise his staff and release the watery walls.

With a strong wind, God hurled the remaining soldiers into the sea and they sank like lead as it collapsed and surged upon them. Within minutes, the Pharaoh and his terrified army were swallowed up and drowned in the depths of a saltwater grave.

At daybreak, for the Israelites who stood on the eastern shore, the dark threat of slavery in Egypt was finally washed away. The light of God's promise to Abraham 430 years earlier glistened like the water that powerfully sealed their freedom.

The throng who was promised a land they had never seen, and who had never been outside Egypt, now joined in exuberant praise and celebration.[8]

Then, continuing their journey, they would soon hear from God Himself at the mountain of the burning bush!

PRIMARY PASSAGES:

Exod. 12–15; Isa. 51:10; Ps. 78:13

KEY VERSE:

"Then Moses stretched out his hand over the sea; and the Lord caused the sea to go back by a strong east wind all that night, and made the sea into dry land, and the waters were divided. So the children of Israel went into the midst of the sea on dry ground, and the waters were a wall to them on their right hand and on their left. And the Egyptians pursued and went after them into the midst of the sea, all Pharaoh's horses, his chariots, and his horsemen." —Exod. 14:21–23

WRAP UP:

"Heavenly Father, when all hope was gone and their murderous enemy was upon them, You made a way for the myriad Israelite men, women, and children to escape an impossible situation. By Your nighttime fire, they rushed between two towering walls of seawater. And hours later, when the last Israelite set foot on shore, You released the suffocating ocean on the warriors thundering across the seabed. With their Egyptian pursuers drowned and a new day dawning, Your people celebrated and sang praise to You. Lord, help me to trust Your plan and never to forget Your mighty power!"

-19-
TEN COMMANDMENTS AND A GOLDEN CALF

c. 1491 B.C.

For over two hundred years, the Israelites were slaves to Egyptian taskmasters. Now free, it was easy to forget what God had done!

Six weeks after escaping from Egypt, the throng of Israelites began to fear starvation, and their need for food had not taken God by surprise. In addition to the cloud by which He led them, God began to miraculously supply manna, an amazing food that could be prepared many ways.[1]

Now with ongoing sustenance, their journey continued. After another six weeks, the throng arrived at Mount Sinai, the same mountain called Horeb where God spoke to Moses from the burning bush only about four months earlier.[2]

Before Moses climbed the mountain to receive the Ten Commandments, the Lord told him to first remind the Israelites how He freed them from the Egyptians. They were to consecrate themselves and wash their clothes in preparation for hearing from God.[3]

Exodus 19 and 20 tell that after two days, God gave a terrifying display and reminder of His power. First, a dark cloud enveloped the top of the mountain. Terrifying thunder and lightning were followed by extremely loud trumpet blasts. Then thick smoke covered Mount Sinai from top to bottom, and a great earthquake struck. The people trembled with fear. When invisible trumpets blasted long and became louder and louder, Moses called out and God answered him by voice. God spoke the Ten Commandments to all the people that day.[4]

When Moses finally climbed the mountain to receive the written Commandments, he was gone for nearly six weeks, and he fasted the entire time — not eating or drinking anything.[5]

God engraved the two stone tablets with his own finger.[6] They include: have no other gods but God, never worship an idol, never use God's name as a curse word or in silly banter, set apart a day every week to God and rest on that day as the Lord did when He created everything in six days and rested on the seventh, honor your parents, never murder, never commit adultery, never steal, never lie, and be content with what you have.[7]

We have disobeyed God's commands many times. This is called sin.

Before Moses came down the mountain, the Israelites convinced his brother

Aaron to make an idol, which he fashioned to look like a calf.

When Moses returned, the people were dancing and decadently worshiping the idol. They had promised that they would honor and obey God[8] so he could hardly believe what he was seeing. In extreme anger, he threw the tablets and they shattered. When he confronted his brother, Aaron replied with a ridiculous excuse, "When I tossed their gold into the fire, out came the calf!"

Then Moses commanded, "Whoever is on the Lord's side, come to me!" He told them to immediately go throughout the huge camp and execute God's judgment by sword. Within hours, 3,000 were killed.[9] Surely the drunken revelry abruptly changed to shrieks of horror as relatives and friends died.

Moses ground the idol to powder, spread it on the water, and made the Israelites drink it. He fell face down on the ground and began another 40-day fast, this time to plead with God to spare Aaron and the Israelites. Eventually God called him back up Mount Sinai, and again God wrote the Ten Commandments with his own finger. However, this time Moses placed the two tablets in a wooden cabinet known as an ark. They were later moved to the gold inlaid Ark of the Covenant.

God gave the Ten Commandments as an ongoing reminder of our sin. No one is perfect, so it is impossible to "deserve" to go to heaven. Our sin separates us from God, and only Jesus can save us from the penalty we so clearly deserve.

PRIMARY PASSAGES:
Exod. 16, 19, 20, 32

KEY VERSE:

"Then the Lord came down upon Mount Sinai, on the top of the mountain. And the Lord called Moses to the top of the mountain, and Moses went up."
—Exod. 19:20

WRAP UP:

"Jehovah God, You shook the earth and filled the air with dark smoke, supernatural lightning, deafening thunder, and loud trumpets. How can it be that even after You spoke audibly to the throng surrounding Mount Sinai and the Israelite leaders pledged their faithfulness, they were unfaithful? Though You disciplined them, You did not abandon them. You alone are faithful! Then, as now, You gave Your people Your written word. Thank You for the Bible that reveals where we came from, where we went wrong, and how we can be saved from the penalty of our sin!"

The Israelites were dancing and decadently worshipping an idol. In extreme anger, Moses threw the tablets and they shattered.

The Israelites set up the Tabernacle and encamped for years at some places. They moved only when God's pillar of cloud and fire moved.

–20–
FORTY YEARS IN THE WILDERNESS

c. 1491–1451 B.C.

Hard lessons on the way to the Promised Land

Barely 300 miles — a few weeks walk — separated the Nile River in Egypt, from the Jordan River near Jericho. Yet it took Moses' caravan of hesitant followers 40 years to complete the journey. During this period, the former slaves learned much about God's holiness, and their own faithlessness.

After Moses received the Ten Commandments at Mt. Sinai, the myriad Israelites encamped in the desert for nearly a year[1] while craftsmen fashioned the Tent of Meeting and its sacred contents. They also prepared holy anointing oil and incense and made silver trumpets to signal the people.

When it was finally erected, Moses dedicated the holy Tent to the Lord. Then God's cloud descended and His presence filled the place. When the cloud lifted, the people set out with the sacred Ark of the Covenant carried before them. Overlaid with pure gold, the Ark contained the two stone tablets on which God inscribed the Ten Commandments, and on top it had two solid gold cherubim with outstretched wings. Whenever they traveled, the Ark was covered by heavy fabric, animal skins, and a blue cloth.[2]

After leaving Sinai, the throng encamped two more times before reaching Kadesh. On the way, people who were not grateful for the miraculous daily manna grumbled for meat, which enraged the Lord. He sent more quail than they could possibly consume, and when the complainers ate it, they died from an incurable plague.

Nevertheless, the grumbling did not stop. When Miriam complained against God's special servant — her youngest brother, Moses — the Lord struck her with leprosy for a week.[3]

In the middle of their second year, 12 Israelite spies were sent from Kadesh deep into the Promised Land to learn what lay ahead.[4] After 40 days, they returned and 10 of the 12 gave a bad report. Although the land was amazingly fruitful, there were extremely strong and massive people there. Only Joshua and Caleb trusted that God would overcome the giants. The others grumbled, spread fear, and began a mutiny. Enraged, God killed the 10 faithless spies and decreed that the Israelites would be in the wilderness 40 years. Those 20 or older would perish before entering the Promised Land.[5]

Soon after, when a frustrated leader named Korah and two others led a rebellion,[6] the Creator split open His earth. It swallowed alive all three men and their families, then closed over them. Fire consumed 250 other leaders who also rebelled, and everyone near ran in terror. Even so, the very next day all the Israelites began to rebel, so God sent another judgment, and within minutes nearly 15,000 died.

The Bible records fewer than 20 times that the assembly broke camp in the 38 years after the spies' bad report.[7] Clearly, the Israelites were not constantly on the move, and they did not roam aimlessly. They encamped, set up the Tabernacle, and waited for years at some places, moving only when God directed. It was during their wilderness existence that Moses wrote down the books of Genesis, Exodus, Leviticus, Numbers, and Deuteronomy.

God provided the people manna and water,[8] and did not allow their clothes or sandals to wear out.[9] As four decades passed, the rebellious generation eventually died.

In the 39th year,[10] the new generation of Israelites was in the wilderness near Kadesh, like the previous generation decades before. God directed Moses to speak to a solid rock to bring forth water. Instead, he struck it, and did not give God the glory.[11]

God still made water miraculously surge forth, but here, only a short distance from the Promised Land, His beloved prophet Moses learned that he too would die and not enter in.

PRIMARY PASSAGES:

Exod.; Num. 10–15 and 20; Ps. 90

KEY VERSE:

"You gave them bread from heaven for their hunger, And brought them water out of the rock for their thirst, And told them to go in to possess the land Which You had sworn to give them." —Neh. 9:15

WRAP UP:

"During their 40 years in the wilderness, You constantly reminded the Israelite families — with a pillar of cloud by day, a pillar of fire by night, and sweet manna from heaven — that You were their protector and provider. Even so, many did not have faith that You could protect them and defeat the 'giants' of the Promised Land. Lord, I don't want to miss out on the good things You want to give me. Please help me to please and honor You, and never to assume that my challenges are too big for You to solve!"

–21–
GREEDY BALAAM
AND HIS TALKING
DONKEY

c. 1452 B.C.

God knows what
you are thinking!

Nearly all of the original, rebellious generation had passed away in the decades since the bad report of the ten Israelite spies. After many years in only a few places, God moved the new generation methodically toward the Promised Land, and Moses led them in defeating scores of fortified cities plus many settlements. They even destroyed the army of King Og, a man-giant whose iron bed was over 13 feet long.[1]

Now encamped in Moab only a few miles across the Jordan River from Jericho, there were many thousands of tents and other shelters, and God's cloud and fire remained over the Tabernacle for months.

The Israelites great number, and undoubtedly their reputation in warfare terrified the Moabite king. Therefore, he devised a plan. If he could get someone to curse the horde, it might then be possible to overpower them in battle. Urgently, the king sent royal messengers to Balaam,[2] a false prophet known for his curses. The king of Moab was willing to pay Balaam whatever he wanted if he would direct a great evil upon the Israelites.

Balaam refused. Surprised, the king sent an even more impressive group of royal messengers.

God came to Balaam at night and told him to go, but to say only what God would tell him. Balaam saddled his donkey and together with the royal Moabite messengers and two servants of his own, set out for the king.

However, Balaam loved money more than God.[3] To him a curse was a commodity, like grain or produce that he could sell to satisfy his self-interests. Like most people, he apparently did not truly believe that one day he would stand before God and be sent either to heaven, or to eternal torment with the devil in hell. Evidently, as he rode on his donkey, Balaam thought more and more about the riches the king of Moab had offered. Somewhere along the way, he decided in his heart to disobey God and curse the Israelites.

But God knew what Balaam was thinking[4] and became very angry. He sent an angel to oppose Balaam. As Balaam rode along, the angel of the Lord stood in his path with his sword drawn. The donkey saw the danger and turned into a field. But God did not reveal the angel to Balaam and he beat the animal to get her back on the road.

Soon the angel appeared again, this time on a narrow part of the path with walls on both sides. The donkey pressed close to the wall, crushing Balaam's foot. Embarrassed, infuriated, and still unable to see the angel himself, Balaam beat her again.

Farther along, the angel stood in front of the donkey in a place where the animal had nowhere to go, so she lay down under him. Balaam was so furious that he struck the animal with his sturdy walking staff.

Then the Lord made the donkey talk in a human voice,[5] but Balaam was apparently so angry that he did not recognize its sudden ability to speak as strange. The donkey said, "What have I done to you? Why do you keep beating me? You have ridden on me for years! Have I ever acted this way before?" Balaam replied that he was so angry that, if he had a sword, he would have killed her.

At that moment, The Lord opened Balaam's eyes and he saw the angel, holding a sword!

Realizing that God sent the angel and that it was by God that the donkey

spoke, he bowed to the ground before the angel. Balaam agreed to speak only what God told him to and continued on.[6]

PRIMARY PASSAGES:

Num. 22–24, 31:8; Deut. 23:3–6; 2 Pet. 2:15–16; Rev. 2:14

KEY VERSE:

"Forsaking the right way, they have gone astray. They have followed the way of Balaam, the son of Beor, who loved gain from wrongdoing, but was rebuked for his own transgression; a speechless donkey spoke with human voice and restrained the prophet's madness."
—2 Pet. 2:15–16 (ESV)

WRAP UP:

"Father in Heaven, You knew Balaam's plan had changed. You knew Balaam intended to curse the Israelites that Moses was leading, and You sent an angel to stop him. But You allowed the animal, not the human, to see that immortal messenger. You used Balaam's faithful donkey to reveal his evil heart and Your great mercy. Lord, You know the intents of my heart, and You can read my mind. You can send angels to help guide me in the path of righteousness. I'm a sinner like Balaam, Lord, and I need You. Thank You for Your grace!"

The Lord made Balaam's donkey talk in a human voice, but the sinful prophet fumed with anger and wanted to kill her!

Trumpets blasted, 40,000 warriors shouted, and God broke the towering walls of Jericho. Only Rahab and her family were spared.

–22–
THE MYSTERY OF THE WALLS OF JERICHO

c. 1451 B.C.

The power of obedience

Moses was 120 years old and still strong when his appointed days on earth[1] were complete. This man, who led the Israelite slaves out of Egypt and received the Ten Commandments from God on Mt. Sinai, now told the new generation of the Creator's commands one last time.[2] Soon after, he climbed Mount Nebo east of the Jordan River and the Lord allowed him to see but not enter the Promised Land.[3] Then, Moses breathed his last.

After the appointed 30 days of mourning for Moses — and the confrontation between Satan and Michael the archangel for his body[4] — his successor Joshua told the Israelites to prepare to cross the Jordan. They would enter the Promised Land in just three days!

Joshua also sent two spies to Jericho, where they found protection in the house of Rahab, a harlot. She hid them on her roof, then helped them escape by lowering a rope through a window in her home, which was part of the city wall.

The spies reported to Joshua that the people of Jericho were dreadfully afraid. Archaeologists have discovered that this "city of palms" had stocks of grain, an underground spring, and two thick walls, which towered over 40 feet in the air and completely encompassed the nine-acre city.[5] Though panicked by the Israelites' horrifying reputation for conquest, the wicked Canaanites[6] must have desperately prayed to their man-made gods that their walls would protect them. With perhaps thousands of people and livestock inside, they secured the gates and waited.

Meanwhile, about five miles east, the Israelites broke camp. Mothers likely felt both joy and fear for their children when Joshua delivered God's command to go to the flooding Jordan River and cross. All their lives, Israelite families had looked forward to when they would enter the Promised Land. That day had arrived!

Carefully keeping more than half a mile separation from the sacred Ark of the Covenant, the people watched 12 priests carry it to the Jordan's edge.[7] When the priests' feet touched the water, the river miraculously stopped. They went to the midst of the dry channel and held the Ark while the people crossed.[8] After all had passed, one man from each of the 12 ancestral tribes came and lifted a large stone from the riverbed. That night Joshua erected the 12 stones as a reminder for all who would come after — God parted the Jordan![9]

When the Lord told Joshua that He was about to deliver Jericho into his hands, Joshua did exactly as the Lord said. Joshua 6 documents that every morning for six days, the Ark was carried once around the city while seven priests blew rams' horn trumpets and 40,000 armed men silently marched. The people of Jericho wondered and worried.

Then on the seventh day, the 40,000 warriors and the priests rose early and carefully marched with the Ark of the Covenant seven times around the city. The first six times the trumpets sounded, but the walls stood firm. Suddenly in a miraculous display of God's power at the end of their seventh time around — when the trumpets gave a long blast and Joshua commanded the people to shout — God broke the towering walls, and they crashed to the ground![10] All the men encircling Jericho immediately charged up over the rubble of the fallen walls. They burned the buildings and killed every living thing, except Rahab and her family.

Rahab was spared because she had faith in God and tied a scarlet cord in her window, as the spies directed. As a result, she is listed in the line of both King David and Jesus.

We too can be spared from the eternal judgment we deserve, but only if we repent and receive in faith Jesus' gift of salvation.

PRIMARY PASSAGES:

Deut. 34; Josh. 1-6; Heb. 11:30

KEY VERSE:

"And Joshua spared Rahab the harlot, her father's household, and all that she had . . . because she hid the messengers whom Joshua sent to spy out Jericho." —Josh. 6:25

WRAP UP:

"Seven days of pent-up anticipation must have driven adrenaline into the blood of the 40,000 Israelite soldiers that morning. With the blast of the ram-horn trumpets and the deafening victory shout of those euphoric, battle-ready men, You supernaturally shattered the high walls of Jericho into nothing more than falling bricks and rising dust. That ear-splitting cry was immediately followed by the clamor of the soldiers who ran up over the bricks and into the exposed city, where every human and animal was slain — all except the woman Rahab and her family. Lord help me to always seek to be on Your side!"

-23-
DEBORAH AND BARAK; THE PROPHETESS & THE WARRIOR

c. 1285 B.C.

Deborah was a prophetess, counselor, and judge who used her gifts to honor God and help bring freedom to the Hebrew people.

In about 1285 B.C., the region we now know as Israel was home to 12 loosely connected tribes, named after the sons of the patriarch Jacob. It was a land of abundant resources, "flowing with milk and honey"[1] and given by God to Jacob-Israel's descendants after they were delivered from slavery in Egypt.

Yet the land was also occupied by Canaanites and other ruthless idol-worshipers who settled there in the centuries following the dispersion at the Tower of Babel. Just over 200 years had passed since the Israelites were rescued from Egypt. Nearly 200 years in the future, Saul would be anointed as Israel's first king. However, until then, a series of warrior-judges would be empowered by God to slowly force the idol worshipers out of the land.

Deborah was a mother who lived with her husband Lappidoth near Bethel, about 20 miles from Jebus, later called Jerusalem. Her love for the Israelite families, her accuracy in communicating God's words, and her wisdom reflect that she was highly regarded at a time when Israel was deteriorating spiritually. People came seeking guidance and judgments from Deborah, often meeting with her under a palm tree that was apparently very near her home, since the Bible says that she dwelled there.[2]

The northern tribes of Israel had done evil in the sight of God and were suffering harsh oppression as a result. They cried out to the Lord for help. God called the warrior Barak to stand against the king of Canaan, but Barak had not yet obeyed. Perhaps he felt that it was impossible to win against the enemy's multitude of warriors and iron chariots;[3] we do not know. But God gave Deborah a message for Barak. She sent word roughly 75 miles and told Barak that he needed to meet with her. When he arrived, Deborah showed that she spoke on God's authority, not her own, when she asked, "Hasn't the Lord commanded you . . ." to take 10,000 of your troops and fight the Canaanite general and his 900 chariots, at the River Kishon? And hasn't He promised to give you victory?

Ten thousand troops probably seemed a small number against the Canaanites and their high-tech war machines — iron chariots.

Barak obviously lacked faith at that time

and said he would only go if Deborah accompanied him. She was respectful of God's "creation order principle" of male leadership[4] and prophesied that if she went along, the glory would go to a woman. But he felt that Deborah's presence was essential, perhaps to bolster his troops' morale by assuring them that God really was with them. She responded "yes" and accompanied him.

The multitude of extremely well-armed Canaanites was truly formidable. Humanly speaking, the Israelites should not have been victorious. In the end, Deborah watched and probably prayed as Barak led his men into hand-to-hand battle. The supernatural acts of God in nature[5] combined with the faith, courage, and leadership of Barak during the battle itself brought deliverance to Israel.[6]

Although Deborah accompanied the army at Barak's request, she did not attempt to lead the soldiers into battle. Instead, she strongly encouraged Barak to obey God and fulfill his role.

The Bible leaves no doubt that Barak was the military leader. As a judge in the "warrior" sense of the word, vanquishing the foes of Israel, it is Barak — not Deborah — who is included in

Hebrews 11. Deborah exhorted and encouraged Barak into his proper role, Barak and his warriors killed the Canaanite army, and later that day a courageous woman named Jael killed the Canaanite general by hammering a tent stake through his head.[7]

PRIMARY PASSAGES:

Judg. 4:1–5:31

KEY VERSE:

"…let all your enemies perish, O Lord; But let those who love [You] be like the rising of the sun in its might.' And the land was undisturbed for forty years."

Judg. 5:31 (NASB)

WRAP UP:

"Thank You for women who encourage men to obey You; women of wisdom and honor. Deborah, a prophetess, was so well respected that people came from near and far for counsel and judgments. Thank You that she challenged and encouraged the army commander Barak to obey You and go into battle. Thank You for speaking truth and inspiration through Deborah when Barak was withering in fear just before the fight. She carefully spoke up, yet she did not attempt to do Barak's appointed job for him! Please help me to discern and undertake the role You have appointed, not the roles of others."

Though the enemy's army appeared invincible, Deborah exhorted Israel's commander, Barak, to lead his 10,000 men into the battle.

In the middle of the night, Gideon's 300 men blew their trumpets, yelled a great battle cry, and watched.

GIDEON'S AMAZING SHRINKING ARMY

Like men and women today, the people of ancient Israel had their spiritual highs and lows. Around 1245 B.C., they were near the bottom.

It had been two hundred years since the Israelites entered the Promised Land and witnessed the miraculous tumbling walls of Jericho. For a while, the people worshiped God, but eventually fathers stopped reminding their families of His mighty works. The peoples' reverence of the Creator faded, and God allowed their land to be overrun.

Now, the Israelites lived in extreme fear. For seven years, a throng of ruthless invaders from the deserts south and east plundered the fruitful land of promise, forcing the Israelites to abandon their farms and villages. They survived wherever they could hide, even mountain crevices and caves.

One day, a man named Gideon was secretly threshing wheat for his family.[1] An angel of the Lord appeared and told him that God was going to use him to save Israel from the brutal Midianite invaders. Gideon wondered how this could be, since many other Israelites were stronger. But after the Lord demonstrated His power, Gideon worshiped God and showed that he would do whatever was asked of him.

So in great faith,[2] empowered by the Holy Spirit, Gideon sounded the trumpet and sent messengers throughout the region; 32,000 men came. They made camp not far from the 135,000 invading Midianites who had overtaken the fertile valley of Jezreel, near Nazareth.

Israel must have no doubt that it was God who rescued them — not their strength or skill. So the Lord told Gideon to let any soldiers who were fearful return home, and 22,000 departed. But even the 10,000 that remained were too many. God told Gideon to take them down in the valley to drink, and 300 apparently cupped water in their hands and then lapped it like a dog as they stood upright.[3] God told Gideon that with just those 300 He would defeat the Midianites.[4]

To reassure Gideon, the Lord allowed him to sneak down to the enemy camp late that night. There he heard a Midianite interpreting a comrade's dream; "Your dream means that God is with Gideon, and the Israelites are going to crush us!"

In the darkness, Gideon bowed in worship. Then he returned to his 300 men. Each was given a strange set of weapons: a ram's horn trumpet, a torch, and a clay pitcher to hide the torch. In faith, Gideon told them that God was about to give the enemy horde into their hands. He said to follow his lead and do exactly as he did.

At around three a.m., the Israelites broke into three companies around the huge encampment of Midianites and their camels. Gideon's men waited in the darkness for the signal. Suddenly, Gideon blew his trumpet, broke his clay pot, and thrust his flaming torch into the air, shouting "The sword of the Lord, and of Gideon!" Immediately the 300 did as he did.

Perhaps God made the trumpet blasts, the battle cries, and the breaking pitchers extra loud. We do not know. Regardless, the Midianite army was so terrified as they suddenly awoke that they ran in horror, 120,000 killing each other in their mass confusion while Gideon's men watched God's plan unfold.

The Israelites pursued the surviving invaders, forcing them out of the Promised Land. The jubilant Israelites exalted Gideon and pleaded with him to rule over them. However, Gideon knew that the people needed to honor and worship God, not him, so he declined their plea and returned to his home.

PRIMARY PASSAGES:

Judg. 6–8

KEY VERSE:

" 'O Lord, how shall I deliver Israel? Behold, my family is the least in Manasseh, and I am the youngest in my father's house.' But the Lord said to him, 'Surely I will be with you, and you shall defeat Midian as one man.' " —Judg. 6:15–16 (NASB)

WRAP UP:

"Lord, when You called Gideon, You called a very ordinary man; a father who was trying to feed his family while his country was being overtaken. He was a farmer, not a war hero. And Gideon was slow to take on the task You assigned. Yet You assured him of Your call, and when he finally bowed in faith that You would smite the Midianites, You proved yourself mighty! You used what appeared to be an impossible plan to vanquish an immense army in Your power, not his. Lord, help me to live in such a way that You get the glory!"

-25-
RUTH, NAOMI AND GOD'S PROTECTION

c. 1175–1165 B.C.

"Where you go, I will go, and where you stay I will stay. Your people will be my people and your God my God."

During the time when Judges ruled Israel, about 80 years before Saul was anointed as the first king, a severe famine gripped the land. Meanwhile, across the salty lake known as the Dead Sea, in the highlands of Moab, food was more plentiful. A farmer in Bethlehem named Elimelech and his wife Naomi moved to Moab with their two sons. They expected to return once the famine ended. However, while there, Elimelech died. This left Naomi alone with their sons, who eventually married Moabite women. But before their wives Ruth and Orpah became pregnant, the young husbands also died. Suddenly Naomi was a widow who faced a fearful future, because it was through family — especially sons — that God designed for women to be cared for in their old age.

When the drought finally ended, Naomi set out for Bethlehem. Ruth and Orpah started the journey with her, but soon Naomi decided that it would be better for them to stay in Moab, where the culture was familiar and they might more easily re-marry and enjoy children of their own.

However, Ruth was deeply concerned for Naomi. She lovingly refused to remain in her own homeland. She wanted Naomi's God to be her God, and committed that she would go with Naomi wherever she went, and only death would separate them. Seeing Ruth's determination, the two women continued to Bethlehem.

Ruth and Naomi were destitute; among the poorest of the poor. For food, Ruth began following harvesters, picking up any grain that was dropped. God's Law allowed this so that able poor could survive.

The owner of the field noticed the young woman. His foreman told him that this was Ruth, the Moabitess. The owner had heard of her kindness toward Naomi and told Ruth to stay close to his servants, and to drink the water and eat the food provided for his workers. After she went back to the field to continue gleaning, he told his harvesters to drop extra grain to make her task easier.

That night when Ruth returned to Naomi with more grain than expected, Naomi asked where she had gleaned. Ruth told of the kind owner named Boaz. Then, possibly for the first time since the loss of her sons, Naomi began to feel a lightening of the bitter load the Lord had allowed in her life. She happily shared that Boaz was a close relative, a kinsman redeemer; one of few men who had the right to purchase her dead husband's land, which they had to leave ten years earlier.

After more days of gleaning, Naomi told beloved Ruth she wanted to find a husband for her. She suggested that since Boaz was a good and respected man, Ruth should make herself appealing and express in the tradition of the day that she desired that Boaz consider her for his wife.

That night, Ruth did all that Naomi suggested; bathing, perfuming, and adorning herself with her best dress. Then she went to where the men were threshing. She waited. When Boaz had eaten, he went to sleep. Ruth came gently to where he was and lay down at his feet. In the middle of the night, Boaz awoke and asked who was there. Ruth revealed her name and asked him to spread the corner of his garment over her. This would be a sign that he would marry her and redeem his right to purchase the land of Naomi's husband.

Boaz blessed Ruth and honored her because she desired to be his wife when others would have gone after younger men. He shared that all Bethlehem recognized her noble character. He desired her, but there was an even closer kinsman redeemer who must first turn down his right to purchase Naomi's land and marry Ruth. Boaz assured her that he would gladly marry her if that relative turned down the opportunity.

Before sunrise, Ruth returned to Naomi. She shared all that had happened and together they waited. At the same time, Boaz went to the city gate. When the kinsman redeemer he told Ruth about came along, Boaz met with him. The nearer redeemer relinquished his right to purchase the land and take responsibility for the childless women.[1]

Boaz married Ruth, who now worshiped the one true God. She bore a son named Obed, and he became the father of Jesse, who became the father of David — who became king over Israel after Saul. It was from the line of King David that Jesus was born many years later, in the same city — Bethlehem! God blessed Naomi and Ruth by leading them to Boaz their "redeemer." God also blesses us, by leading us to our redeemer, Jesus!

PRIMARY PASSAGES:

Ruth 1–4

KEY VERSE:

"But Ruth said, 'Do not urge me to leave you or turn back from following you; for where you go, I will go, and where you lodge, I will lodge. Your people shall be my people, and your God, my God.'" —Ruth 1:16 (NASB)

WRAP UP:

"Father, it is clear that You had a plan for the care of widows. It required the obedience of Your people; the oldest son was to see that his mother was cared for in her elderly years. But today we tend to transfer our personal responsibility to government programs. Regardless of whether the necessary resources come from taxes or savings, we must give care and love to our parents. Help us to realize the special responsibility we have to the woman through whom You provided food, shelter, and guidance to us as children."

The young widow, Ruth, was destitute. For food she followed harvesters, picking up any grain that was dropped.

When the blind strong-man prayed, God granted his request and the roof of the coliseum crushed thousands of Philistines.

–26–
SAMSON — STRONGMAN IN GOD'S PLAN

c. 1155–1117 B.C.

Samson was an astonishing man of immense physical strength and extremely poor discernment.

More than 11 centuries before Christ came to earth as a baby, an angel visited a barren Jewish woman. She lived with her husband in a village near Jerusalem. The angel told her that God would soon bless her with a son. She was to name him Samson, and he must not drink wine, eat anything unclean, or allow his hair to be cut.[1] God would use Samson to continue delivering the Jews from the idol-worshiping Philistines.

As Samson grew, God blessed him. But Samson did not always do what God wanted. When he was probably about 18, he saw a Philistine girl and was so taken with her beauty that he disobeyed God's command not to marry idol-worshipers.

During their week-long wedding banquet, Samson's bride was threatened by her countrymen. They would kill her if she could not get her groom to tell the answer to a riddle he had bet 30 Philistines they could not solve. Exasperated by her crying and pleading, Samson finally told her the answer, which she in turn revealed. In great anger, Samson killed 30 other Philistines and used their belongings to settle his wager. Then he returned to his parents' home rather than to his bride.

Sometime later, Samson wanted to be with his bride, but her father was so convinced Samson hated her that he had already given her in marriage to someone else.

Furious, Samson blamed his situation on the Philistines. He caught 300 foxes, tied them together with a torch between their tails, and released them to wipe out their crops and orchards.

In retaliation, the Philistines burned to death Samson's bride and her father.

Samson repaid their evil with more evil, viciously slaughtering many and in so doing carrying out more of Jehovah's plan to loosen the enemy's grip on His chosen people. When the Jews were about to give in to the Philistines' demand that Samson be turned over for execution, God intervened and gave him extra strength, because it was not yet his appointed time to die. Samson broke the ropes that bound him, and as a throng of Philistine warriors ran at him shouting, he used the jawbone of a donkey to slay a thousand of them.

After this, Samson was even more feared and honored. For 20 years, he carried out God's judgment on Israel's oppressors. And though God continued to protect him, Samson continued to make poor decisions, especially concerning alluring females.

When he was about 38, Samson fell in love with another Philistine, a treacherous woman named Delilah. She accepted a bribe to get Samson to tell the secret of his strength, then hounded him until he revealed that if his head was shaved his strength would be gone. When he fell asleep, a man shaved off his seven braids, and the strength of the Lord left him. The Philistines then seized Samson, gouged out his eyes, and forced him to grind grain on a prison millstone.

But God was still at work, and Samson's hair began to grow again.

Judges 16 relates that one day thousands of Philistines, including all their leaders, were gathered at their pagan temple. Samson was led up from the prison so the crowd could mock him.

The blind strongman prayed one last time. He asked God to give him strength to kill the pagan Philistines in revenge for his eyes. God granted Samson's prayer and when he knocked the two central pillars off their pedestals, the roof crashed down. At least 3,000 Philistines were crushed.[2] Finally, God's plan for Samson was complete.

The death of so many Philistines that day was a major turning point in the Israelite's conflict with their archenemies. Although Samson had obvious cracks in his character, God called him to a specific role in preparing His chosen people for the future birth of Jesus.

PRIMARY PASSAGES:

Judg. 13–16; Heb. 11:32–34

KEY VERSE:

"Then Samson called to the Lord, saying, 'O Lord God, remember me, I pray! Strengthen me, I pray, just this once, O God, that I may with one blow take vengeance on the Philistines for my two eyes!' . . . Then Samson said, 'Let me die with the Philistines!' And he pushed with all his might, and the temple fell on the lords and all the people who were in it." —Judg. 16:28, 30

WRAP UP:

"Father in Heaven, thank You that You can use us in spite of ourselves! You gave Samson supernatural strength with fearsome abilities to kill, but his carnal yearnings for beautiful women led to his downfall. You made Samson the strongest man in the world, but he was spiritually weak and blind many years before he lost his eyes! Like so many men today who refuse to obey Your commands, sexual sin bound Samson and blinded him. At the end, he turned back to You and You used his imperfect faith. Lord please use me, in my imperfections, too!"

–27–
THE DESPERATE PROMISE OF A CHILDLESS WIFE

The birth and life of Samuel the boy prophet.

Eli the priest was shocked. *How dare this woman come to this place of worship, drunk!*

As he sat by the doorpost of the tabernacle at Shiloh, he could see that the woman, Hannah, was mouthing words yet saying nothing. Convinced that she had been drinking too much wine, he rebuked her. She was surprised and trembled, then said, "Sir, I am not wicked. I am praying in my heart to God because I am unable to have children."

Hannah's husband had taken two wives, which was not in keeping with God's creation plan of one man for one woman. She was barren, and the other wife had cruelly mocked and humiliated her for years. Weeping bitterly, she prayed: "God Almighty, if you will give me a son, I will dedicate him to your service for his entire life, and his hair will never be cut."

Eli saw her earnestness, blessed her, and gently sent her home. Soon, Hannah conceived and God gave her a son! She kept her promise and brought Samuel to Eli to serve the Lord after he was weaned and able to eat solid food.

Years later when he was a youth, the Lord spoke directly to Samuel.[1] One night when Eli was nearly asleep God called young Samuel. But Samuel did not recognize that the voice was that of the Lord. Running to Eli, he said "Here I am, you called me." But Eli said "I did not call, lie back down."

Soon the Lord called a second time, and Samuel again went to Eli. However, Eli said, "I did not call you, son. Go back to bed."

Then, the Lord called the boy a third time, but again he went to Eli. The Jewish historian Josephus suggests that Samuel was about 12 years old.[2] Now, Eli perceived that the Lord had called Samuel, and said, "If you hear the voice again, say, 'Speak Lord, for I am listening.' "

God did call again. He revealed to Samuel that because of the shameful sins of Eli's two adult sons, and because Eli did not restrain them, Samuel would replace him as the spiritual leader of the 12 tribes of Israel.

Sometime later the Israelites went to war against the Philistines, but 4,000 Israelites were killed. They went out again, and this time took the Ark of the Covenant. But they treated it more like a good luck charm than the sacred place where the Covenant was stored and the Lord Almighty was enthroned. Therefore, God allowed it to be captured by the Philistines, and 30,000 more Israelite soldiers were killed — 98-year-old Eli and his sons also died.

Samuel replaced Eli as God said, and he began leading Israel while still a youth.[3]

Many years passed and Samuel was a godly leader. But when he was old, the people insisted on a king, not another priest. They wanted to be led like the pagans. So God chose Saul, and Samuel anointed him.

Saul was tall, very handsome, and about 30 years old. He started out well and was humble. During his decades as king many battles were fought but, sadly, he eventually chose to lead his own way rather than carefully follow the Lord. Therefore, God sent Samuel to secretly anoint a shepherd named David as Israel's future king.

Before ascending a throne, however, about a decade would pass. Young David would confront a giant in battle and then spend years on the run from Saul, growing in his faith and his dependence upon God.

PRIMARY PASSAGES:

1 Sam. 1–16

KEY VERSE:

"Then she made a vow and said, 'O Lord of hosts, if You will indeed look on the affliction of Your maidservant and remember me, and . . . give Your maidservant a male child, then I will give him to the Lord all the days of his life, and no razor shall come upon his head.'"

—1 Sam. 1:11

WRAP UP:

"Father God, when old Eli told Samuel to listen again for Your call, he gave the youth excellent advice: 'If you hear the voice again, say, "Speak Lord, for I am listening."' Yet it was because Eli had not guided his own sons in Your ways that You woke Samuel that night and told him to get ready to take over for Eli! So often, I know Your will, but I don't do the right thing myself! You soon stopped calling on Eli, and started calling on someone who was ready and willing to obey. Help me to be ready and willing whenever You call, Lord."

Eli perceived that the Lord called Samuel, and said, "If you hear the voice again, say, 'Speak Lord, for I am listening.'"

BONUS
The Problem of Polygamy

The practice of multiple women marrying or being treated as the wife of one man, even due to extreme situations, was a clear deviation from the Creator's original Garden of Eden design. But for various reasons, including lust, the desire for children, aligning of kingdoms, and warfare that often led to sudden increases in widows and fatherless children, the acceptance of a man having multiple wives had persisted for millennia.

God's perfect one-woman-for-one-man design for marriage had apparently become optional in the minds of many, even some who genuinely feared and worshiped God.

The all-powerful Creator's intent for marriage and sexuality was established on day 6 of creation week, when He easily made one woman from one rib and joined her to one man for life.

In Genesis 2:24 the Bible says that a man shall be united to his wife (not wives) and they will become one flesh. This is monogamy, and Jesus affirmed it in Matthew 19 and Mark 10. In the New Testament era, one of the requirements for spiritual leadership within the Church is noted in 1 Timothy 3:2 and elsewhere — a man must be the husband of only one wife.

Distortions of marriage began early in history. Genesis 4 tells of a man named Lamech who was born only six generations after Adam who had two wives. This was outside of God's created order, and Lamech defied God in his sin.[1]

The biblical record makes it clear that those living in multi-spouse households often experienced significant conflict.[2] However, God did not disallow the practice. Though we do not know exactly why, it is important to remember that we live in a terribly fallen world that is only a shadow of its original design. It may be at least partially because women were otherwise more likely to be destitute and physically abused, and to become slaves or prostitutes in order to feed and shelter themselves and their children.

Clearly, God's original perfect design for marriage, where one man and one woman are joined for the remainder of their natural lives, is the only design endorsed and blessed by Jesus.

In most civilized cultures today, the basic and most fundamental needs of widows and orphans are provided by extended family, churches and through taxes upon society at large — a practice born from biblical tenets.

In faith David ran at Goliath, placed one stone in his sling, and threw it. God delivered the fatal blow!

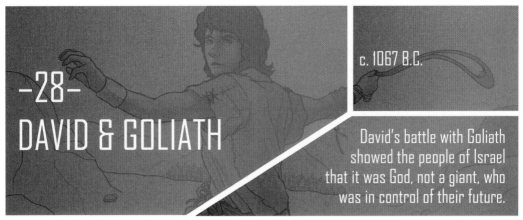

—28—
DAVID & GOLIATH

David's battle with Goliath showed the people of Israel that it was God, not a giant, who was in control of their future.

The Bible records that before ever fighting Goliath, David was a mighty man of valor, a warrior who was smart, handsome, and godly. He had already served as both a musician and an armorbearer for King Saul.

The ruddy young man was evidently about as tall as King Saul[1] and by God's power had killed both a lion and a bear without sword or spear. The courageous, youngest son of Jesse was not a skinny-armed little shepherd boy.

While his three oldest brothers were encamped with Saul and his army against the Philistines, David returned to his home near Bethlehem. There he protected and ranched his family's sheep. One day, David's elderly father sent for him and told him to go to the place of battle a few hours away to deliver roasted grain, bread, and cheeses to his brothers and their commander.

When David arrived, the taunting voice of a huge Philistine who was nearly ten feet tall boomed across the valley.

David was certain the Lord would give Israel victory, so he did not hide his dismay that Saul's soldiers were afraid to fight the giant. The king summoned

David to his tent. There David offered to fight the giant himself, confident that the God whom Goliath taunted would deliver both the giant and the Philistine army into the hands of the Israelites.

After Saul reminded David that he was young and inexperienced, at least compared to Goliath, God softened Saul's heart.[2] The king offered his armor, but David turned it down and expressed his confidence that the absence of armor or sword or spear would help the whole world to see that God gave the victory, not the tools of man.

As he walked down the hillside, David stopped at a brook and chose five smooth stones. The Israelite warriors surely worried that David would soon die and that they too would be killed or taken as slaves.

When David walked onto the battlefield, Goliath cursed boldly and declared that he would feed the young man to the birds of the air and the beasts of the field. But David declared his faith in God for all to hear, "You come against me with sword and spear and javelin. They are nothing. I come against you in the name of the Lord Almighty, whom you have defied.

Today the Lord will hand you over to me, and I'll strike you down and cut off your head. I will feed you and your idol-worshiping army to the birds of the air and the beasts of the field, and the whole world will know that God is for Israel. Everyone will know that it is not by sword or spear that I slay you. The battle is the Lord's!"

When the giant began to move toward David, the vulnerable warrior did not waver. Instead, he ran at Goliath! Then he placed one stone into the pouch of his sling, threw it, and struck Goliath so hard that it lodged into his forehead and he fell on his face to the ground.

David immediately drew Goliath's huge sword from its sheath and cut off his head.

When the stunned Philistines saw their champion collapse and David lifting the blood-dripping head, they suddenly ran for their lives. But Saul's army immediately rose up shouting in victory and chased them, killing many as the Philistines fled nearly 20 miles toward the Mediterranean coast.

Just as the Creator used an ill-equipped but willing young man to rout an entire army, so also God would one day provide an unlikely Savior for those who trust Him rather than the world's wisdom!

PRIMARY PASSAGES:

1 Sam. 16:14–17:58

KEY VERSE:

"You come to me with a sword, with a spear, and with a javelin. But I come to you in the name of the LORD of hosts, the God of the armies of Israel, whom you have defied. This day the LORD will deliver you into my hand, and I will strike you and take your head from you . . . that all the earth may know that there is a God in Israel.'"

—1 Sam. 17:45–46

WRAP UP:

"On the day that David delivered food to his brothers at the battle lines, he knew he was Israel's anointed future king. Still, Lord, it clearly took great faith for that young man to walk out on the battlefield and face a massive giant who was covered by heavy armor. Goliath held all the fearsome tools of battle. All David had was a sling and faith that he would live to become king. Goliath's rancid taunts against You disturbed David greatly. Soon, the stone You directed ended the scoffing. Please grow my faith to live boldly for You, like young David!"

JONATHAN & DAVID

c. 1067–1055 B.C.

Jonathan's unwavering commitment to God's man, and God's plan.

David walked into Israel's camp carrying the blood-dripping head of Goliath the giant. After speaking with King Saul, David was honored by the warrior Jonathan, Saul's oldest son.

Because of Jonathan's great love and respect, he made an extraordinary pledge of loyalty and protection to David, the Israelites' next king. Jonathan gave David the robe off his back plus his sword, bow, and belt. The Bible reveals that God had knit Jonathan's soul to the soul of David.[1] His commitment would be tested repeatedly in the years ahead.

As Saul's warriors were returning home from the battle, the women and dancers of the towns met the men with joyful songs, tambourines, and stringed instruments. But they sang greater praise to David than the king, and Saul burned with jealousy.

The next day[2] as David played the harp for Saul at his palace home in Gibeah, a spirit of sadness came upon Saul and he tried to spear David, but the young hero escaped.

Soon, Saul sent David to war, hoping the enemy would slay him. Yet in every battle, David had great success because the Spirit of the Lord was with him.

Eventually, Saul ordered Jonathan and others to kill David. However, Jonathan warned his friend, and then reasoned with his father, reminding him of David's faithfulness, and Saul relented.

War again broke out, but David struck the enemy with such force that they fled for their lives, and the people revered David even more. Nevertheless, when he returned, the jealous king again tried to spear him. David's wife, Michal, a daughter of Saul, truly loved David and warned him that he must run that very night for his life. She let him down to the ground through a window and he escaped to the prophet Samuel, at Ramah. In anger, King Saul annulled their marriage and gave Michal to another man.

David was forced to live as a fugitive. After a time, Jonathan was hopeful that his father no longer intended to kill David. He would check, and then reveal Saul's answer by shooting arrows into a field where David was hiding.[3] Depending on where Jonathan shot, David would know whether to run, or return. Jonathan's secret warning again saved the life of his friend, and David continued to hide.

In Saul's rebellion against God, he had many priests and their families cruelly murdered.[4] He was obsessed with killing David, yet even when David had opportunities to assassinate Saul — once in a cave while he was relieving himself, and once while he was sleeping — he would not.

Year after year, Saul promised not to slay David, yet his jealousy continually drove his pursuit of the fugitive hero.

After more than a decade, 600 fighting men and their families had banded with David. They hid from Saul deep in Philistine territory. The men raided, killed, and seized bounty from wicked Canaanite tribes, which were Philistine allies.

Finally, an ominous night arrived when the entire Philistine army assembled for battle against Israel. King Saul, who was about 70 years old, disguised himself and in a final major disobedience of God, sought out a medium, the witch of Endor. Her news could not have been worse. The next day Saul would die and the army of Israel would fall.

Within hours, Philistine archers slew Jonathan and two of his brothers in a fierce battle on Mount Gilboa. King Saul, mortally wounded, hurried his own death by falling on his sword to escape torture.

To Jonathan's dying breath, he kept his covenant pledge to protect David, and Israel's Messiah, Jesus Christ, was eventually born through David's line!

PRIMARY PASSAGES:

1 Sam. 18-31

KEY VERSE:

"Then Jonathan and David made a covenant, because [Jonathan] loved him as his own soul. And Jonathan took off the robe that was on him and gave it to David, with his armor, even to his sword and his bow and his belt." —1 Sam. 18:3–4

WRAP UP:

"Lord, King Saul started out humble, but eventually he chose to do things his way, not Yours. And that reminds me of prideful King Nebuchadnezzar who found out the hard way that it is You who establishes the leaders of nations. Some You place as presidents and prime ministers by Your direct action. Others You allow this sin-cursed world to choose, even though they may be very sinful. Please help me to long for leaders who will submit to You. And in the areas of my own life where You give me authority, please help me to lead Your way!"

David hid in a field. Depending on where Jonathan shot the arrow, David would know whether to run away or return.

David wanted the beautiful Bathsheba, but she was the wife of one of his most faithful soldiers. Even so, he refused to resist his ungodly passions.

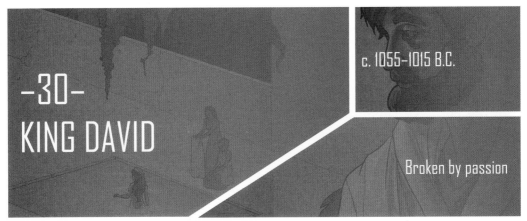

–30–
KING DAVID

Broken by passion

After years on the run, David was 30 when Israel's first king, Saul, died in battle. David was a beloved leader and ruled Judah from Hebron, while Saul's surviving son, Ishbosheth, ruled the north. But peace was elusive and there were many merciless deceptions and battles.[1]

After a long war, David became king of all 12 Israelite tribes. Now about 38, he led warriors 20 miles north to conquer the fortified city of Jebus. His invasion force entered by stealth, surprising the arrogant idolaters by climbing up through an underground water shaft. Victorious, Jebus was renamed Jerusalem and became known as the City of David when his regal palace was built there.[2]

Life had changed significantly for the former shepherd from Bethlehem who fought and killed the giant Goliath for the glory of God. By the time he was 50, David had conquered many fierce enemies. He was very rich, highly respected, and greatly feared. Jubilant because of God's favor, he even led the people in bringing the awe-inspiring Ark of the Covenant to Jerusalem.

However, one spring evening when his army was off to war and he was walking on the roof of his palace, David watched a beautiful woman bathe at her home.[3] It was Bathsheba, the wife of Uriah, one of David's elite mighty men. Though the powerful king already had numerous wives and concubines, and surely could have fulfilled his awakened passions with almost any of them, he had Uriah's wife brought to him, and she became pregnant.

The intimacy stolen by King David greatly altered his life and legacy from that night forward — a reality reflected in many of the Psalms.

As his baby grew in the womb of Uriah's wife, David tried urgently to conceal his sin. He called Uriah back from battle and encouraged him to spend a night with Bathsheba. The king even got Uriah drunk, yet the devoted soldier refused to enjoy his wife while his comrades were encamped at war.

Finally, in a desperate strategy, David sent a message back with Uriah to his commander. "Put Uriah in the front line where the fighting is fiercest. Then withdraw from him so he will be struck down and die."[4] Bathsheba's husband was killed, but God knew David's detestable secret.

The pregnant widow soon became another of David's wives. But after the baby was born, Nathan the prophet informed the king of God's severe displeasure. "Your baby will die, and God will give your wives to someone close to you to humiliate you before the eyes of all Israel."

David was broken. He repented of the sins of his adulterous passion, then fasted and pleaded for the child. Nevertheless, God took him.[5]

Though the Lord did not slay David, He sent great adversity.[6] David's virgin daughter Tamar was raped by his son Amnon. In retribution, David's son Absalom murdered Tamar's rapist, then Absalom led an insurrection and sexually assaulted ten of his father's concubine wives on the roof of David's palace.[7]

Many other sorrows beset the king, yet God gave him another son by Bathsheba. His name was both Jedidiah and Solomon.

The Bible reveals that when David became old, he went out to war but fainted and never returned to battle again. Feeble and unable to stay warm, he appointed his teenage son Solomon as his successor and died when he was 70.

Nearly a thousand years later, Jesus was born of David's line, reminding us of the undeserved second chance that God gave to this truly repentant adulterer and murderer. Today, through grace, God provides soul-saving redemption for the broken, like David.

PRIMARY PASSAGES:

2 Sam. (all); 1 Kings 1

KEY VERSE:

"Blessed is he whose transgression is forgiven, Whose sin is covered. Blessed is the man to whom the Lord does not impute iniquity, And in whose spirit there is no deceit.... You are my hiding place; You shall preserve me from trouble; You shall surround me with songs of deliverance."

—Ps. 32:1–2, 6–7

WRAP UP:

"Father, when You sent the prophet Nathan to confront King David for taking Bathsheba and killing her husband Uriah, David truly repented. However, his sin had repercussions, including tragedies in his household. First, when the child of his adultery was born, You struck the infant with sickness, and he died. Then in the years that followed there was tremendous heartache for David and his entire family. Father, I still sin, too! Please remind me often that nothing in my heart or among my actions is hidden from You."

–31–
THE WISEST MAN IN THE WORLD

c. 1016–975 B.C.

From young and wise, to old and foolish.

Solomon was born after his father David's glory years were over, and as he grew there was extreme family conflict and civil unrest.

In separate rebellions, two of Solomon's older brothers attempted to snatch the kingdom from David, and Solomon was with his parents when they were forced to flee Jerusalem. He probably felt both sorrow and relief when his mutinous brother Absalom was killed during a battle, after being caught by his head in the tangled branches of a tree.

Solomon survived three terrible days when 70,000 Israelites died in a judgment caused by his father's lack of faith.[1] This was especially sad because, as a youth with only a sling and a stone, David had unflinching faith in God's miracle-working might. Yet decades later, with a myriad of battle-ready men, he nervously counted soldiers rather than counting on God.

As David's health declined, he appointed Solomon as coregent king, and the young father was only about 19 when David died.

Now the lone ruler, Solomon felt the weight of the daunting responsibilities before him, and one night God appeared to him in a dream.[2] The Creator promised to give Solomon whatever he wanted. Yet rather than ask for riches or power, the young man requested wisdom and knowledge to govern justly.[3] This pleased God, who rewarded him far beyond his request.

As an example of Solomon's wisdom, the Bible tells of two harlots who came before him with a baby.[4] Both claimed to be the mother and accused one another of lying. It was impossible to know who was telling the truth, so the king ordered that a sword be brought and the babe divided in two. One woman was spitefully pleased with the solution, while the other begged that the child be spared and given to her adversary. At that, Solomon knew that the woman who cried for mercy was the mother.

The Book of 1 Kings says that Solomon's wisdom and understanding were exceedingly great, and dignitaries came from all nations to hear him speak.

Four years into his reign and nearly 500 years after the Exodus, Solomon began construction of a great Temple, based on detailed plans David received from the Lord.[5] Seven years later — with the labor of more than 180,000[6] quarry workers, lumbermen, carriers, mariners, carpenters, sculptors, painters, goldsmiths, and others — it was completed. The structure was majestic, with gold-covered walls and ceilings, beautiful art, and fragrant cedars from Lebanon. In the most sacred room — the cube-shaped Holy of Holies where only the high priest could go, and only on the annual Day of Atonement — the outstretched wings of two glorious golden cherubim 15 feet tall spread from wall to wall above the Ark of the Covenant.

When the Temple was complete, Solomon passionately dedicated it before a vast number of Israelites. He praised and worshiped the God of creation, whose cloud of glory suddenly and visibly filled the place.[7]

Early in Solomon's reign he loved the Lord and kept His decrees. During his life he wrote the Song of Solomon, Proverbs, and Ecclesiastes.[8]

Yet by the end of his 40-year rule, the wisest and richest king in the world had foolishly disobeyed God's commands by marrying 700 wives and taking 300 concubine lovers.[9] He worshiped their detestable deities, and they turned his heart away from the Lord. Solomon no longer worshiped only the one true God.[10] He sank from rapturous and exclusive reverence to leading the people in sacrificing to the idols of his foreign wives.

The magnificent temple designed by God and built by Solomon stood in Jerusalem for nearly 400 years. However, because of Solomon's idolatry God brought adversaries and Israel split into two warring kingdoms soon after he died.

PRIMARY PASSAGES:

1 Kings 1–11; 2 Sam. 15-24; 1 Chron. 29:21–25; 2 Chron. 1–9

KEY VERSE:

"Trust in the Lord with all your heart, And lean not on your own understanding; In all your ways acknowledge Him, And He shall direct your paths. Do not be wise in your own eyes; Fear the Lord and depart from evil."

—Prov. 3:5–7

WRAP UP:

"My Lord, the mess Solomon made of his life is mind-boggling! He ruled the most important kingdom in the entire world. You gave him more money and wisdom than anyone else on the planet. Yet he soon allowed his carnal cravings and his desire to please others more than You, to turn him from world leader to world loser. I want to please others too, Lord! Please, save me from myself; help me to want to honor and please You more than I want to look good in the eyes of the people around me."

Two harlots fought over a baby. It was impossible to know which one was the mother, so Solomon ordered that the babe be divided in two. The reaction of each woman revealed the truth.

After Elijah called on the Lord, God sent fire from above. It consumed the drenched sacrifice, even the stone altar.

-32-
ELIJAH'S FIRE FROM HEAVEN

The miracle-filled life of Israel's most-wanted fugitive!

Five years into the reign of Solomon's evil son Rehoboam, God caused the Promised Land to be broken into two kingdoms. The ten tribes north of Jerusalem were called Israel, and the two in the south were called Judah. Over the next one hundred years, numerous other kings ruled, but few worshiped the Creator.

When wicked Ahab became king of Israel, he married the Phoenician princess Jezebel. She was domineering and probably a priestess of the gods Ashtoreth and Baal.

Jezebel tried to kill off all the prophets of The Lord, but God protected Elijah. He went to King Ahab and said, "The Lord God of Israel has sent me to tell you that as surely as He lives, there shall not be dew or rain for years, except at my word." Then God sent Elijah to hide in a ravine east of the Jordan River. God provided for him by sending ravens with meat and bread twice each day, and he drank from a brook.

When it dried up, God guided Elijah to the coastal city of Zarephath. As he arrived, he asked a widow for a little water and bread. Now God had commanded her to provide for him, but

she was fearful. She had barely enough flour and oil to make a tiny meal for her son and herself and expected them to starve. Elijah assured her that if she did as he asked, her flour and oil would not run out. She obeyed, and for three years the fugitive prophet was safe in her home.

Meanwhile, Ahab aggressively hunted Elijah. He even sent search parties to other nations to capture the "trouble-maker" who pronounced the crushing drought, then disappeared.

After three and a half years, God sent Elijah back to the wicked king. Ahab was furious, yet desperate for rain. He agreed to call Jezebel's prophets of Baal and Ashtoreth and people from throughout Israel to Mount Carmel.

There Elijah outlined an impossible challenge for miraculous fire — Baal against God. All day, 450 prophets pled, prayed, danced, and even stabbed and cut themselves to get Baal to light a fire and burn their sacrifice. There was not even a spark.

Finally, toward evening Elijah stopped the exhausted, bleeding priests. He took 12 stones, built an altar to the Lord, killed a bull, and saturated both the wood and the sacrifice with 12 pots of water. Then, after calling on the Lord, fire fell and consumed the drenched sacrifice, even the stone altar. How amazing that moment must have been! The hearts of the people turned to the Lord, and they fell face down in fearful worship.

The 450 false prophets were seized, taken to the valley below, and executed.[1] Then God ended the terrible drought with a heavy rainstorm that very night.

When Ahab told Jezebel all Elijah had done, she vowed to quickly kill him. Though he had just experienced God's miraculous power, he fled over 100 miles south to Beersheba.

In the wilderness, emotionally overwhelmed, Elijah prayed to die.[2] However, God sent a ministering angel and provided food and rest. Then Elijah went 40 days to Horeb, also called Mount Sinai.[3] There, the Creator again displayed tremendous power and sent Elijah back to Israel, where he ministered for years alongside his successor, Elisha.

In time, God honored Elijah in an astounding way! As he and Elisha were walking, a fiery chariot drawn by blazing horses came down and separated them. In a whirlwind, Elijah was suddenly taken up into heaven.

Gone, but not deceased, Elijah would appear some 900 years later with Moses at the glorious Transfiguration of Jesus!

PRIMARY PASSAGES:

1 Kings 17–2 Kings 2

KEY VERSE:

"Then the fire of the Lord fell and consumed the burnt sacrifice, and the wood and the stones and the dust, and it licked up the water that was in the trench. . . . Elijah said to them, 'Seize the prophets of Baal! Do not let one of them escape!' So they seized them; and Elijah brought them down to the Brook Kishon and executed them there."

—1 Kings 18:38, 40

WRAP UP:

"Elijah was emotionally spent. You knew that, Father, and in Your mercy You sent an angel to feed and encourage him when he felt so alone and feared for his life. He witnessed Your consuming fire on Mt. Carmel and then led the execution of 450 false prophets. He even witnessed the amazing way You ended the drought that evening with a miraculous rainstorm. Yet when he heard that Queen Jezebel was coming to kill him, he forgot Your power and ran many miles in desperate fear. Father, I'm quick to forget Your power, too. Please keep reminding and encouraging me, as You did Elijah."

-33-
JONAH AND
THE GREAT FISH

The pitiless prophet

Again and again, the merchant ship broke through dark, thundering waves and plunged heavily to the bottom of each tall swell. Terrifying wind and pounding surf nearly broke the wooden vessel apart[1] as saltwater surged across the deck and poured below, drawing the craft deeper into the frothing sea.

The ship's crew cried out to their gods to save them. Desperate, they threw cargo overboard to lighten the load so that they might not die in the punishing tempest.

Meanwhile below deck, a prophet named Jonah who boarded at Israel's main port of Joppa, somehow slept through the dreadful mayhem.

God had instructed Jonah to warn the people in Assyria's capital city, Nineveh, of the impending judgment on their wickedness. However, Jonah silently refused because Assyrians were Israel's enemy — among the most viscous of ancient peoples.[2] Rather than obey God and give the Ninevites a chance to repent, he attempted to run from God and was bound for Tarshish, over two thousand miles in the opposite direction.[3] However, God knows our thoughts, so Jonah's were never hidden.

The captain woke Jonah and demanded that he cry out to his God, as well. In despair, the crew cast lots to determine who was responsible for this calamity. The lot fell to Jonah, and he revealed what the true God of heaven, earth, and sea had required of him. He told the sailors to throw him overboard to calm the storm.

At first, they pitied Jonah and rowed with all their strength for shore, but the deep Mediterranean became even more wild. Finally, they cried out for mercy from Jonah's God and then cast Jonah into the raging sea. As he sank into the watery darkness, the gale grew calm. The sailors feared Jonah's powerful God so much that they sacrificed and made vows to Him.

The Creator had prepared a great fish to swallow Jonah, and he was inside the sea creature for three days. Though the Bible does not say what kind of fish it was, Jesus taught that it was real. In fact, Jesus referenced the account as actual history when he compared Jonah's three days in the fish to the three days that He would be in the "heart of the earth" before His Resurrection.[4]

From inside the fish, Jonah earnestly

pleaded and made promises to God. At last, the creature vomited him onto dry land. God was giving the wayward prophet another chance, and this time Jonah obeyed.

Nineveh was in the region now known as Iraq, hundreds of miles east of Israel's coast. When Jonah arrived, he began proclaiming that the city would be overthrown in just 40 days.

To Jonah's great disappointment, the people repented, fasted, and put on sackcloth. Nineveh turned from evil. God relented, but Jonah was angry. He told God that he would rather die than see the Assyrians live.

To teach the pitiless prophet a lesson, God made a shade-plant grow up overnight. Jonah enjoyed its relief from the intense sun as he watched and hoped for Nineveh's destruction. But the next day God sent a worm that killed the plant.

Jonah again complained, and God exposed Jonah's lack of concern for the 120,000 people of Nineveh. Just as Nineveh did not deserve God's mercy, Jonah did not deserve God's merciful provision of the shade-plant.

God's mercy at that time to the Assyrians of Nineveh helped Jonah and all Jews to see that He is concerned about people everywhere, not just the chosen people of Israel. The amazing true account of Jonah reminds us today of the undeserved grace that God freely offers to all who repent and receive it, through the death and Resurrection of His only Son, Jesus!

PRIMARY PASSAGES:

The Book of Jonah; Matt.12:40

KEY VERSE:

"Now the Lord had prepared a great fish to swallow Jonah. And Jonah was in the belly of the fish three days and three nights." —Jon. 1:17

WRAP UP:

"It must have been terrifying to be cast into the surging sea and then swallowed by a creature so big that a man could be inside it three days yet remain whole! Lord, Your reluctant prophet Jonah didn't pray in some unemotional way. The Bible says he cried out. I would have cried too! He ran away when You told him to warn the Ninevites. He forgot that You knew both his thoughts and his location. Please keep reminding me that You know and see all. Please help me to live as You call us to, in the Bible!"

As Jonah sank into the watery darkness, the ferocious gale grew calm and the terrified sailors worshiped Jonah's powerful God.

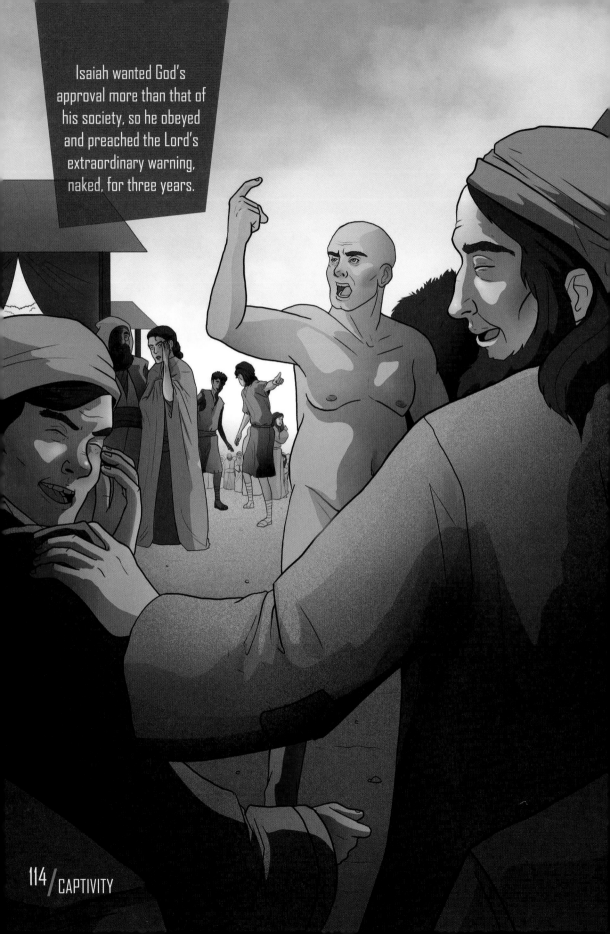

Isaiah wanted God's approval more than that of his society, so he obeyed and preached the Lord's extraordinary warning, naked, for three years.

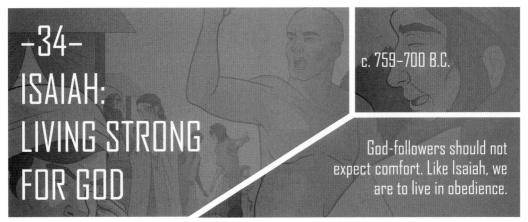

-34-
ISAIAH:
LIVING STRONG
FOR GOD

c. 759–700 B.C.

God-followers should not expect comfort. Like Isaiah, we are to live in obedience.

A book of mysteries is tucked in the middle of the Bible. Sixty-six chapters written hundreds of years before Jesus was born contain accounts of supernatural judgment, an amazingly accurate prophecy of the Messiah's virgin birth, details of Jesus' crucifixion, and much more.

Within only two centuries after the reign of King Solomon, nearly everyone had turned away from the Creator and worshiped lifeless stars and statues. As was the case with Solomon, fathers failed to live out and pass down the teachings of the Scriptures, so love for God and knowing what He has done were quickly being forgotten. Thankfully, there was a small remnant in the southern kingdom of Judah who still worshiped the Creator.

God was angry at the idolatry of His chosen people. Therefore, He called Isaiah, a husband and father in the city of Jerusalem to warn King Hezekiah to turn the nation back to God or face judgment. If they placed their trust in God rather than political alliances with other countries, they could avoid enslavement by the merciless world power, Assyria, the same enemy that

God sent Jonah to only about 50 years earlier.

Isaiah, a prophet, was genuinely concerned for Jerusalem. Though he may have been of noble birth, his mission was far from easy. At one point God directed him to remove his tunic and prophecy naked — something most people would have attempted to avoid. However, Isaiah placed his relationship with God above the respect of his society, so he obeyed and went unclothed and barefoot for three years.[1] The Lord used this as an extraordinary warning that no nation could save them from Assyria. They would have to call upon and trust the one true God.

Isaiah's willingness to minister in such an unorthodox way emphasizes the profound commitment of this man. Though only three years out of several decades, it was surely an exceptionally difficult time for him and his family.

After Assyria conquered the fortified cities throughout Judah, their massive army camped outside Jerusalem and demanded that Hezekiah surrender. Things looked bleak. In the midst of this despair, God sent Isaiah to deliver another message to the king of Judah. This time, it was good news.

Because Hezekiah had placed his trust in God rather than heathen nations, the Lord promised to save Judah from the myriad warriors who were ready to attack. The next morning, shocked men awoke to find 185,000 corpses. The angel of the Lord had silently decimated the ruthless Assyrian army, which was prepared to besiege and enslave Jerusalem.[2]

Other remarkable accounts and prophesies of future events are included. Yet because Isaiah moves repeatedly from present to future and back again, it has long been one of the more challenging portions of the Holy Scriptures. Once we understand the big picture message — that man cannot save himself, and the Messiah's sacrificial death is the only way our sins can be forgiven — the seemingly disconnected topics are joined.

For anyone who does not accept that Jesus Christ is the prophesied Messiah, much of the book remains a mystery. This includes most Jews. They do not believe that a perfect final sacrifice has been made and can save them from the penalty of their sins. Nevertheless, their debt and ours was paid-in-full when Jesus was crucified over 700 years after Isaiah foretold it! [3]

Isaiah's lifetime of warning and calling people to trust God ended around 700 B.C., about a century before the beginning of Jerusalem's 70-year captivity in Babylon. Some historians feel that he died a martyr's death. Regardless, he lived an exemplary life of death to self, for the glory of God.

PRIMARY PASSAGES:

1 Kings 11; Isa. (all)

KEY VERSE:

"Behold, God is my Salvation; I will trust and will not be afraid; for the LORD GOD is my strength and my song, and [H]e has become my salvation." —Isa. 12:2 (ESV)

WRAP UP:

"Isaiah's faith and his commitment to You humble me, Lord. Would I have been willing to remove my clothes and preach naked in front of my neighbors and my wife and children — to obey You like he did? I realize that Your purpose was to visually warn the people of Jerusalem, day after day, not to put their faith in earthly alliances. Please Lord, help me never to forget that You are the one in control, not my government leaders or others. Help me to trust in You, and to choose to obey even Your faith-stretching commands, like Isaiah did!"

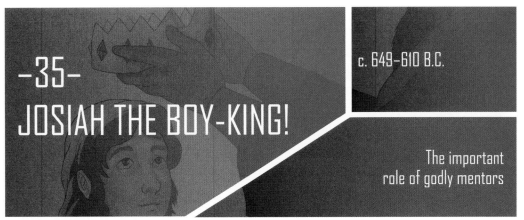

-35-
JOSIAH THE BOY-KING!

c. 649–610 B.C.

The important
role of godly mentors

Two books in the Bible tell the amazing account of Josiah, the little boy who became king in Jerusalem and did great things for God. But why would an 8-year-old, with all the power and wealth he could imagine, choose to follow and worship the Lord? The answer may have much to do with Josiah's grandfather, Manasseh.

The bloodthirsty, evil king Manasseh reigned for 55 years after the time of Hezekiah and the prophet Isaiah. For most of his life, Manasseh corrupted the holy places and set up idols throughout the land. He consulted mediums, worshiped stars, even sacrificed his own sons. He practiced sorcery, divination, and witchcraft, committing detestable sins. Manasseh led the Israelites into even more evil than the nations the Lord had destroyed before them.

Manasseh refused to heed God's warnings. Finally, the Lord caused the Assyrian army to take Manasseh prisoner. They put a ring in his nose, bound him with shackles, and took him hundreds of miles to Babylon.

There, Manasseh was greatly distressed and finally cried out to the Lord. God was moved by his plea and restored him

to his kingdom. From that time on, the repentant Manasseh did everything he could to right the horrendous wrongs of his life, yet the tentacles of his evil reign were deeply rooted throughout the land, including his own family.

When Manasseh died and his son Amon became king, Amon chose the evil, idolatrous ways of his father's earlier life. After only two years, Amon's own officials assassinated him, and young Josiah became king.

Perhaps it was 8-year-old Josiah's mother, Jedidah, or a godly government official who helped guide the boy to admire and follow the repentant ways of his grandfather rather than the idolatrous path of his father.[1]

While we know from the Scriptures that Josiah already had at least two children by the time he was 14, the Bible also reveals that by the time he was 16, he had fathered at least four children. Second Chronicles 34 reveals that it was at age 16 that Josiah began seeking God, rather than rebelling against Him.[2]

When he was 20, he began to purge the land of its many idols and altars to false gods.

At age 26, King Josiah commanded that the Temple built by Solomon be restored. During repairs, the lost book of the Law of the Lord was found.[3] When it was read to him, Josiah was shocked and frightened. He tore his clothes and wept because he realized the great gap between his efforts and God's requirements.

So Josiah assembled all Jerusalem. Standing beside the Temple, he read the book aloud[4] and committed to follow the Lord and keep His commandments. He cleaned out the Temple and all Judah, removing every vestige of idol worship, even slaying and burning pagan priests.

Then he commanded that the Passover feast described in the book be celebrated with great care, more completely than in hundreds of years. Josiah even provided 33,000 of his own animals to sacrifice for the families.

The Bible says that no king before or after Josiah turned to the Lord as he did, with all his heart and soul and might.[5] Therefore, it is surprising that at 39, his life suddenly ended. He stood against the pharaoh of Egypt at Megiddo, a fortified city north of Jerusalem, but the pharaoh claimed that God sent him to help Assyria against the Babylonians and if Josiah tried to stop him, Josiah would die. Josiah did not believe him and evidently did not seek proper counsel; he struck out against Egypt's pharaoh, who really was sent by God, and he was killed.

Josiah is an inspiring model of passion for God. From the earliest records of his life as a teen, to his actions after discovering the Book of the Law, Josiah was unwavering in his obedience. Only the Messiah, Jesus, will be a more-perfect king.

PRIMARY PASSAGES:

2 Kings 21:1–23:30; 2 Chron. 33:1–35:27

KEY VERSE:

"Josiah was eight years old when he became king, and he reigned thirty-one years in Jerusalem. His mother's name was Jedidah the daughter of Adaiah of Bozkath. And he did what was right in the sight of the Lord…" —2 Kings 22:1–2

WRAP UP:

"Lord, would I make the same mistake as Josiah? Did he fail to seek godly counsel? When the pharaoh claimed that You sent him, did Josiah think, 'He is lying! The holy scrolls we discovered in the Temple tell that when our people were enslaved by a pharaoh, God used ten plagues to bring victory over him. Surely I will win against this pharaoh, like Moses did. After all, I've done so much for God. He surely would have told me if He was going to use a pharaoh rather than me!'? Father, please remind me to seek godly counsel."

Perhaps it was 8-year-old Josiah's mother Jedidah, or a righteous government official who helped guide the boy to seek after God.

Shadrach, Meshach, and Abed-Nego worked in Nebuchadnezzar's kingdom, but they worshiped Jehovah God. They were ready to die rather than bow to the idol.

–36–
SHADRACH, MESHACH, AND ABED-NEGO

c. 607–590 B.C.

Jerusalem's exile
and Babylon's fiery furnace

Three years after the battlefield death of godly King Josiah, the Jewish people again worshiped idols — and the prophesied 70-year exile soon began.

Babylon's army set a siege and Jerusalem's king surrendered without a fight. Israelites of the royal family and nobility were captured and forced hundreds of miles to Babylon. There, the finest young men — healthy, wise, well-educated, and handsome lads trained in God's ways mainly during Josiah's reign — were educated for King Nebuchadnezzar's service. Among the young men were Daniel, Shadrach, Meshach, and Abed-Nego.[1]

One night, the tyrannical Nebuchadnezzar had a troubling dream. No one could interpret it, so in great frustration he ordered the execution of all his wise men. But God, in response to the earnest prayers of Daniel and his three friends, revealed both the dream and its interpretation. Then Nebuchadnezzar promoted all four young men to positions of honor and found them to be ten times wiser than all his other wise men.

Sometime later, perhaps 15 years or more, King Nebuchadnezzar erected a towering golden image 90 feet tall.[2] Officials throughout the kingdom were summoned to its dedication. They were commanded to bow down and worship it as soon as they heard the sound of musical instruments. If anyone refused, they would be thrown into a blazing furnace.

The instruments sounded, and all the officials who were there fell to the ground and worshiped the image — but not Shadrach, Meshach, and Abed-Nego.

Some men went to Nebuchadnezzar and reported that three of his high officials refused to worship the idol. Enraged, Nebuchadnezzar summoned Shadrach, Meshach, and Abed-Nego. He warned of the fiery doom that awaited, then gave them one last chance.

The three said, "If we are thrown into the blazing furnace, the God we serve is able to save us from it, and He will rescue us from your hand. . . . But even if He does not, we want you to know, O king, that we will not serve your gods or worship the image of gold you have set up."

Now in full fury, Nebuchadnezzar

ordered the furnace heated seven times hotter. He demanded that several of his strongest soldiers tie up the three Jews, who were still wearing their robes, trousers, turbans, and other clothes. The king's command was so urgent that the fire killed the soldiers as they threw them into the blazing furnace.

Immediately a fourth figure appeared, walking unbound with the three in the fire. Nebuchadnezzar said the fourth looked like a son of the gods and called the three men out. When they emerged from the inferno, many stunned officials who had been worshiping the golden image crowded around and saw that not a hair of their heads was singed, their clothes were not scorched, and there was no smell of fire on them!

Astonished, the most powerful king in the world[3] said, "Praise be to the God of Shadrach, Meshach and Abed-Nego, who sent his Angel and rescued his servants who trusted in Him!" Nebuchadnezzar was amazed that the three were willing to suffer a terrifying death rather than worship the image.

Perhaps they remembered living under King Josiah and were greatly inspired by his passion for God and his stand against idolatry.

Regardless, the account of Shadrach, Meshach, and Abed-Nego reminds Christians today that, although we live in the world, we too are in exile awaiting the day when we will be rescued.[4] Just as God sent the fourth figure in the furnace to rescue them from Nebuchadnezzar's wrath, He sent Jesus Christ nearly 600 years later to rescue us from the terrible fires of eternal punishment in hell.

PRIMARY PASSAGES:

Jer. 25 and 29; Dan. 1–3

KEY VERSE:

"our God whom we serve is able to deliver us from the burning fiery furnace, and He will deliver us from your hand, O king. But if not, let it be known to you, O king, that we do not serve your gods, nor will we worship the gold image which you have set up." —Dan. 3:17–18

WRAP UP:

"Father God, what was it like for these three men when they landed inside the furnace, unsinged by the blazing fire? Did they hear the death screams of the soldiers whose bodies must have burst into flames as they threw them in? Were they surprised that Your messenger was there beside them? Nebuchadnezzar was surprised! And so were many among the hundreds of officials who had been bowing to the idol. Thank You for your miraculous rescue of Shadrach, Meshach, and Abed-Nego when they obeyed Your Second Commandment by refusing to bow and worship — even outwardly — any god but You!"

-37-
NEBUCHADNEZZAR'S ANIMAL INSANITY

From tyrannical king to God-praising follower!

In the years after God saved Daniel's three friends from the fiery furnace, He allowed Nebuchadnezzar's vast realm to grow even bigger. Yet the king continued in his hard-hearted, tyrannical ways.

When Nebuchadnezzar was around 65 years old, he had a dream of an immense tree. Its leaves were beautiful, everyone in the world could see it, and it provided shelter and abundant fruit for all the creatures of earth. Then a messenger from heaven commanded that the tree be cut down. Its trunk and roots remained, but its branches were destroyed.

The mighty Nebuchadnezzar was terrified by what this dream might mean.

As with another of the king's dreams over 30 years earlier, God again enabled only Daniel, one of the Jews exiled from Jerusalem, to interpret it.

However, this time Daniel was distressed at the meaning. The king implored, "Let not the dream or the interpretation alarm you." Daniel replied, "My Lord, if only the dream applied to your enemies, and its meaning to your adversaries."

Daniel then revealed that because Nebuchadnezzar would not acknowledge that the God of heaven rules the earth and gives its kingdoms to whomever He wants, the mighty ruler would go insane and be driven away from men. He would eat grass with cattle and live in the fields among the dew-drenched beasts. He would be cut down like the great tree in his dream.

Daniel advised the king, "Break off your sins by practicing righteousness, and your iniquities by showing mercy to the oppressed, that there may perhaps be a lengthening of your prosperity." But Nebuchadnezzar refused.

For a year, nothing happened. As the months passed, it must have appeared to the prideful king that Daniel was wrong. However, God's timetable is perfect, and often different than we expect.

One day when Nebuchadnezzar was walking the roof of his royal palace, admiring his vast kingdom and praising himself aloud, a voice from heaven suddenly pronounced, "This is what is decreed for you, King Nebuchadnezzar. Your royal authority has been taken from you."

All the things Daniel had revealed would now happen.

Within minutes, the king was driven away from people. He ate grass like oxen. His skin was drenched with the dew of heaven until his hair grew thick like the feathers of an eagle, and his nails grew like the claws of a bird.[1]

It appears that seven long years passed as Nebuchadnezzar existed in the wild like an animal. Finally, the humbled king raised his eyes toward heaven and his sanity miraculously returned. He declared, "Now I, Nebuchadnezzar, praise and exalt and glorify the King of heaven. Everything he does is right and all his ways are just. And those who walk in pride he is able to humble."

Nebuchadnezzar was restored as king and became even greater than before. Like the Apostle Paul who would write of his own transformation some 600 years later, the high point in Nebuchadnezzar's life came by being brought to an all-time low. Daniel chapter 4 is the text of a letter Nebuchadnezzar sent to rulers worldwide. The transformed tyrant warned kings and princes everywhere to acknowledge that God chooses and empowers the rulers of the world, not the leaders or their mighty armies.

Even by the record of Nebuchadnezzar's wilderness years, when he was made insane and believed he was an animal, it is obvious that salvation is by grace. The powerful king did not deserve God's mercy, but his life and heart were transformed when he repented of his pride and acknowledged God's sovereign authority. Then, through Nebuchadnezzar's transformation, God's name was glorified among the nations.

PRIMARY PASSAGES:

Dan. 4

KEY VERSE:

"Now I, Nebuchadnezzar, praise and exalt and glorify the King of heaven because everything He does is right and all His ways are just. And those who walk in pride He is able to humble." —Dan. 4:37 (NIV)

WRAP UP:

"The mighty King Nebuchadnezzar of Babylon was extremely proud, cruel, and unteachable. You sent humble Daniel to warn him to repent, show mercy, and live righteously. Nebuchadnezzar obviously didn't think You could take him down, but You did. You took him all the way down to his knees, and on the wet ground he ate what cows eat. He lost his ability to reason, and his prestige. You showed him, and the whole world, that You oppose the proud. Then when Nebuchadnezzar finally repented, You showed grace. Lord, help me to never think of myself more highly than I should."

Within minutes the proud king was driven away. He existed like a wild beast until he truly understood that it is God who is in control — not the rulers or their armies.

God sent his angel to shut the mouths of the ravenous lions. They did not hurt Daniel because he was innocent and trusted God fully.

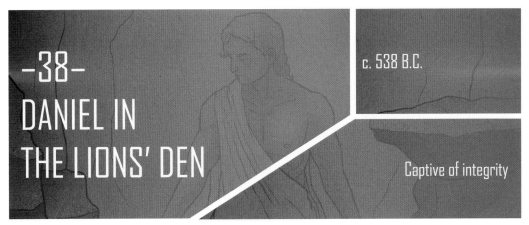

Daniel was a highly esteemed advisor to King Nebuchadnezzar of Babylon. His reputation was well regarded, even two decades after Nebuchadnezzar's death. The Babylonian Empire finally fell when Cyrus of Persia captured the mighty capital city and appointed Darius as a subordinate king.

In Darius's realm, there were 120 governors, and Daniel was one of three presidents over them. His remarkable qualities were vital to King Darius, who intended to promote him to be second only to Darius himself.

But the other officials conspired against Daniel's promotion, possibly because he would not participate in their bribes and other dishonesty. However, there was no corruption or negligence to charge him with, so they devised a plan to use his deep commitment to God against him.

Officials went to Darius and said that all the presidents and governors agreed that, for 30 days, everyone throughout the kingdom should be required to pray only to Darius himself. If anyone prayed to any other god or man, he would be cast into the lions' den. Darius agreed

and signed a decree.

We can only imagine what thoughts passed through Daniel's mind as he went to his house that day. Now over 80 years old, he walked upstairs to a room where the window faced Jerusalem — his homeland that still lay mostly in ruins. Daniel got down on his knees and prayed, as he always did. This time, however, he knew that ferocious, hungry lions awaited him.

The conspirators easily found Daniel asking God for help. They went to King Darius and reported that the exiled Jew continued to pray three times a day. Greatly distressed, Darius searched for a way to rescue Daniel from the fate that Darius' own decree demanded.

At nightfall, the evildoers returned and reminded the king that, according to the law of the Medes and Persians, the decree could not be changed.

Finally, Darius gave the order that Daniel be cast into the lions' den, a terrifying place with one basic purpose — to savagely execute anyone who dared to break a decree such as this. The powerful king accompanied Daniel, but admitted that Daniel's fate was beyond his control. It was up to Daniel's God to rescue him. Then a stone was laid over the opening, and the king's own signet ring, and others, sealed it shut.

All night Darius was greatly troubled. He did not eat, refused to be entertained, and could not sleep. Finally, at the first rays of dawn he hurried to the lions' den and sorrowfully called out to the man he trusted and was so important in his kingdom. "Daniel, has the God whom you constantly serve, saved you?"

Even before the stone was removed, Daniel exclaimed, "Oh king, live forever! My God sent his angel and he shut the mouths of the lions. They have not hurt me, because I was found innocent." Darius was overjoyed and ordered that Daniel be lifted out. He was unharmed, because he trusted God fully.

Then Darius had the conspirators and their wives and children thrown in the lions' den.[1] The powerful beasts crushed their bones before they even reached the floor.

News of Daniel's steadfast, living God was sent by Darius to his entire kingdom.

As we read the Old and New Testaments today, we see that, like faithful Daniel, Jesus was unjustly accused by enemies who wanted him executed. Like Daniel, the Redeemer was sealed in a hole in the ground. And like Daniel, Jesus came forth when the stone was removed. However, there the similarities end.

Only Jesus Christ conquered death so that we could live forever in heaven!

PRIMARY PASSAGES:

Dan. 6

KEY VERSE:

"Now when Daniel knew that the writing was signed, he went home. And in his upper room, with his windows open toward Jerusalem, he knelt down on his knees three times that day, and prayed and gave thanks before his God, as was his custom since early days."
—Dan. 6:10

WRAP UP:

"Lord, Your servant Daniel was exemplary in many ways, especially his prayer life. As an exile from Jerusalem, where Your grand Temple once stood, he made sure that he got on his knees and faced that city-in-rubble no less than three times a day. He bowed, praised, and prayed. He was committed to a deep relationship with You, so he met with You more than one thousand times each year, for decades. Even when he knew he would be torn limb from limb for praying, he prayed! Lord, please help me to love and honor You like Daniel did!"

-39-
ESTHER, THE ORPHAN QUEEN

c. 518–509 B.C.

...for such a time as this.

The book of Esther tells the amazing true account of an orphaned maiden, and how God used her to rescue countless Jews from certain death.

Around 20 years had passed since tens of thousands of Jewish exiles returned to the Promised Land to begin rebuilding God's temple at Jerusalem, and the villages of Judah. But many thousands more continued living throughout the other provinces of the Persian Empire.

The city of Susa, in the region we know as Iran, had become the center of Persia's royal elite. During a feast with much wine, King Ahasuerus became drunk. While showing off his possessions, he commanded the queen, Vashti, to come to where the men were celebrating. Ahasuerus wanted to display her extraordinary loveliness and her crown. To his surprise, she refused. The humiliated king burned with anger and removed her from her royal position.

Later, his advisors suggested that he have the most beautiful young virgins from across his vast Persian empire gathered and kept as a harem. He would select a new queen from among them, and the others would be his concubines.

Four years after Vashti refused to expose herself to the degrading party of drunken men, maidens from the king's 127 provinces were selected, taken to Susa, and given a full year of beauty treatments. Then they awaited their opportunity to win the king's affections.[1]

One of the lovely young women brought by the king's officers was Hadassah, a Jewish orphan raised by her older cousin, Mordecai. To protect her, Mordecai had given Hadassah the Persian name Esther, which hid her Jewish heritage.

Eventually, Esther was summoned from the harem to be with the king, and she pleased him greatly. We know she won the warmth of his heart, because the Bible says that Ahasuerus loved her more than all the other women. He crowned her the new queen of Persia and celebrated her with a long and lavish banquet.

After another five years, the king's top official, Haman, devised a horrific plot to exterminate all the Jews throughout the empire. Men, women, and children were to be murdered and their possessions plundered on a single day.[2] The unalterable edict was dispatched in all the languages to all the provinces, so that everyone knew the date set to kill the Jews among them.

When Mordecai learned of the coming massacre, he fasted, wept in sackcloth, and sent word to Esther. He challenged his cousin to immediately reveal that she was a Jew, to hopefully thwart Haman's plan to slaughter all her people. Mordecai encouraged Esther, saying it was perhaps "for such a time as this" that she had such favor with the Persian king.[3]

The Bible reveals in the book of Esther how the fearful young queen repeatedly put her life at great risk. It tells of her dangerous approach to Ahasuerus' throne and the banquets she prepared in order to expose the murderous plan of Haman. It also reveals how the king ended up hanging Haman from the same high gallows that Haman had built to humiliate and execute Mordecai.

After Haman's death, the Persian king distributed a second edict. This time he decreed that the Jews within his empire could defend themselves, and defend they did! Over 75,000 attackers were killed, instead of the Jews that Haman intended to exterminate.

During the time of Queen Esther, and for several decades afterward, God made it possible for the former Jewish exiles who were nearly 1,000 miles away in Judah to rebuild the Temple, the homes, and eventually the walls surrounding Jerusalem itself.

Then, more than 400 "silent years" passed before another young Jewess was blessed to become the mother of the most honored and reviled baby of all time!

PRIMARY PASSAGES:

Esther; Ezra 1–2

KEY VERSE:

"Then Mordecai told them to reply to Esther, 'Do not think to yourself that in the king's palace you will escape any more than all the other Jews. For if you keep silent at this time, relief and deliverance will rise for the Jews from another place, but you and your father's house will perish. And who knows whether you have not come to the kingdom for such a time as this?'" —Esther 4:13–14 (ESV)

WRAP UP:

"Lord, throughout the Old Testament, You are the hero! You parted the Red Sea, You knocked down Jericho's wall, You killed Goliath, You closed the mouths of the lions. It wasn't Moses or Joshua or David or Daniel. But each of these people had to choose to honor You by standing firm for You. You worked through their faith and obedience. Thank You, Lord, for the example of Esther and how You saved the Jewish people from Haman's murderous plan when she chose to divulge her dangerous secret. Please, raise up more 'Esthers' for such a time as this!"

Queen Esther put her life at risk when she revealed that she was a Jew. She asked the king to save her people from the murderous plan of Haman.

BONUS
— 400 Years of Silence
(c. 398–5 B.C.)

The prophet Malachi wrote the final book of the Old Testament about 100 years after the time of Esther, the Jewish queen of Persia. After Malachi, God did not send another prophet for nearly four centuries. Although this period is commonly seen as 400 years of silence, it was far from uneventful. In fact, the New Testament blazes to life with extra clarity when we are aware of some of the key happenings that took place in the time between Malachi and Matthew.

By about 331 B.C., on the plains of modern-day Iran, a 20-year-old Grecian king named Alexander the Great conquered the armies of the Persian Empire. Alexander was prophesied centuries earlier. Rather than simply conquer and enslave, he also re-educated the nations he captured, as advised by Aristotle his personal tutor. This tactic greatly accelerated the shift of world power from East to West.

During the 400 years before Christ, Israel was repeatedly squeezed between powerful empires north and south. The people suffered under Greece, Egypt, Syria, Rome, and others. The ideologies and armies of Julius Caesar, Ptolemy, Antiochus Epiphanes, Pompey, Marc Antony, Cleopatra, and Augustus demoralized the people of the Promised Land, and they yearned for the Messiah.

Clearly, God orchestrated human activity in preparation for the arrival of His Son, Jesus.[1] Greek became the primary language throughout countries surrounding Israel and the Mediterranean Sea, and the entire Old Testament was translated into that language by order of the Egyptian king, Ptolemy II. The task of translation took place in the Greek city of Alexandria on the shore of Egypt. An amazing network of ancient and Roman-engineered roads and aqueducts connected former enemies, and both commodities and communication moved rapidly via land and sea.

Then, near the end of the silent years, the brutal Rome-appointed king of Judea, Herod the Great, expanded Zerubbabel's Temple (widely known as the Second Temple) at Jerusalem. It again became the center of Jewish worship, and synagogues that sprang up in most cities throughout Israel became the centers of Jewish community.

Finally, in about 5 B.C., the messenger that Isaiah had prophesied 700 years earlier was born. He would be "one crying in the wilderness," warning all who would listen to prepare for the coming of the Lord. We know that messenger as John the Baptist.[2]

Six months later, when the stage was completely set and the "time had fully come, God sent forth his Son, born of a woman, born under the law, to redeem those who were under the law..."[3] However, the arrival of Jesus the Christ — the Messiah — would occur in an altogether unexpected way!

Imagine the joy-filled peace experienced by Mary and Joseph in the hours after the incredible testimony of the shepherds!

-40-
THE ANNOUNCEMENT AND BIRTH OF JESUS

c. 5–4 B.C.

In a fleeting moment, in the angel's presence, Mary had to decide whether she really trusted God.

It had been four thousand years since Adam sinned in the Garden of Eden. Now, God's plan for the redemption of mankind was focused on Nazareth, a village about 75 miles north of Jerusalem.

There, an angel appeared to a Jewish maiden, a virgin engaged to a godly carpenter named Joseph.[1] The angel said, "Do not be afraid, Mary, for you have found favor with God." He told her that she would bear a son, and to name him Jesus.

When Mary became pregnant, Joseph did not believe her when she explained that an angel told her that, by God's Holy Spirit, she would give birth to a son. Joseph was probably reeling from deep disappointment and other overwhelming feelings. Yes, he was betrothed to Mary, but her story was impossible, so he intended to quietly end their engagement.

Then in a dream, an angel assured him that Mary's news was true. From that moment, the burden of mistrust toward his beloved lifted, and Joseph took on the role of protector of both Mary and the Messiah in her womb.

His obedience to God and his role as provider for Jesus was crucial.

Although Joseph and Mary were descendants of King David, the couple was of humble means. What set them apart was their trust in God.

In God's sovereign plan, Joseph had to travel to Bethlehem to be counted in a Roman census. The Bible does not say that Mary rode a donkey. Nor does it say that they arrived on the day of Jesus' birth. Nowhere does it say that a hotel manager turned them away or that there were any hotels at all.

It does say that while they were at Bethlehem the time came for Jesus to be born, and there was no room in the "inn." Now, many homes included space for animals on the ground level, and an upper room for guests, called a kataluma. This was the "inn." Extra guests often slept in the downstairs stable. It is likely that others, perhaps elderly relatives, were given the upper room. After all, many other relatives were also arriving at Bethlehem and Mary's farfetched pregnancy story was surely scoffed and disbelieved.

Luke 2 reveals that on the night Jesus

was born, Mary wrapped him and laid him in a manger — a feeding trough.

That same night, a group of shepherds was keeping watch over their sheep. First, they were visited by just one angel, who told of the birth of Jesus and that they would find Him wrapped in cloths, lying in a manger. Then a multitude of angels suddenly appeared, praising and giving glory to God! The shepherds were probably dirty, stinky, and disheveled, but they hurried to Bethlehem anyway.

At the place where Jesus was born, they found a Jewish maiden who had recently experienced the joy and pain of childbirth. They also found tiny Jesus wrapped and lying in a manger, just as the angel told them. However, the Bible does not mention a special star that night above where Jesus lay. No camels, glowing halos, or wise men on that first night. It does not even say that the angels sang.[2]

But surely the excited shepherds encouraged Mary when they told her of the great company of angels. Then they went throughout Bethlehem and the countryside telling of the throng of angels and the Savior that had been born!

The excitement of their joyous report must have been a huge blessing to Mary and Joseph, and an amazing confirmation to their relatives and others that the girl everyone assumed to be unchaste truly was the chosen virgin-mother of the long-awaited Messiah!

PRIMARY PASSAGES:

Matt. 1:18–25; Luke 2

KEY VERSE:

". . . and she brought forth her son — the first-born, and wrapped him up, and laid him down in the manger, because there was not for them a place in the guest-chamber."
—Luke 2:7 (YLT)

WRAP UP:

"Father, it is hard to imagine the joy and relief felt by Mary and Joseph on the night that Jesus was born. The angel's promise of a boy-child had come true and both mother and baby were safe! Then, You sent an unexpected group of men; shepherds who joyously and probably boisterously told of being visited by a multitude of angels who confirmed that the child in the manger was the long-awaited Messiah. What a beautiful gift You gave the young couple, whose story regarding Mary's supposed 'virgin pregnancy' was supernaturally confirmed."

–41–
STAR-GAZING WISE MEN AND A POWER-CRAZED KING

c. 5–4 B.C.

The arrival on earth of the One who spoke the universe into being was suddenly emblazoned across the heavens.

In a country east of Israel, scholars known as magi carefully studied the heavens. To their surprise, one night they observed a new star mysteriously rising. Fascinated, the magi found that the star was prophesied hundreds of years earlier, to mark the arrival of a very special Jewish king.[1]

Meanwhile, in Bethlehem, perhaps 600 miles due west across the desert, the fire glow that illuminated the place of Jesus' birth was erased by the morning sunrise. Although the angel's announcement shared by the shepherds was exciting and surely led to visits by numerous townsfolk, basic daily responsibilities had to continue. The small family with the amazing story probably soon found a better place to stay and left the feeding-trough-manger behind.

In obedience to the Scriptures, Joseph had Jesus circumcised when he was eight days old. During the weeks and months that followed, Joseph apparently found work at Bethlehem, where loved ones heard the eyewitness account of the shepherds and now wondered in amazement, *Could Mary's absurd testimony about her virgin-pregnancy actually be true?*

Meanwhile the magi prepared for their historic trek — perhaps with a caravan that included servants, soldiers, riding animals, and pack animals loaded with gifts, shelters, food, and other provisions. The goal — to locate and worship the extraordinary king whose birth was heralded by a star!

Forty days after Jesus' birth, Joseph took Mary and Jesus to Jerusalem to fulfill the Law of Moses requiring a sacrifice for the new mother's purification. Only about six miles from Bethlehem, it was likely an easy walk on the much-traveled road to the capital city. During their time at Jerusalem's stately temple, more about Jesus was shared, first by the jubilant Simeon, then by the elderly prophetess, Anna.

Sometime after that day, possibly when Jesus was around one year old,[2] the magi arrived at Jerusalem. It was here, in the city of the Jewish Temple that they expected to find the future king of the Jews. The esteemed magi received an audience with King Herod the Great and told of the star and its meaning. Herod inquired of his chief priests and scribes, who confirmed that, yes, a king was to be born, but in Bethlehem of Judea, not Jerusalem.[3]

Herod directed the magi to the nearby town. He told them to report back to him as soon as they found the child, supposedly so he too could go and worship. The magi rejoiced greatly that the very special star — a supernatural phenomenon — guided them and came to rest over the home where Jesus was.[4] They fell down and worshiped the child, presenting Him with valuable gifts of gold, frankincense, and myrrh.

Then, because they had been warned in a dream not to report to Herod, they returned to their country by another route. In a dream that night, the Lord told Joseph to get up, take Mary and Jesus, and immediately escape to Egypt, because Herod was about to search for Jesus to kill Him.

Joseph obeyed without delay, but Herod became furious that he had been outwitted by the magi. Likely to help ensure the future king's death, ruthless Herod ordered the execution of every male child up to two years old in Bethlehem and the surrounding region.

Joseph stayed with Mary and Jesus in Egypt until an angel appeared again in a dream and told him to return to Israel. On his way to Bethlehem, Joseph was warned again, in another dream. So he turned and went to the region of Israel known as Galilee, and it was there in the village of Nazareth that Jesus was raised — as the Scriptures foretold.

PRIMARY PASSAGES:

Matt. 2; Luke 2; Lev. 12:2–6

KEY VERSE:

"… behold, the star that they had seen when it rose went before them until it came to rest over the place where the child was… they rejoiced exceedingly with great joy. And going into the house, they saw the child with Mary his mother, and they fell down and worshiped him. Then, opening their treasures, they offered him gifts, gold and frankincense and myrrh."

—Matt. 2:9–11 (ESV)

WRAP UP:

"God, when I picture the magi I envision stately, aloof men. I do not imagine a group of leaders who are ecstatic, rejoicing with exceeding great joy. But the Bible describes some sort of euphoric state that night as the supernatural star led them to the house where Jesus was. Your lovingkindness must have been an exceptional encouragement to Mary and Joseph as regal representatives from a faraway nation actually fell before Jesus and worshiped Him! Thank You for supplying for the needs that Joseph and Mary would face in their urgent departure only a few hours later."

After months of travel, the wise men worshiped Jesus and presented Him with valuable gifts of gold, frankincense, and myrrh.

What might it have been like to be able to see what was happening in Israel, and Persia, at the very same time on the night of Jesus' birth and during the days and months that followed? It may have been that. . . .

As angels filled the nighttime sky near Bethlehem, announcing the arrival of the long-awaited Jewish Messiah, a new star captured the imaginations of a small group of wise men in a country hundreds of miles to the east.

As amazed shepherds near Bethlehem rushed to find the baby in a manger, magi studying the nighttime sky in Persia rushed to reveal to their colleagues the discovery of what looked like a brand new star![1]

Within hours, sunrise erased the fire-lit scene at the Savior's birthplace. The countryside near Bethlehem echoed with the joyous news from eyewitness shepherds about angels and a newborn king. . . . Meanwhile, in Persia, wise magi clustered in discreet excitement of their own, anxious to understand the meaning behind the star that suddenly appeared from nowhere.

It seems likely that townsfolk in Bethlehem came to Mary to see for themselves the newborn baby whose angelic announcement had transformed dirty, smelly, often profanity-spewing shepherds into God-praising worshipers. In a span of hours, the quiet couple who only yesterday were seen as deceitfully covering their immorality were now VIPs whose honor had been confirmed by messengers from God Himself.

A guestroom was probably soon made available at the home of a relative or a neighbor. And the manger made famous by modern Christmas carols may have been needed only for a night, then soon became simply a feeding trough once again.

But even with all the excitement and happiness surrounding Mary's impossible reality, the essential duties of everyday life soon stole the astonished townsfolk away from their visits with the virgin mother and her carpenter husband. They marveled at the full account, beginning with the angel Gabriel's announcement to Mary, Joseph's dream, Mary's visit to her relative Elizabeth, and of course the amazing events of the night Jesus was born!

It is likely that the actual time of year of Christ's birth was late spring, not December.[2] The villagers were busy in the surrounding fields, and in cooking, sewing, shearing sheep, grinding grain, nurturing children, and more.

Joseph found work to sustain his small family. They stayed in Bethlehem beyond the eighth day when Jesus was circumcised. By the day following the 40-day cleansing sacrifice required after the birth of a male child, the couple returned to small Bethlehem.

One night, perhaps about a year later, it was at a house in Bethlehem that the magi found and worshiped the young child they knew to be the King of the Jews. Their star had guided them the final hour or so from Jerusalem and stopped above the house of Jesus.

We can only imagine the events that transpired in Persia beginning the night of the sudden occurrence of the star in the western sky. From their place hundreds of miles away, likely in the region now known as Iraq and Iran, they studied the sky west of them toward the Mediterranean Sea. Surely the learned men went almost immediately to the source of so much of their information, the scrolls and writings of Daniel and others stored in their vast library.

And their plan to visit the future king — whose birth was announced by a star — was born!

On the third day, Joseph and Mary found Jesus at the Temple sitting among the religious scholars. The teachers were amazed at His understanding.

-42-
JESUS — HIS BOYHOOD, BAPTISM, & EARLY MIRACLES

c. A.D. 8–30

From astonishing student to miracle-working Messiah

The hills surrounding Jerusalem were alive with Jewish travelers, makeshift tents, and animals for sacrifice. Every spring this city of tens of thousands suddenly hosted hundreds of thousands! And every spring, Jesus' parents traveled there for Passover.[1] When He was 12, Jesus came too.

When his parents started their return trek — at least 75 miles back to Nazareth — Jesus lingered behind. That evening, Joseph and Mary discovered their son was not among their relatives and friends. Worried, they returned to Jerusalem and after three days finally found the boy at the temple, sitting among the religious scholars. The teachers were amazed at his questions, answers, and understanding. Mary chided Him for causing them worry, but Jesus said that they should have expected He must be in His Father's house. They did not understand,[2] but returned together to Nazareth.

Eighteen years later Jesus was about 30 and, according to Matthew 13, had at least six brothers and sisters.[3] Now mature both physically and in wisdom,[4] the carpenter's son was well liked.[5] But the time for His ministry had come.

Jesus left Nazareth and went east to the Jordan River.

There, an unusual prophet named John — who dressed in camel's hair and ate locusts — was baptizing and teaching multitudes of people. They were repenting of their sins and John was turning the hearts of the fathers to the children, to prepare the people for the coming of the Lord.[6]

Jesus asked to be baptized, and the writer of Matthew recounts a brief but amazing conversation between the two men. They were relatives, born only six months apart, but Jesus grew up in Nazareth while John grew up several days south in the hills of Judah. John knew Jesus well enough that he felt unworthy even to carry His sandals. He was surprised, and said, "I need to be baptized by you, and you are coming to me?"

Nevertheless, John did as He asked, and immediately as Jesus came up out of the water the heavens opened and the Spirit of God came down on Him as a dove. Then a voice from heaven said, "You are my beloved son, in you I am well pleased." Perhaps a host of angels in the heavens praised God at that moment, as they did when Christ's birth was announced to a small group of shepherds three decades earlier.

Then the Holy Spirit led Jesus into the desert[7] and for 40 days, He fasted. The devil, who tempted Adam and Eve to disobey God in the Garden of Eden, now repeatedly enticed God's own Son to join forces with him. Yet, though weak from hunger, He stood firm and Satan's desperate temptations were put down.

Many knew Jesus as the son of Joseph from Nazareth. They would now be given the opportunity to grasp that he was also the long-awaited Messiah, the Christ!

By the time Jesus performed His first sign, turning six large pots of water into wine during a wedding feast in Cana, five men that He personally called to follow Him were there as well. At the wedding that day, Jesus revealed a tiny glimpse of His glory and His miracle-working power. By His presence, Jesus celebrated the marriage of one man to one woman, as designed by God in the Garden of Eden.

Over the next several months, Jesus went throughout Galilee, preaching with authority in the synagogues, teaching in the villages and countryside, and driving out many demons. He made time to pray alone and, filled with compassion, Jesus healed many people of sickness, disease, deformity, and even paralysis.[8] As He did, the excited crowds came from everywhere, and the number of disciples and other followers kept growing!

PRIMARY PASSAGES:

Luke 1–2; Mark 1; John 1–2

KEY VERSE:

"Now after John [the baptizer] was put in prison, Jesus came to Galilee, preaching the gospel of the kingdom of God, and saying, 'The time is fulfilled, and the kingdom of God is at hand. Repent, and believe in the gospel.'" —Mark 1:14–15

WRAP UP:

"Father, I love the passages that paint a picture of the human side of Jesus. He was born to the virgin Mary when she was engaged to Joseph, a carpenter. As He grew He was well-liked, and He had four brothers and at least two sisters. His intellect and wisdom were great, but to His siblings He was just the perfect oldest brother, literally. They played and worked and slept beside Him, but it was not until after His Crucifixion, that His own brothers recognized Him as Messiah. Thank you, Father, for revealing that at least James and Jude eventually believed."

-43-
JESUS THE SUBMISSIVE MIRACLE WORKER

God in the flesh . . . teaching, healing, submitting.

As the Creator of the universe, Jesus is all-powerful and eternal. When He was sent to earth by God, He became fully human[1] and submitted to His Father's will. In His humanity, He experienced exhaustion, temptation, pain, sadness, thirst, hunger, and death.

The prophet Isaiah tells us that Jesus was average looking.[2] And we know that when He was alone He easily and repeatedly blended in to ordinary crowds, unnoticed.[3] Yet as He walked the rural hillsides and city streets of Israel, throngs came to see the many incredible miracles that gave evidence of His complete identity. He spoke with bold authority and continually called the people to repent of their sins.

Several months after his baptism, Jesus was at the holy temple in Jerusalem. It was here, when only 12, that He astonished the religious teachers. Now, in righteous anger He made a whip and drove out the moneychangers who turned animal sacrifice into a business that profited peddlers of convenience and cheapened true worship.

One night, a ruler and teacher of the Jews, a Pharisee named Nicodemus came to Jesus. He said he knew that Jesus was sent by God, but had questions. When Jesus told him that no one can enter heaven unless he is born again, Nicodemus asked, "How can a man be born when he is old? Can he enter a second time into his mother's womb?"

Jesus explained that rebirth is spiritual, not physical. Then, perhaps looking deep into Nicodemus' eyes yet pointing at Himself, Jesus told him, "God loved the world so much that He sent his only Son, so that whoever believes in Him will not perish but have eternal life."[4]

In the months afterward, the legalistic Pharisees became very nervous because so many Jews were believing that Jesus was the prophesied Messiah. So He left Judea and headed north for Galilee, but led His disciples through the land of the despised Samaritans. It was here, hundreds of years earlier during the northern captivities, that Israelites who remained behind intermarried with idol-worshiping Gentiles. The full-blooded Jews considered the Samaritans half-breed "dogs," and they hated each other.

Even so, Jesus knowingly broke social and religious norms when He asked a Samaritan woman, who was getting water at a well, for a drink from her jar.[5] Surprised, she asked him deep questions. He told her about the living water of everlasting life and soon revealed that He knew all about her, her five husbands, and even her current boyfriend. Then Jesus revealed to her that He was the Messiah.

His disciples were stunned that He was talking to her, but she believed and then shared throughout her town all that had happened. Within only two days, many more Samaritans believed, and it all started with someone that society treated as a castoff. Christ's love for all lost people, regardless of their background, was obvious.

During the next two years, Jesus continued the mission His Heavenly Father required.

- He forgave and healed a cripple who was lowered through the roof of a house.

- He prayerfully chose and then gave special authority and power to 12 of His disciples.

- He taught and healed multitudes, including at the Sermon on the Mount.

- He calmed the raging sea by the command of His voice.

- He drove out demons.

- He fed 5,000 with only the lunch of a boy.

- He walked on water.

- And He did many other signs, too numerous to record.

Even so, many followers deserted Him the day after he fed the 5,000. They struggled with His teachings and did not truly believe.[6]

PRIMARY PASSAGES:

John 1–6

KEY VERSE:

"And truly Jesus did many other signs in the presence of His disciples, which are not written in this book; but these are written that you may believe that Jesus is the Christ, the Son of God, and that believing you may have life in His name."
—John 20:30–31

WRAP UP:

"God, Your miracle-working Son, Jesus, is my Savior. I have repented and I believe that only the blood of a perfect spotless lamb can forever blot out my sins and rescue me from eternal punishment in hell, which I deserve. I believe that Jesus is that spotless lamb. But God, help me to live all the days You give me on earth in ever-increasing submission to Your Word, the Bible. Please continue to convict me of my sin, strengthen my faith, and change me from the inside out. Fix my eyes on Jesus, and my heart on heaven!"

Jesus' many miracles — like walking on water and raising Lazarus from the dead — were signs that He truly was the long-awaited Messiah, the Son of God!

BONUS– John the Baptist

It is hard to overstate how important John the Baptist was in God's eternal plan. Jesus even said that among all men on earth, none was greater. None.[1] Beginning with his conception, the account of John the Baptist reveals the undeniable hand of God.

Consider the situation in Israel in 5 B.C.

Augustus Caesar of Rome controlled much of the known world, and in God's sovereign plan the Promised Land had not escaped Roman occupation. A growing network of Roman-engineered roads connected many of Israel's strategic cities, and one of the main international trade routes was within only a few miles of Nazareth, the boyhood hometown of Jesus. Carpenters and stonemasons busily constructed roadways, public buildings, and homes for the Jewish people and their Roman rulers.

In Jerusalem, Herod the Great magnificently expanded and restored the "second temple."

At the same time, in the Judean[2] hills west of Jerusalem, a godly, elderly woman named Elizabeth lived with her husband Zacharias, a respected priest. Elizabeth was barren. They had no children.

To Zacharias's very great surprise, the angel Gabriel appeared to him while he was serving in the Temple at Jerusalem. Gabriel told the old man that his wife, Elizabeth, would bear a son. He was to name the boy John and never allow him to drink wine or any other fermented drink, or even eat grapes or raisins. Still reeling and fearful, Zacharias found the angel's announcement almost beyond belief, so as confirmation God made the elderly father-to-be deaf and mute until after his son was born.[3]

When he returned home to Hebron in Judea, Elizabeth became pregnant and went into seclusion. After five months, her young relative Mary came from Nazareth, pregnant with the Messiah whom Elizabeth's son would one day proclaim and baptize.

What remarkable realities the two women shared! Both were impossibly pregnant. Both knew their child's gender. Both would bear sons tasked with soul-saving journeys. Both sons were named by God, and both women's sons would die by violent brutality.

Decades later, when John and Jesus were both about 30, John had lived in the wilderness for years. He was widely known as an outspoken and unusual prophet. His mission was to call the people of the city of Jerusalem, the desert of Judea, and the region of the Jordan River to "Repent," because "the kingdom of heaven is at hand!"[4]

Perhaps this desert-dweller was seen as a crazy wild man with his camel hair garment, his diet of locusts and wild honey, and possibly very long hair. Undoubtedly, there were scoffers, but many people — probably thousands — streamed out to the wilderness where he was.[5] Though he did not perform miracles, they responded to his message of warning. They confessed their sins and were baptized by him in the Jordan River.

Jewish religious leaders also came, but with wrong motives. John spoke quite plainly. He told these Pharisees and Sadducees they were like a brood of vipers and that they must truly repent. Simply being born a Jew, a descendant of Abraham, was not enough. If they did not bear good fruit they would be cast like chaff into the unquenchable fire. This was a clear declaration in the hearing of the people that, like everyone else, even religious leaders will burn in the fires of hell if they do not truly repent.

Jesus' face changed shape and shone bright. Suddenly God's voice said, "This is my beloved Son, in whom I am well pleased. Hear Him!"

-44-
JESUS' TRANSFIGURATION; THE TURNING POINT MIRACLE

c. A.D. 32

Preparing the Apostles
for the unthinkable!

In the months after He fed at least 5,000 with only a boy's lunch, Jesus continued calling the Jews to repent and believe the good news.[1] Multitudes were amazed and flocked to Him with their blind, lame, diseased, and demonized. They wanted the healing power of His touch.[2]

As He preached to the masses, Jesus also prepared the disciples to stand firm in the hard days to come. They were between villages north of the Sea of Galilee when He asked them, "Who do you say I am?" Peter spoke up and replied, "You are the Christ, the Son of the Living God."

Finally, after at least three years with Jesus, Peter and probably several of the others, truly believed that He was the long-awaited Messiah![3]

This marked the essential turning point in Jesus' earthly ministry. He commended Peter for his answer, which had been given to him by God, but then described the opposite of everything the disciples expected of their Messiah. He would not crush Israel's enemies. He would not restore Jerusalem to King David's superpower status or King Solomon's splendor. Instead, He would

suffer many terrible things from the Jewish religious leaders and die, then rise on the third day.

It probably felt like the air was suddenly knocked from their lungs. In fact, Peter was so shocked that he took Jesus aside and began to rebuke Him. "Far be it. . . . this shall never happen to You!"

However, as if shaking sense into the man He had just commended, Jesus reproved Peter in the disciples hearing. Peter was obstructing God's mission, like Satan, and Jesus demanded he get out of the way.[4]

Considering Christ's unconcealed rebuke, the next few days were probably very hard for Peter. Yet Jesus still loved him greatly, and after a week, He took Peter, James, and John up a high mountain — probably the 9,200-foot Mount Hermon — to pray.

Little did they know, something terrifying was about to happen.

Like the astounding metamorphosis of a caterpillar into a beautiful butterfly, Jesus literally changed before their eyes![5] His face shone like the sun and His clothes became dazzling white and glistened on His radiant, glorified body.

Moses and Elijah suddenly appeared with Jesus, talking with Him about His coming death. Then a bright cloud enveloped them and God's voice from heaven said "This is my Son, whom I love. . . . Listen to him!" The declaration struck terror in the disciples, and they fell face down on the ground.[6] Afterward, Jesus touched them and said, "Get up, and do not be afraid."

This phenomenal event known as the Transfiguration is described in Luke 9 and elsewhere. It was a glimpse at the true nature and fearsome glory and authority of Jesus. Some Bible scholars consider it the most important miracle in the New Testament prior to the Resurrection.

Near the end of Peter's life, he left a permanent record of the momentous event. His co-witness John was still alive when Peter wrote in 2 Peter 1, that, "…we did not follow cleverly devised myths … but we were eyewitnesses of his majesty. For when He received honor and glory from God the Father, and the voice was borne to him by the Majestic Glory, 'This is my beloved Son, with whom I am well pleased,' we ourselves heard this very voice borne from heaven, for we were with Him on the holy mountain."

By making Peter, James, and John eyewitnesses of Jesus' heavenly glory, Jesus equipped them to communicate with even greater passion the soul-saving reality of His Messiahship. The Transfiguration was a bedrock event in the preparation of Peter, in particular; the man chosen to lead the early Church in proclaiming the gospel message after Jesus' soon-coming death and Resurrection!

PRIMARY PASSAGES:

Mark 8:27–9:8; Matt. 16:13–17:8; Luke 9:18–36; 2 Pet. 1:16–18

KEY VERSE:

"For we did not follow cleverly devised myths when we made known to you the power and coming of our Lord Jesus Christ, but we were eyewitnesses of his majesty. For when he received honor and glory from God the Father . . . we were with him on the holy mountain."
— 2 Peter 1:16–18 (ESV)

WRAP UP:

"Jesus, You took just Peter, James, and John up on a mountain to witness something more amazing than any other miracle. There, as You prayed, Your face morphed and became brighter than the sun. Moses and Elijah were beside You, and all three disciples fell to the ground, terrified when the voice of the Heavenly Father declared, 'This is My beloved Son…Hear Him!' Then, You touched them and told them to keep what they saw secret, until Your Resurrection. Jesus, please remind me that it is Your Word that holds authority over all others, as You did for Peter, James, and John."

-45-
JESUS' FINAL WEEKS

Welcoming the Messiah,
seizing the Savior

After Jesus came down the mountain of His transfiguration, many who saw Him were awestruck and immediately ran to Him.[1]

In the midst of the miracle seekers, a desperate father fell to his knees. With tears streaming from his eyes, he pled for Jesus to heal his demonized son, who was thrashing on the ground and foaming at the mouth before them. In compassion, Jesus rebuked the unclean spirit that had inhabited the boy for years. He ordered it to come out and never return. As the demon departed, it shrieked and convulsed the lad violently. When he suddenly appeared lifeless, many gasped "He's dead!" but Jesus took him by the hand and raised him up.[2]

As weeks passed, Jesus continued to teach and heal, even raising a man from the dead, and His fame spread even farther.

After passing through a crowd in Jericho — where a dishonest tax collector named Zacchaeus repented and was saved[3] — Jesus' final week on earth began. He and the 12 arrived at Bethany, the hometown of his friends Lazarus, Mary, and Martha, about two miles outside Jerusalem.

On Sunday, five days before His crucifixion, the holy city overflowed with untold thousands of Passover visitors, and Jesus' presence caused jubilant celebration to break out. He was ushered into Jerusalem on a young donkey,[4] and many who witnessed His amazing miracles triumphantly praised their Messiah.

The euphoria was infectious. Many yelled, "Hosanna! Blessed is the King who comes in the name of the Lord!" They spread cloaks and leafy branches before His donkey[5] and expected that He would soon overthrow the harsh Roman oppressors, perhaps that very week!

On Monday, Jesus again forced animal sellers and dishonest moneychangers out of the Temple. Then He healed more blind and lame.

On Tuesday, He returned to the Temple and answered the questions of jealous religious leaders about taxes, divorce, and more.[6] When He saw a poor widow donate two small coins, He gathered the disciples and revealed an unseen reality; the widow had given more than all the rich people, because she gave everything. That night He stayed at the Mount of Olives, not far from the Temple, and taught privately about coming signs of the end times.

By Thursday, the dreaded culmination of His life-mission was imminent. Jesus and the 12 arrived at the upper room of a home for the Feast of Unleavened Bread, and He demonstrated servant-hood by washing their feet. Later, while they were still reclining and eating, Satan entered Judas Iscariot, and Judas left. After the first communion Jesus taught and they prayed, and then they sang a hymn. When their last supper together ended, they walked to the Mount of Olives and Jesus shared that all of them would abandon Him that very night. Shocked, Peter intensely vowed that He would never disown Jesus.[7]

Finally, the Lord took three of His closest disciple-friends to the Garden of Gethsemane.[8] Knowing what lay ahead, He was in emotional agony and even sweat blood as He knelt alone in prayer. Repeatedly, however, the three disciples fell asleep. Then, when Judas arrived with many armed soldiers he betrayed Jesus with a kiss.[9]

As all the disciples fled, envious religious leaders had Jesus bound and taken to the courtyard of Caiaphas the high priest. Through the cold night, Caiaphas and the others relentlessly sought false evidence against Jesus. Finally, just before dawn, they charged Him with blasphemy, spit in His face, blindfolded Him, and struck Him with their fists.

All the while, Peter watched. In fear, he cursed and repeatedly denied knowing Jesus. The third time, when a rooster crowed, Jesus looked across the court-yard directly at Peter, who ran in shame and wept bitterly.[10]

PRIMARY PASSAGES:

Mark 9:9 – 14:72; Mat. 26:6–67; John 13–17

KEY VERSE:

"And what shall I say? 'Father, save Me from this hour?' But for this purpose I came to this hour."
—John 12:27

WRAP UP:

"How quickly the excited crowds changed! As long as You kept healing the sick, the crowds grew. As You moved slowly toward the Holy City, many thousands screamed their excitement. They waved palm branches and threw garments in front of the donkey on which You entered Jerusalem. But the massive crowds and even Your twelve special disciples, the Apostles, deserted You when You allowed Yourself to be arrested and beaten. The whole purpose for which You became human was about to be horribly played out. Jesus, thank You so very much for obeying God's plan to redeem me. I'm sorry, Lord."

When the rooster crowed, Jesus looked across the courtyard directly at Peter, who ran in shame and wept bitterly.

When Jesus breathed His last and the earth quaked, the terrified centurion admitted, "Surely this was the Son of God!"

-46-
JESUS' CRUCIFIXION

The terrible suffering and death of the Savior.

At His arrest hours earlier, Jesus told a disciple to put away his sword. After all, at least 72,000 angels — 12 legions — stood ready to rescue Him.[1] Even so, Jesus continued to obey God's plan to pay the penalty for humanity's sin. His battle was not against soldiers but against unseen principalities and spiritual forces of evil, which began in the Garden of Eden.[2]

Now, shortly after dawn, the scheming religious leaders delivered their bludgeoned prisoner to Pontius Pilate. However, this Roman governor found no basis for execution.

Herod Antipas, who ruled Galilee, was in Jerusalem at the time so Pilate sent Jesus, a Galilean, to him. Herod's soldiers mocked Jesus and dressed Him in fine garments to humiliate Him even more, then returned Him to Pilate.

Although he wanted to release Jesus, Pilate gave the raging mob a choice — Jesus, or a murderer named Barabbas. The Jewish religious leaders provoked the people to such frenzy that they cried, "Crucify! Crucify him!" In great frustration, Pilate washed his hands before them and declared himself innocent of Jesus' blood.

Horrific tortures were added to Christ's beatings and humiliations. Sometime before about nine in the morning, Jesus was mercilessly scourged. In this savage punishment, Roman soldiers inflicted vicious lashes with lead and bone-tipped whips.[3] They ripped open the naked flesh of the back, shoulders, and legs and left veins and bones exposed. Jesus was probably barely able to stand when they threw a purple robe on Him, then pushed a crown of thorns on His skull. Mocking, the soldiers forced Jesus to hold a reed like a king's scepter, then spat upon and struck Him. Still, the crowd demanded crucifixion. The soldiers tore the robe from His open wounds and dressed Him again.

At first, He carried His cross, but soon a foreigner was forced to carry it the rest of the way as a multitude of onlookers followed.[4]

When He finally reached Golgotha, soldiers stripped Jesus again, and this time nailed Him to the dreadful timbers. As the Cross was raised, and probably dropped into place, the horrific process of crucifixion began. With spikes hammered through His hands and feet,[5] our bleeding Savior pushed, arched, and pulled His disfigured body upward for every agonizing breath. Even so, He prayed, "Father, forgive them, for they do not know what they do."[6] The punishment for the sins of the world was on Jesus. It is only by the blood of the Lamb of God that we can be saved from the penalty of our sin.

A sign nailed above His ravaged body sarcastically read, "Jesus of Nazareth, the King of the Jews." As soldiers gambled for His garments, spectators and religious leaders reviled and cursed Him. Soon, however, one of the criminals dying beside Him confessed his own guilt and pleaded, "Lord, remember me when you come into Your kingdom." Jesus replied, ". . . today you will be with me in Paradise."[7]

Then, beginning at about noon, an unnatural darkness fell. At three o'clock, Jesus screamed, "My God, My God, why have You forsaken me?" and then soon, "It is finished! Father, into your hands I commit my spirit." In the blackness that midday, the world's sin-debt was paid.[8]

When Jesus breathed His last, the earth quaked.[9] Rocks split and the terrified centurion keeping guard over Jesus admitted, "Surely this was the Son of God!"

When His side was pierced, water and blood flowed out. The Messiah was dead, and the curtain of the Temple tore from top to bottom.

The day of Christ's execution ended with a hasty burial in a borrowed tomb.[10] Legions of demons may have roared in demented celebration of their apparent victory.[11] However, as all would soon realize, nothing could be further from the truth.

PRIMARY PASSAGES:

Matt. 27:1–61; Mark 15; Luke 23; John 18:24–19:42

KEY VERSE:

"Greater love has no one than this, than to lay down one's life for his friends." —John 15:13

WRAP UP:

"Dear God, was there ravenous excitement among the unseen demons at Golgotha that terrible day? As the life of Your Son pulsed out of His veins, drop by drop, did Satan's demons rejoice? When Christ's side was pierced, did they laugh and scream in delight? As His limp body was wrapped and buried, were they euphoric? When the dejected disciples hid in great fear, did Satan's minions follow them like prowling lions, seeking to devour their faith? Father, thank You that Satan did not and will not win. Please help me to live in obedience to Your Word and not give him any opportunity to drag me in to sin."

BONUS —
The Frustrated Pharisees

In the hours after Jesus' execution, the concerns of Jerusalem's power hungry Pharisees and other religious leaders mounted.

What would they do with the blood money — 30 pieces of silver — that Judas remorsefully threw into the Temple after Jesus was condemned?

How would they explain the eerie and frightening reality that, at the very moment of Jesus' death the veil in the Temple suddenly tore nearly 60 feet from top to bottom?

Why was Jesus' body removed from the Cross on Friday evening and then entombed rather than left hanging for the animals and the elements to slowly consume in the sight of all?

How would Pilate respond on Saturday when the chief priests and elders demanded that the tomb be secured by Roman guards and the stone sealed?

How could it be that on Sunday morning a strong earthquake would rock the countryside and the bodies of many dead saints would rise and walk throughout Jerusalem?

And what about the soldiers who shook in fear and fainted after watching a lightning-white angel descend from heaven and roll away the huge stone that sealed Jesus' tomb? Would the soldiers accept a bribe and agree to say that the disciples came at night and stole the body while they slept, though they knew He had risen?

A house of cards had been constructed, and the religious leaders knew that their tenacious grasp on power could quickly collapse!

Forty days after His Resurrection from the sealed tomb, Jesus blessed the Apostles and ascended up through the clouds into heaven.

–47–
ALIVE AGAIN! RESURRECTION TO ASCENSION

c. A.D. 33

Forty days with the risen Savior[1]

Before sunrise on Sunday, a great earthquake shook Jerusalem's countryside. As darkness slowly gave way to dawn on the morning we now joyfully celebrate as Easter, a group of women made their way to Jesus' tomb to complete the burial preparations of His body. But when they arrived, the stone that had covered the opening was already rolled away.[2]

The women did not know that soldiers, who were on duty only minutes earlier, trembled and fainted when a mighty angel who looked like lightning rolled the huge rock from the door.[3] They did not know that the guards scattered when they awoke and saw a gleaming white being atop the stone, in clothes as bright as snow.[4]

Instead, the women only saw the open tomb, and assumed Jesus' body had been stolen. Mary Magdalene, a leader among them, immediately ran to tell Peter and John. But the rest of the women looked inside the open sepulcher. To their great surprise, there were two angels, and one shared the most important fulfilled prophesy of all time — *Jesus had risen!*[5] Death could not hold Him, for He truly was the Son of God, Christ the Messiah!

With joy and fear, the astonished women ran to tell the other disciples.[6] As they dashed *away* from the tomb, likely east to Bethany, Peter and John raced *toward* the tomb, probably from nearby Jerusalem west of the Garden. Mary Magdalene followed. The two men immediately went inside, but saw only the grave clothes and quickly left.

Now alone and still thinking Jesus' body was stolen, Mary Magdalene stood weeping. However, when she bent and looked in, two angels in white were sitting where His body had been. Then when she turned, there was Jesus! Mary Magdalene was the first person to whom Jesus appeared. Then while she ran to tell the disciples, he appeared to the group of women as well.

Within minutes, the disciples began to hear reports of Jesus' missing body, accusations that they had stolen it, and astonishing news of His appearance to various women. Scripture even reveals that immediately after Jesus arose, numerous dead saints arose from their graves as well. They walked throughout Jerusalem, appearing to many![7] The terror and jubilation that ensued must have spread the news of Jesus' Resurrection like wildfire.

Later that same day, two of Jesus' followers were going from Jerusalem to a village called Emmaus. As they talked about the incredible things that had happened, Jesus joined them. While they walked, He explained what the Old Testament says about Him, but they were prevented from recognizing Him until dinner that evening. Then He vanished, and the two disciples immediately returned to Jerusalem. There, great excitement was in the air because Jesus had also appeared to Simon Peter. All of the Apostles except Thomas and the betrayer Judas Iscariot were there behind locked doors, fearful of the Jewish leaders.[8] While the disciples were talking about these things, Jesus suddenly appeared in their midst. Now, thinking Him a spirit, they were even more terrified![9] But He calmed them, showed them His wounds, and ate with them.[10]

A week later, Jesus came to the disciples again, and now Thomas believed.[11] During the next month, He appeared to Peter and six others as they fished from a boat in the Sea of Galilee. Later, the 11 met with Him on a Galilean mountain. That may have been the occasion Paul references in 1 Corinthians, an amazing day on which over 500 brethren saw the risen Jesus at one time. After that, He appeared to His half-brother, James.

Then in Jerusalem, Jesus appeared to the Apostles one last time and commissioned the 11 to go into all the world.[12] Finally, He led them out to Bethany at the Mount of Olives and there, 40 days after His Resurrection, He lifted His hands, blessed them, and ascended through the clouds into heaven.

As they stood watching, two angels appeared and revealed that Jesus will return in the same way He was taken up.[13] Those who know Jesus as Savior eagerly anticipate that amazing day!

PRIMARY PASSAGES:

Matt. 28; Mark 16; Luke 24; John 20; Acts 1

KEY VERSE:

"And he said to them, 'Do not be amazed; you are looking for Jesus the Nazarene, who has been crucified. He has risen; He is not here; behold, here is the place where they laid Him.'" —Mark 16:6 (NASB)

WRAP UP:

"Jesus, Your Resurrection — Your victory over death — is the key to life here and in heaven! Without it, Christianity would be just another religion launched by a man who is now dead. But if we repent and receive You as Savior, You give salvation. Though the process of dying may be frightening — especially if we experience pain, which is the result of the Fall — death is a defeated foe. You took the sting and Your blood covers our sin, forever! Thank You for suffering and dying for me, Jesus!"

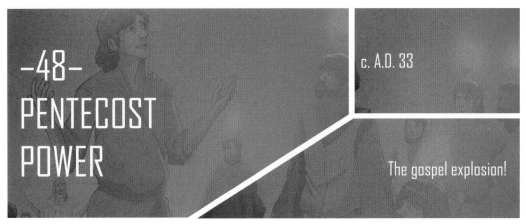

-48-
PENTECOST POWER

c. A.D. 33

The gospel explosion!

As Jesus returned to heaven and took His glorified position of honor at God's right hand, the joyous Apostles returned to Jerusalem.

Jesus had promised that the Holy Spirit would soon come to guide them and give them great power.[1] But first, Peter led his co-laborers in determining a replacement for Judas, who betrayed Jesus and then hung himself.[2] The new Apostle would need to have been with the others throughout Jesus' ministry, and to have witnessed the living, resurrected Lord. Two men were put forward for God's decision, which would come through the casting of lots. The lot fell to Matthias, and he became the new 12th Apostle.[3]

All during the week after Jesus' ascension, the Apostles and others were at the Temple praising and blessing God. Then, on Pentecost when they were together in one house, there was suddenly a sound from heaven like a mighty wind, and tongues like flames of fire rested on each of them.[4]

In part reversing the confusion that started over two millennia earlier at the Tower of Babel when God changed one language into many, the Holy Spirit now gave the 12 Galileans the miraculous ability to communicate in tongues they did not know. Immediately, the Apostles shared the gospel of Jesus with foreign Jews, speaking with great power in at least a dozen different languages.[5] Amazed that everyone could hear in their own birth language, they joined in praise to the Lord!

Of course, there were scoffers. Some said the Apostles were drunk, but Peter told the crowd the many miraculous proofs of the life, death, and Resurrection of Jesus the Messiah. Also, news of the saints who arose from the dead on the morning of Jesus' Resurrection was undoubtedly still being shared by the many witnesses who saw them! Cut to the heart, the people asked what they should do. Then Peter — whom Jesus promised to make a "fisher of men" barely three years earlier — told them to repent and be baptized in the name of Jesus Christ. Acts 2 states, "That day about three thousand souls were added to them."

In the weeks and months following, the believers lived in exceptional unity. When one was in need, another would sell his possessions for the benefit of the brethren. And "continuing daily with one accord in the temple, and breaking bread from house to house, they ate their food with gladness and simplicity of heart, praising God and having favor with all the people."

The Apostles met daily on the Temple grounds and multitudes of men and women became believers. They healed great numbers of the sick and demonized, including many who were carried out and placed on beds and couches in the streets so that Peter's shadow might fall on them as he passed.[6]

All these miracles greatly angered the Jewish authorities. Yet the Apostles determined to obey God rather than men, so they continued preaching the Resurrection of Jesus from the dead. They were seized and thrown in prison, but an angel of the Lord rescued them. On another day the authorities had them severely beaten, yet again they obeyed God.

In an alarming display of God's expectation of honesty, Peter delivered God's judgment against a deceptive husband and wife. Ananias and Sapphira sold property, but when they presented their offering for those in need, they lied and kept a portion to make it look like they gave the full price.[7] As a result, each immediately fell dead when Peter confronted them, and all who heard of it greatly feared the power of God.

The Church grew by thousands more in the months after Pentecost. Every day in the temple, and from house to house, the Apostles taught and proclaimed the good news of Jesus, our Savior.

PRIMARY PASSAGES:

Acts 1–5

KEY VERSE:

"And suddenly there came a sound from heaven, as of a rushing mighty wind, and it filled the whole house where they were sitting. Then there appeared to them divided tongues, as of fire, and one sat upon each of them." —Acts 2:2–3

WRAP UP:

"The excitement in Jerusalem after You sent the Holy Spirit at Pentecost was infectious, Father. But the religious leaders were fearful of losing their power. Thousands of Jews believed the Romans crucified their Messiah and that He would return in glory! Christ-followers were praising You in the temple and sharing food in one another's homes. And they were learning so much under the 'unlearned' fisherman Peter. The Apostles kept preaching and healing even after being imprisoned and beaten. Father, help me to be willing to share about Jesus and stand firm for You!"

The Holy Spirit arrived with a sound like a mighty wind, and tongues like flames of fire. The Spirit gave the 12 Apostles the ability to speak in languages they did not know, and that day thousands believed!

BONUS— Who were the 12 Disciples?

Most of us assume that Matthew, Mark, Luke, and John were among the disciples that Jesus' later called Apostles. But were they?

Matthew 10:1-4 lists the 12 that Jesus originally chose from among the many who followed Him. There were many disciples, but only these 12 did He also call Apostles. Most of them may have been only teenagers when they began following Jesus.[1]

The Bible helps us to see that the Apostles were average, ordinary Jews.

1. Simon Peter was a fisherman and the older brother of Andrew. The impetuous Peter walked on water and witnessed the transfiguration, yet denied Jesus three times. The Jewish historian Josephus recorded that Peter was martyred by crucifixion in about A.D. 67–68, and Origen says his crucifixion was upside down. He may have been the only member of Jesus' 12-man inner circle who was over 20, since it appears from Matthew 17:27 that only Jesus and Peter were responsible to pay the temple tax (and Exodus 30:13–14 notes that tax was only charged to those over 20). Peter was definitely married, because his mother-in-law was healed of a fever by Jesus.

2. Andrew was also a fisherman. The younger brother of Simon Peter, Andrew was initially a disciple of John the Baptist but left him to follow Jesus, and then led Peter to Christ. Like Peter, Andrew was evidently martyred by crucifixion.

3. James the Greater was a son of Zebedee and Salome (Mark 15:40; Matt. 27:56), who may have been a sister of Jesus' mother Mary. James was a fishing partner of Simon Peter (Luke 5:10) and the brother of John, called "Son of Thunder." He witnessed the transfiguration, and was martyred by sword in A.D. 44 (Acts 12:2).

4. John, like the three called before him, was a fisherman by trade. He too was a son of Zebedee and Salome (Mark 15:40; Matt. 27:56) and partner of Simon Peter (Luke 5:10). John was the brother of James the Greater, also called a "Son of Thunder." He too saw Jesus' amazing transfiguration. It appears that he died of old age, sometime between A.D. 89–120 (long after both his brother James, and Peter, who both witnessed the transfiguration with him).

5. Philip. Occupation unknown. He is said to have been martyred in Asia Minor.

6. Bartholomew is probably the same man known as Nathaniel. Occupation unknown. Some traditions indicate that he may have been martyred by crucifixion upside-down in Albania.

7. Thomas, also called Didymus. Nickname, "Doubting Thomas." Occupation unknown. Possibly martyred.

8. Matthew, also called Levi. He was a tax collector. Possibly martyred.

9. James the Less, the son of Alphaeus. Occupation unknown. Cause of death unknown.

10. Jude or Thaddeus. Occupation unknown. Possibly the brother of James the Less, possibly martyred by crucifixion or clubbed to death in Edessa of modern Turkey.

11. Simon the Zealot, a Canaanite per Mark 3:18. Occupation unknown. Possibly spread the gospel in Egypt and martyred in Persia.

12. Judas Iscariot. Occupation unknown. Traitor. Treasurer for the disciples. Committed suicide by hanging, then his bloated body fell when the branch or rope broke and he burst open after hanging in the hot sun for some time. Replaced by Matthias.

The day after Jesus fed 5,000 men and their families with only a boy's lunch, a large number of followers — people who were only looking for another free meal or other easy benefits — left when He challenged their motives. Among those who remained were the 12 men He had prayerfully chosen (above). Those 12 he now called Apostles and gave authority and power to heal every kind of illness and cast out evil spirits.

After Jesus' death and Resurrection, the followers known as disciples quickly exploded to thousands and soon to tens of thousands. The few who were identified as Apostles in the New Testament are the 12 above, plus the five noted below.

13. Matthias (who replaced Judas, Acts 1:20–26)

14. Paul (2 Corinthians 11:5, 2 Corinthians 12:11, and elsewhere)

15. Barnabas (Acts 14:14)

16. James, the brother of Jesus (Galatians 1:19)

17. Jesus is THE Apostle (Hebrews 3:1)

They stoned him even as he knelt and asked God to have mercy on them. Stephen's martyrdom launched the gospel from Jerusalem to the uttermost parts of the earth.

—49—
THE STONING OF STEPHEN

The martyr's bridge between Peter the evangelizer and Saul the exterminator.

Jerusalem pulsed with excitement and distrust.

In the months after Pentecost, thousands more Jewish men and women repented and their families were being transformed. They sincerely believed that Jesus, the carpenter's son from Nazareth, was also the prophesied Messiah, so they no longer trusted the powerful religious authorities who had demanded His Crucifixion.

To signify their repentance and commitment to obey Christ's commands, throngs were baptized in His name. There was great delight as the gospel of Jesus and the power of the Holy Spirit spread like wildfire[1] and burned in the bosoms of those who were learning daily under the teaching of Peter and the other Apostles.

However, tensions inevitably arose, and Acts 6 documents a situation that brought disharmony to Christ's followers.

Foreign-born, Greek-speaking believers complained that the widows among them were being overlooked in the daily distribution of food. They blamed the Aramaic-speaking believers of Jerusalem. This caused the 12 Apostles to call the thousands of disciples together.

The Apostles directed that seven men full of wisdom and the Holy Spirit be chosen to deal with this situation. One of the seven was Stephen. The Apostles prayed and laid their hands on them.

Filled with faith and power, Stephen taught among the people and did great wonders and signs. There soon arose heated debate from foreign Jews who did not believe the gospel of Jesus.[2] Yet the wisdom that the Holy Spirit gave Stephen was too much for them. So they stirred the people to anger, seized godly Stephen, and forced him to appear before the Sanhedrin. There, they falsely accused him of blasphemy.

In a scene reminiscent of the trial of Jesus, the high priest asked, "Are these charges true?" Surely aware that this could be his last opportunity to share the gospel, Stephen went straight to the Scriptures. He summarized all that led to the origin of Israel and the Jewish people through Abraham, Isaac, and Jacob; their centuries of multiplication and oppression in Egypt; their exodus and wilderness years with Moses;

their entry into the Promised Land with Joshua; God's driving out of the Gentiles until the time of David; and Solomon's construction of the majestic Temple for God.[3]

Then, looking beyond the painful death that he surely expected would follow, Stephen challenged the leaders. He called them stiff-necked and uncircumcised where it really matters, their heart and ears. He condemned them as betrayers and murderers of Jesus, the just One whom the prophets foretold. He declared that although they knew the Law, they did not keep it.

The truth cut them to the heart, and their anger was so intense that they literally gnashed their teeth at him. When he looked up into heaven and saw the glory of God and Jesus standing there, and told them what he saw, all at once with violent fervor they screamed, covered their ears, and ran at him. They cast him out of the city and stoned him, even as he somehow knelt and asked God to have mercy on them. The bludgeoning continued and soon his broken and bloody body lay still and lifeless in the dirt.

All the while a young Pharisee named Saul watched and approved the death of this peaceful, spirit-filled man by the hate-filled mob.[4]

By his martyrdom, Stephen's Jesus-focused testimony launched the gospel from Jerusalem to the uttermost parts of the earth. Chosen by Peter and the Apostles, then murdered at the feet of Saul — who would later be called Paul — Stephen was the first of thousands at that time and millions through the centuries who have been killed for their faith in Jesus Christ.

PRIMARY PASSAGES:

Acts 6–8

KEY VERSE:

"And they stoned Stephen as he was calling on God and saying. 'Lord Jesus, receive my spirit.' Then he knelt down and cried out with a loud voice, 'Lord, do not charge them with this sin.' And when he had said this, he fell asleep."
—Acts 7:59-60

WRAP UP:

"Stephen had unwavering faith. He was a man of great intellect who performed miraculous signs and wonders. And when he was falsely accused of blasphemy, he did not cower. Instead he stood before the Sanhedrin and shared the amazing true story of the Jewish people. Then, when he accused his accusers of killing the righteous Jesus, they exploded in murderous fury. Even so, as their stones pummeled him, Stephen prayed, 'Lord, do not charge them with this sin.' Father, please help me to love those who hate You, like Stephen did."

In the decades after the great Pentecost awakening, the Holy Spirit lit a fire that would soon blaze in hearts worldwide.

Acts 8 reveals that soon after Stephen's broken body was buried, a terrible persecution was launched at Jerusalem. The high priest and other Jewish religious leaders had declared that calling Jesus the Messiah, the Son of God, was blasphemy. Therefore, throngs of believers were savagely hunted, beaten, imprisoned, and even executed.[1] This led to the scattering of countless Christ-followers throughout Judea and Samaria. Even so, their number continued to multiply.

They were still Jews, and they worshiped where other Jews worshiped. They believed the Scriptures of old, but they also believed that Jesus of Nazareth truly was the prophesied Messiah. They quickly became known as "the Way" of Jesus, and about a decade later as "Christians."[2] Powerful Jewish authorities sought to stamp out the fire of the Holy Spirit that spread through the homes and synagogues across the land. The leader of that terrifying assault was a hate-filled young Pharisee known as Saul of Tarsus.

Because of the scattering, many converts shared the gospel far beyond Jerusalem. Their lives were at stake, yet as they spread out, they told that Jesus was the long-awaited Messiah. And many more believed.

During these days, there was a disciple named Philip. Like the martyr Stephen, he was one of the seven men commissioned by the 12 apostles, and he too performed miracles. At a city in Samaria he cast out many shrieking demons and healed many paralytics, which caused the crowds to pay close attention when he preached of Jesus.

After that, an angel told Philip to go south to the desert road that led from Jerusalem to Gaza near the Mediterranean Sea. There the Holy Spirit told him to run and catch up to the chariot of the treasurer of all Ethiopia.[3] Philip heard the Ethiopian reading aloud from Isaiah's prophesies about Jesus. But the powerful dignitary did not understand and asked Philip to come up beside him and explain the scroll.

Soon the Ethiopian truly believed that Jesus was indeed the Messiah. When he saw some water he earnestly asked, "What hinders me from being baptized?" Philip replied, "If you believe with all your heart, you may," and the Ethiopian answered, "I believe that Jesus Christ is the Son of God." So Philip immediately baptized him, then suddenly disappeared as they came up out of the water. The new believer — who had just learned the answers to his questions about the Messiah from a man who now vanished before his very eyes — went on his way rejoicing.[4]

Although God was showing His miraculous power through the 12 apostles and some of the disciples, the murderous Saul refused to be swayed. He and a force of men authorized by the chief priests went about terrorizing and imprisoning believers, men and women alike, throughout Israel and even foreign cities.[5] However, the situation was not unseen by the Almighty, sovereign Creator.

When Saul and his companions were near the large foreign city of Damascus, about 150 miles north of Jerusalem, a stunning light brighter than the sun suddenly encompassed them and all fell to the ground.[6] Blinded, Saul heard a voice say, "Saul, Saul, why do you persecute me?" He asked, "Who are you, Lord?" Then came the reply that would change both his life and his eternity. "I am Jesus, whom you are persecuting."

Astonished and trembling, the ruthless Pharisee now fearfully asked, "Lord, what do you want me to do?" Jesus said to get up and "go into the city, and you will be told."

PRIMARY PASSAGES:

Acts 8–9, 26:9–20

KEY VERSE:

"…many of the saints I shut up in prison, having received authority from the chief priests; and when they were put to death, I cast my vote against them. And I punished them often in every synagogue and compelled them to blaspheme; and being exceedingly enraged against them, I persecuted them even to foreign cities."

—Acts 26:10–11

WRAP UP:

"Imprisonments, beatings, and executions of Christ-followers became so common that families dispersed in every direction. In his ravenous pursuit, Saul the Christ-hater went north to the city of Damascus. Before he arrived, however, a light even brighter than the sun knocked him and the men with him to the ground! There, You, Jesus, spoke to him. You did not accuse him of persecuting Stephen, or coming to Damascus to persecute Christ-followers. No, You asked, 'Saul, Saul, why are you persecuting Me?' Jesus, please blind me to the things of this world, so I can see more of You!"

A stunning light brighter than the sun suddenly encompassed them and all fell to the ground. A voice said, "I am Jesus, whom you are persecuting."

Jews and soldiers plotted to kill Saul. Late one night, he was lowered through a window in the city wall and escaped to Jerusalem.

−51−
THE SECRET THAT COULD NOT BE KEPT

c. A.D. 35 and after

Reaching the world!

Now blind, Saul the terrorizing persecutor had to be led like a toddler into Damascus.[1] There he prayed for three days, not eating or drinking anything. In his darkness, one truth was clear: the crucified Galilean was not dead.

In a blinding flash, Saul's world had crashed upon him. Yet, through the hands of one of the Christ-followers he so vehemently despised, God restored his sight![2]

Like the 12 men who walked the dusty roads of Israel with Jesus, Saul received the gospel directly from the Savior, probably during his blindness. He believed, was immediately baptized, and then began sharing the many infallible proofs that the same Jesus he formerly blasphemed truly is the long-awaited Messiah.[3]

Three years after he started preaching, exasperated Jews conspired to kill him. They and a garrison of soldiers kept watch at the gates of Damascus. However, in a daring escape he was lowered at night in a basket through a window in the city wall.[4]

He fled to Jerusalem, but the disciples there were afraid and suspicious. Had

the Pharisee who led the murderous persecution of so many brethren actually repented?

Into this tense situation, God sent a trusted disciple named Barnabas. He took Saul to the Apostles and testified of his miraculous conversion and bold witness. So they accepted Saul and he lived among them and preached in Jerusalem, until yet another group attempted to kill him. When the brethren heard, they whisked Saul to the Mediterranean and sent him north to Tarsus, in modern-day Turkey.

Once the aggressive evangelist was gone, a period of peace settled upon Judea, Galilee, and Samaria.[5] Soon all of the Apostles except Saul had married and 1 Corinthians chapter 9 reveals that their wives were also believers and traveled with them.

During his six years or so at Tarsus, Saul preached the gospel, defending the faith he once tried to destroy. Meanwhile, hundreds of miles to the south, Peter healed the sick and raised the dead, and the number of Jews who believed in Jesus multiplied.

Through a vision, God showed Peter

that the gospel was not only for Jews.[6] It must be shared with others as well, and the Apostles soon gave their blessing to the dangerous journeys of Saul — who would now be called by his Roman name, Paul. He and his co-laborers Barnabas, Mark, Timothy, Luke and many others shared the gospel and taught believers from Israel to Italy.

At Athens, he encountered philosophers with an altar "to the unknown god." They knew little of Christianity, so he did not begin with Jesus. Rather, he first told about the Creator of all things and our need to repent for salvation through the one God raised from the dead.[7]

At the same time, Peter and other Apostles, plus many other believers, also took the gospel to people near and far. While on the Roman island of Patmos, the Apostle John was given an amazing experience that we know as the Revelation.

Before the end of the first century A.D., various writers documented the travels, challenges, and life-ending martyrdoms of the Apostles and other disciples. Since then, many people have attempted to eliminate the Holy Scriptures and annihilate all who share the soul-saving gospel of Jesus Christ. But God's Word cannot be destroyed.[8] It is unstoppable.

In the late 1400s, translations of the meticulously preserved Testaments began to be printed in large numbers using a revolutionary new technology, Gutenberg's movable type printing press. Within about two generations, many churches and some households throughout England, Germany, Spain, France, and elsewhere had their own copy of the Bible in their everyday language.[9]

Since then, thousands more languages have been translated and countless multitudes have believed upon their Savior, Jesus, the Christ, the Messiah, the only begotten Son of God!

PRIMARY PASSAGES:

Acts 9 and 13–28; Gal. 1; 2 Cor. 11

KEY VERSE:

"…I also count all things loss for the excellence of the knowledge of Christ Jesus my Lord, for whom I have suffered the loss of all things, and count them as rubbish, that I may gain Christ." Phil. 3:8

WRAP UP:

"As the number of Christ-followers grew, places to meet and worship sprang up in countries near and far. Over the centuries, millions of Christians were martyred, and it even continues today, but Your Word never dies. The gospel of Jesus has been spread by everyone from illiterate peasants to highly educated world leaders via sermons, scrolls, books, radio waves, and plasma screens. Lord, please help me to be a conduit of Your truth and grace!"

–52–
THE HOPE OF HEAVEN

It has been two thousand years since the Resurrection of Jesus, and myriads of believers worldwide expectantly await His return.

The ultimate destination of Christ's followers is heaven, but that incredible place remains sealed in a spiritual realm. Even the most powerful super-telescopes cannot peer beyond the physical limits of our mortality.[1] Thankfully, the Bible reveals numerous facts about this otherwise mysterious place.[2]

Most important, all who repent and receive Jesus Christ as Lord and Savior will live forever[3] in heaven with our Redeemer and people we love.[4] We will have new, imperishable bodies. There will be no sin, loneliness, suffering, or death; no disease, deception, envy, or injustice.

Heaven will be even more amazing than God's original creation. We cannot adequately imagine what it might be like, for "eye has not seen nor ear heard" the things God has prepared for those who love Him.[5] The Bible mentions its many mansions, splendid music, plentiful foods, and crystal-clear water. Theologians even write of joy-filled work, amazing creatures, and incredible explorations. And it is possible that heaven will be eternally fresh and new to us. Like a bride prepared for her groom, God may continually reveal inexhaustible beauties and details, ever stirring us to euphoric, delight-filled worship!

To understand the essentials of what happens when people pass into the afterlife, we must simply read what the Bible clearly states. In the past — during the four millennia between the Fall of Adam and the Resurrection of Jesus — when a person died their body went to the grave[6] and their spirit to the place called Sheol.[7] Most people do not go to heaven,[8] so Sheol had two distinct parts. The wicked were sent to punishment in the part called hell, while the saved were given peace in paradise.

In the present, since Jesus' Resurrection, our Savior's home is the present heaven. The souls of all who receive Him as Savior go there to be with Him. But all who fail to repent and believe that God raised Jesus from the dead suffer in hell, awaiting the final judgment.[9]

The Bible also reveals that the angels rejoice when a sinner repents, but it does not state that a deceased spouse can watch a living spouse, or that deceased parents watch over their living children.[10] Heaven is a place of peace, not worry or regret.

In the future, Jesus will return! We do not know exactly when, but the Bible clearly states that the spirits of Christ's followers will come down with Jesus from heaven to the clouds.[11] There will be a great trumpet blast and an arch-angel will declare the return of Jesus with a mighty shout. The remains of the dead in Christ on earth will rise and be united in the clouds with their spirits. In the twinkling of an eye new, eternal bodies will immediately materialize.[12] Lastly, every born-again believer alive on earth will also rise[13] and meet the Lord in the air.

Everyone who has ever lived, from the wicked multitudes before the worldwide Flood to the billions living today, will bow to Jesus. Satan and everyone whose name is not in the Book of Life will be cast into the eternal Lake of Fire,[14] and with a loud roar the original heavens and earth will burn up and melt away.[15] Redeemed people from every language group will experience an amazing new life in the perfect new heaven on the new earth.[16] The Bible describes it as having an immense and beautiful walled city, the New Jerusalem.[17] And God will be worshiped forever for His glory, honor, and power.[18]

Imagine the joy of Adam and Eve,[19] whose sin brought suffering and death into the once-perfect world. Finally, they will again eat the fruit of the Tree of Life, as the Creator originally designed for them in the Garden of Eden. God's merciful restoration and redemption will be complete and the gospel fulfilled.

Indescribable and glorious joy[20] in heaven awaits all who repent of their sins and receive Jesus Christ as Savior![21]

PRIMARY PASSAGES:

The Revelation (all); 1 Thess. 4

KEY VERSE:

"And if I go and prepare a place for you, I will come again and receive you to Myself; that where I am, there you may be also. . . . I am the way, the truth, and the life. No one comes to the Father except through Me."
—John 14:3, 6

WRAP UP:

"Lord Jesus, as humans we know what clouds look like and we know what pain feels like. It is easy to spend more time thinking about meeting You in the clouds and receiving pain-free heavenly bodies, than thinking of what it might be like to live forever in heaven. But You are the ultimate groom, pre-paring a spectacular forever-home. Please help me to consider what an eternity of discovering Your magnificence will be like. Will every moment be like the euphoric hon-eymoon of a strong groom and His beautiful bride? Wow! Please help me not to be so comfortable with earth that I never long for heaven!"

God will be worshiped forever for His glory, honor, and power. Indescribable joy in heaven awaits all who repent and receive Jesus Christ as Savior!

The "Summary First" Bible Read-through Plan

Many people set out to read their Bible straight through, from beginning to end. However, most soon get bogged down and frustrated. The seemingly haphazard sequence of the books within the Bible can be perplexing. And this can cause even well-intentioned commitment to fall by the wayside. Has this ever happened to you?

Possibly one of the greatest benefits of *The 10 Minute Bible Journey* is that it can make the "big Bible jigsaw puzzle" fit together with ease. So, for maximum enjoyment, consider starting your next Bible read-through with just ten minutes or so per day, for 30-days, in these pages. Then follow the special chronological reading plan below. You will have an encouraging and fresh understanding of the big picture of Scripture.

Be careful not to allow the suggested number of minutes per day, or a specific number of months, to spoil your time in God's Word, or to turn it into a legalistic "checkoff" of verses read but not taken to heart. The biggest joy comes by reading at a pace and at a time of day that is comfortable for you. For some that is in the early morning. For others, it will be mid-day, or with their family at dinner. And for still others, an evening timeframe after the rest of the family has headed to bed may be the best option.

As you begin, focus. Ask God to remove the distractions that easily come to mind. Turn off your cell phone or set it to airplane mode. If possible, read out loud. Then journal a note or two in your Bible's margin, or on a separate notepad that you reserve as a diary of what you learn or want to study further.

Before you close for the day, take a few minutes to review and pray about that day's passage, and ask God to help you remember and apply it to your life. After all, whether your Bible read-through takes one year or several, the goal is to honor God and become more like Jesus.

This one is like chronological reading plans promoted by various respected ministries. I've simply taken 12-months of Bible reading and squeezed it slightly to fit it into 11. Nothing is missing.

However, if you prefer to read the Scriptures in the same order that most Bibles are laid out — where the historical books are grouped together, the poetic books are grouped together, the Epistles are grouped together, and so forth — feel free! *The 10 Minute Bible Journey* will give you the big picture overview, and that will equip you to be able to begin pretty much anyplace. Enjoy!

PHASE 1 — *The 10-Minute Bible Journey* book

In the first 30-days (or however long Phase 1 is in your particular situation) read the 52 chronological accounts in *The 10 Minute Bible Journey* to attain a solid overview of the entire Bible in the order that the events actually occurred. Consider including your spouse and/or your older children. Pray for one another, including any concerns raised during your discussion.

PHASE 2 — The Bible (20-to-40 minutes per day)

Now begin your read-through of the Holy Bible itself. Read at a pace that works with your schedule, and check off each passage as you finish it so that you can be encouraged by your progress. This also helps you to not waste time finding where you left off, for those occasions when several days go by between readings. If possible, read aloud, and use a sharp pencil to make notes in your Bible as you go!

__ Genesis 1–7

__ Genesis 8–11

__ Genesis 12–15

__ Genesis 16–21

__ Genesis 22–26

__ Genesis 27–31

__ Genesis 32–37

__ Genesis 38–42

__ Genesis 43–47

__ Genesis 48–50

__ Job 1–5

__ Job 6–13

__ Job 14–20

__ Job 21–28

__ Job 29–34

__ Job 35–39

__ Job 40–42

__ Exodus 1–3

__ Exodus 4–9

__ Exodus 10–15

__ Exodus 16–21

__ Exodus 22–27

__ Exodus 28–32

__ Exodus 33–38

__ Exodus 39–40; Leviticus 1–4

__ Leviticus 5–10

__ Leviticus 11–15

__ Leviticus 16–21

__ Leviticus 22–25

__ Leviticus 26–27; Numbers 1–2

__ Numbers 3–6

__ Numbers 7–10

PHASE 3

__ Numbers 11–15; Psalm 90

__ Numbers 16–17

__ Numbers 18–20

__ Numbers 21–22

__ Numbers 23–25

__ Numbers 26–27

__ Numbers 28–30

__ Numbers 31–32

__ Numbers 33–34

__ Numbers 35–36

__ Deuteronomy 1–2

__ Deuteronomy 3–4

__ Deuteronomy 5–7

__ Deuteronomy 8–10

___ Deuteronomy 11–13

___ Deuteronomy 14–16

___ Deuteronomy 17–20

___ Deuteronomy 21–23

___ Deuteronomy 24–27

___ Deuteronomy 28–29

___ Deuteronomy 30–31

___ Deuteronomy 32–34; Psalm 91

___ Joshua 1–4

___ Joshua 5–8

___ Joshua 9–11

___ Joshua 12–15

___ Joshua 16–18

___ Joshua 19–21

___ Joshua 22–24

___ Judges 1–2

PHASE 4

___ Judges 3–5

___ Judges 6–7

___ Judges 8–9

___ Judges 10–12

___ Judges 13–15

___ Judges 16–18

___ Judges 19–21

___ Ruth 1–4

___ 1 Samuel 1–3

___ 1 Samuel 4–8

___ 1 Samuel 9–12

___ 1 Samuel 13–14

___ 1 Samuel 15–17

___ 1 Samuel 18–20; Psalm 11, 59

___ 1 Samuel 21–24

___ Psalm 7, 27, 31, 34, 52

___ Psalm 56, 120, 140–142

___ 1 Samuel 25–27

___ Psalm 17, 35, 54, 63

___ 1 Samuel 28–31; Psalm 18

___ Psalm 121, 123–125, 128–130

___ 2 Samuel 1–4

___ Psalm 6, 8–10, 14, 16, 19, 21

___ 1 Chronicles 1–2

___ Psalm 43–45, 49, 84–85, 87

___ 1 Chronicles 3–5

___ Psalm 73, 77–78

___ 1 Chronicles 6

___ Psalm 81, 88, 92–93

___ 1 Chronicles 7–10

PHASE 5

___ Psalm 102–104

___ 2 Samuel 5:1–10; 1 Chronicles 11–12

___ Psalm 133

___ Psalm 106–107

___ 2 Samuel 5:11–6:23; 1 Chronicles 13–16

___ Psalm 1–2, 15, 22–24, 47, 68

___ Psalm 89, 96, 100–101, 105, 132

___ 2 Samuel 7; 1 Chronicles 17

___ Psalm 25, 29, 33, 36, 39

___ 2 Samuel 8–9; 1 Chronicles 18

___ Psalm 50, 53, 60, 75

___ 2 Samuel 10; 1 Chronicles 19; Psalm 20

___ Psalm 65–67, 69–70

___ 2 Samuel 11–12; 1 Chronicles 20

___ Psalm 32, 51, 86, 122

___ 2 Samuel 13–15

___ Psalm 3–4, 12–13, 28, 55

___ 2 Samuel 16–18

___ Psalm 26, 40, 58, 61–62, 64

___ 2 Samuel 19–21

___ Psalm 5, 38, 41–42

___ 2 Samuel 22–23; Psalm 57

___ Psalm 95, 97–99

___ 2 Samuel 24; 1 Chronicles 21–22; Psalm 30

___ Psalm 108–110

___ 1 Chronicles 23–25

___ Psalm 131, 138–139, 143–145

___ 1 Chronicles 26–29; Psalm 127

___ Psalm 111–118

___ 1 Kings 1–2; Psalm 37, 71, 94
___ Psalm 119:1–88
___ 1 Kings 3–4; 2 Chronicles 1; Psalm 72
___ Psalm 119:89–176
___ Song of Solomon 1–8

PHASE 6
___ Proverbs 1–3
___ Proverbs 4–6
___ Proverbs 7–9
___ Proverbs 10–12
___ Proverbs 13–15
___ Proverbs 16–18
___ Proverbs 19–21
___ Proverbs 22–24
___ 1 Kings 5–6; 2 Chronicles 2–3
___ 1 Kings 7; 2 Chronicles 4
___ 1 Kings 8; 2 Chronicles 5
___ 2 Chronicles 6–7; Psalm 136
___ Psalm 134, 146–150
___ 1 Kings 9; 2 Chronicles 8
___ Proverbs 25–26
___ Proverbs 27–29
___ Ecclesiastes 1–6
___ Ecclesiastes 7–12
___ 1 Kings 10–11; 2 Chronicles 9
___ Proverbs 30–31
___ 1 Kings 12–14
___ 2 Chronicles 10–12
___ 1 Kings 15:1–24; 2 Chronicles 13–16
___ 1 Kings 15:25–16:34; 2 Chronicles 17
___ 1 Kings 17–19
___ 1 Kings 20–21
___ 1 Kings 22; 2 Chronicles 18
___ 2 Chronicles 19–23

PHASE 7
___ Obadiah 1; Psalm 82–83
___ 2 Kings 1–4
___ 2 Kings 5–8

___ 2 Kings 9–11
___ 2 Kings 12–13; 2 Chronicles 24
___ 2 Kings 14; 2 Chronicles 25
___ Jonah 1–4
___ 2 Kings 15; 2 Chronicles 26
___ Isaiah 1–4
___ Isaiah 5–8
___ Amos 1–5
___ Amos 6–9
___ 2 Chronicles 27; Isaiah 9–12
___ Micah 1–7
___ 2 Chronicles 28; 2 Kings 16–17
___ Isaiah 13–17
___ Isaiah 18–22
___ Isaiah 23–27
___ 2 Kings 18:1–8; 2 Chronicles 29–31; Psalm 48
___ Hosea 1–7
___ Hosea 8–14
___ Isaiah 28–30
___ Isaiah 31–34
___ Isaiah 35–36
___ Isaiah 37–39; Psalm 76
___ Isaiah 40–43
___ Isaiah 44–48
___ 2 Kings 18:9–19:37; Psalm 46, 80, 135
___ Isaiah 49–53
___ Isaiah 54–58
___ Isaiah 59–63

PHASE 8
___ Isaiah 64–66
___ 2 Kings 20–21
___ 2 Chronicles 32–33
___ Nahum 1–3
___ 2 Kings 22–23; 2 Chronicles 34–35
___ Zephaniah 1–3
___ Jeremiah 1–3
___ Jeremiah 4–6
___ Jeremiah 7–9

__ Jeremiah 10–13

__ Jeremiah 14–17

__ Jeremiah 18–22

__ Jeremiah 23–25

__ Jeremiah 26–29

__ Jeremiah 30–31

__ Jeremiah 32–34

__ Jeremiah 35–37

__ Jeremiah 38–40; Psalm 74, 79

__ 2 Kings 24–25; 2 Chronicles 36

__ Habakkuk 1–3

__ Jeremiah 41–45

__ Jeremiah 46–48

__ Jeremiah 49–50

__ Jeremiah 51–52

__ Lamentations 1:1–3:36

__ Lamentations 3:37–5:22

__ Ezekiel 1–4

__ Ezekiel 5–8

__ Ezekiel 9–12

__ Ezekiel 13–15

__ Ezekiel 16–17

PHASE 9

__ Ezekiel 18–19

__ Ezekiel 20–21

__ Ezekiel 22–23

__ Ezekiel 24–27

__ Ezekiel 28–31

__ Ezekiel 32–34

__ Ezekiel 35–37

__ Ezekiel 38–39

__ Ezekiel 40–41

__ Ezekiel 42–43

__ Ezekiel 44–45

__ Ezekiel 46–48

__ Joel 1–3

__ Daniel 1–3

__ Daniel 4–6

__ Daniel 7–9

__ Daniel 10–12

__ Ezra 1–3

__ Ezra 4–6; Psalm 137

__ Haggai 1–2

__ Zechariah 1–7

__ Zechariah 8–14

__ Esther 1–5

__ Esther 6–10

__ Ezra 7–10

__ Nehemiah 1–5

__ Nehemiah 6–7

__ Nehemiah 8–10

__ Nehemiah 11–13; Psalm 126

__ Malachi 1–4

PHASE 10

__ Luke 1; John 1:1–14

__ Matthew 1; Luke 2:1–38

__ Matthew 2; Luke 2:39–52

__ Matthew 3; Mark 1; Luke 3

__ Matthew 4; Luke 4–5; John 1:15–51

__ John 2–4

__ Mark 2

__ John 5

__ Matthew 12:1–21; Mark 3; Luke 6

__ Matthew 5–7

__ Matthew 8:1–13; Luke 7

__ Matthew 11

__ Matthew 12:22–50; Luke 11

__ Matthew 13; Luke 8

__ Matthew 8:14–34; Mark 4–5

__ Matthew 9–10

__ Matthew 14; Mark 6; Luke 9:1–17

__ John 6

__ Matthew 15; Mark 7

__ Matthew 16; Mark 8; Luke 9:18–27

__ Matthew 17; Mark 9; Luke 9:28–62

__ Matthew 18

__ John 7–8

__ John 9:1–10:21

__ Luke 10–11; John 10:22–42

__ Luke 12–13

__ Luke 14–15

__ Luke 16:1–17:10

__ John 11

__ Luke 17:11–18:14

__ Matthew 19; Mark 10

PHASE 11

__ Matthew 20–21

__ Luke 18:15–19:48

__ Mark 11; John 12

__ Matthew 22; Mark 12

__ Matthew 23; Luke 20–21

__ Mark 13

__ Matthew 24

__ Matthew 25

__ Matthew 26; Mark 14

__ Luke 22; John 13

__ John 14–17

__ Matthew 27; Mark 15

__ Luke 23; John 18–19

__ Matthew 28; Mark 16

__ Luke 24; John 20–21

__ Acts 1–3

__ Acts 4–6

__ Acts 7–8

__ Acts 9–10

__ Acts 11–12

__ Acts 13–14

__ James 1–5

__ Acts 15–16

__ Galatians 1–3

__ Galatians 4–6

__ Acts 17:1–18:18

__ 1 Thessalonians 1–5;
   2 Thessalonians 1–3

__ Acts 18:19–19:41

__ 1 Corinthians 1–4

__ 1 Corinthians 5–8

PHASE 12

__ 1 Corinthians 9–11

__ 1 Corinthians 12–14

__ 1 Corinthians 15–16

__ 2 Corinthians 1–4

__ 2 Corinthians 5–9

__ 2 Corinthians 10–13

__ Acts 20:1–3; Romans 1–3

__ Romans 4–7

__ Romans 8–10

__ Romans 11–13

__ Romans 14–16

__ Acts 20:4–23:35

__ Acts 24–26

__ Acts 27–28

__ Colossians 1–4; Philemon 1

__ Ephesians 1–6

__ Philippians 1–4

__ 1 Timothy 1–6

__ Titus 1–3

__ 1 Peter 1–5

__ Hebrews 1–6

__ Hebrews 7–10

__ Hebrews 11–13

__ 2 Timothy 1–4

__ 2 Peter 1–3; Jude 1

__ 1 John 1–5

__ 2 John 1; 3 John 1

__ Revelation 1–5

__ Revelation 6–11

__ Revelation 12–18

__ Revelation 19–22

Congratulations, you have completed your total Bible read-through!

Tips for Use in Family or Small Group Bible Studies

Questions to consider after each account

- What was the most interesting aspect of this account to you? Why did it stand out?

- Name another detail or two that you are still thinking about. Why?

- Can you think of Bible details that were not included in this summary? Let's look them up.

- Did this account reveal anything about God? His Character?

- What did it make you think about regarding mankind?

- How does that apply to you? What do you feel the Lord may want you to adjust in your own life?

Small Group usage ideas

- When introducing the series, tell why you feel *The 10-Minute Bible Journey* can help your family or your group to quickly get a solid overview of the main accounts and characters of the Bible. Tell about how much easier it is to understand the Bible's full storyline by reading its main points in the chronological order that they actually took place.

- Start at the beginning and read each account aloud. Consider having two or three group members take turns. Read with emotion to increase the group's sense of the situations being highlighted.

- Place each account on a linear timeline, as each is read and discussed. Start the group study with a large wide piece of blank paper on the wall. Draw a 6,000-year timeline with 4000 B.C. on the far left and A.D. 2000 on the far right. Emulate the timeline at the back of this book, but only the line and the millenium dates. The leader adds or has a group member add the number and title of each account as it is covered. Roll the paper up and bring it back every week. (Whiteboard not recommended.)

- Have the group open their Bibles to the passages covered (so they are also "in" their Bibles). For the accounts that are based on just a chapter or so, it is fairly easy to follow along. However, accounts based on multiple chapters or pieces from multiple books, will be more cumbersome. Some group members may want to scan the long passages between meetings.

- Discuss the generic all-account questions (pg. 186).

- Draw or show "where" each account takes place on a map of Bible lands. Have a group member show the route or sequence of cities and other places as each is introduced.

- As part of the leader's lesson prep, be sure to read the endnotes and primary passages connected to that lesson.

- Close each discussion with a few minutes of prayer that includes a time of asking God to help the group to change and grow in their relationship with Jesus, and their trust in the truth and authority of the Bible. We all need a continual heart-change. Ask God to accomplish that in you!

This print edition of *The 10 Minute Bible Journey* contains a select group of endnotes. The digital edition includes an expanded reference section with over 1,000 endnotes with documentation and links for videos, articles, and more so you can complete a deeper study. Those notes are searchable and hyperlinked for convenience on your digital device. You can purchase the digital edition from the publisher's website or leading online bookstores.

1. The Beginning

1 Creation from nothing is clear from the early verses of Genesis 1, and expanded upon in the New Testament (John 1:1–3); the worlds were framed by the word of God (Hebrews 11:3).
2 www.answersingenesis.org/articles/nab/why-christians-shouldnt-accept-millions by Dr. Terry Mortenson.
3 The biblical term "kind" is roughly equivalent to the taxonomic term "family" in most instances. See Dr. Gary Parker's article, "Species and Kind," at www.answersingenesis.org/articles/cfl/species-kind.
4 "Monsters" is the most literal translation (YLT, NASB). Most contemporary versions simply state "sea creatures" or similar, which does not adequately denote the immense length and bulk of some of the creatures, both current and in the fossil record.
5 Genesis 1:30

2. God Creates Marriage

1 "Although there are about 668 names of dinosaurs, there are perhaps only 55 different "kinds" of dinosaurs, quoted from "Were Dinosaurs on Noah's Ark?" online at www.answersingenesis.org/dinosaurs/were-dinosaurs-on-noahs-ark/.
2 Genesis 2:7–14. The Bible mentions four main regions before the Fall of mankind and the catastrophic worldwide Flood of Noah's day; the four regions were Havilah, Cush, Asshur, and Eden. Adam was formed from the ground in the region called Eden, which was in the east, and then placed in an extra-special garden God prepared — the Garden of Eden. Once in the Garden, God brought animals to Adam to name.
3 Genesis 2:17 is literally, "dying thou dost die" (YLT). The process of dying began immediately after man's sin.
4 Although millions of species of animals exist today, nearly all are the result of rapid changes within the "kinds" (roughly equivalent to the "family" category). For instance, today we have a multitude of species of dogs, but all of them came from the original canine kind. All the species and breeds of dogs — including all the domesticated dogs, and wild dogs like coyotes, wolves, and dingoes — have come about by the tremendous amount of information and adaptability that God designed into the DNA of the original pair. Dogs do not evolve into other kinds of animals, they adapt (speciate) within the dog kind. God designed DNA to allow for tremendous and rapid adaptation and speciation through the generations of each kind.
5 For example, if Adam had to name 1,000 top-level kinds, and he named one kind every 15 seconds, he could have been done in less than five hours, even allowing 45 minutes for breaks. In research by Dr. Jean Lightner and others, scientists project that there were around 1,000 different top-level kinds of animals [proto-species (genera)] to name. Even so, Adam did not name all the beasts of the earth, but merely a subset of that (the beasts of the field), so he named far less than this number. See Dr. Jean Lightner's *Answers Research Journal* article, https://answersingenesis.org/noahs-ark/determining-the-ark-kinds/.
6 The Bible says that Adam was "alone" (he had no mate). It does not say that he was "lonely" (isolated). A common misconception.
7 Genesis 2:22–23 (in Young's Literal Translation, multiple exclamation marks more fully communicate Adam's intense delight).
8 The married couple was told to have children in a way that required the act of producing them; not only "caring for" them. The created order was male and female, and Jesus defended this in Matthew 19:4–6 and Mark 10:5–9. Homosexuality and homosexual "marriage" is a form of adultery, one of several sins of sexual immorality. With regard to the biblical mandate for parenting, the question is not whether a same-sex couple can love a child, but whether God intended for same-sex couples to be parents.
9 Genesis 3:18
10 Exodus 20:11, 31:12–18. Colossians 2:13–17 indicates that the death of Jesus on the Cross cancelled the Sabbath-keeping covenant that was previously required of the Israelites.

BONUS–Angels

1 Jesus is not an angel. He created the angels, and He was given authority above all angels by God (Matthew 28:18; Ephesians 1:22; Colossians 1:16; etc.). Note that Michael the archangel had to appeal to the Lord (Jesus) to oppose Satan in Jude 1:9.
2 Revelation 12:4 and 12:7–10. See also Jesus' reference to Satan falling like lightning, Luke 10:18.
3 Genesis 3:14–4:2 (Some researchers who agree that Satan's rebellion occurred soon after day 6 feel that it is doubtful that it occurred the very next day, on day 7, since that day was sanctified and made holy by God.)

3. Rebellion And The Curse

1 1 Timothy 2:14; Romans 5:12
2 Romans 5:12 ". . . through one man sin entered the world, and death through sin. . . ."

3   Genesis 3:15

4   Genesis 3:23–24 (and Romans 5:12) emphasize that the blame was laid squarely on Adam, not Eve. It was Adam that God banished from the Garden ("him," v. 23) and it was Adam that God drove out ("the man," v. 24). Both the man and his wife sinned (1 Tim. 2:14) and lived the rest of their lives with the impact of eating the forbidden fruit, but Adam was the one whom God held responsible.

5   Genesis 4:1

6   Adam and Eve's original gene pool was perfect. They had no defects. By God's design, brothers and sisters and cousins married, and their children were free of genetic deformities. It was not until the time of Moses, some 2,500 years after creation and 850 years after the Flood in about 1500 B.C., that God prohibited marriage between close relatives. (Also see "Cain's Wife — Who Was She?" by Ken Ham, at www.answersingenesis.org/articles/nab/who-was-cains-wife.)

7   Acts 3:19–21 (restoration, NKJV & NAS / restore, NIV).

4. Noah Builds the Ark

1   A population of at least hundreds of thousands is likely, and many more are mathematically reasonable. See "What Was the Pre-Flood Population Like?" by Ken Ham, https://answersingenesis.org/noahs-ark/pre-flood-population. Also consider "Population of the Pre-Flood World," by Tom Pickett, www.ldolphin.org/pickett.html, and "Why Don't We Find Human and Dinosaur Fossils Together?" by Bodie Hodge, www.answersingenesis.org/articles/nab/human-and-dino-fossils-together#fnList_1_4. Dr. Henry Morris III of the Institute for Creation Research says, "If one uses a very conservative formula of six children for each family, an average generation of 100 years, and a lifespan of 500 years, there would have been over 235 million people alive at the time of the global Flood. That is probably much too low an estimate. For instance, if the average family size were eight instead of six, the generation was only 93 instead of 100, then the population at the death of Adam (930 years after creation) would have been 2.8 million. At that rate, the population at the time of the Flood would have been over 137 billion!" Henry M. Morris III, The Book of Beginnings (Dallas, TX: Institute for Creation Research, 2012), p. 219 — based on Henry M. Morris, 1970, Biblical Cosmology and Modern Science (Grand Rapids, MI: Baker Books, 1970), p. 87.

2   Acts 3:19–21

3   Genesis 5:32. Noah is 500 when his first son, Japheth, is born (Gen. 10:21). Shem (son 2) was born two years after Japheth. We know this because Gen. 11:10 tells us that Shem was 100 two years after the Flood, and Noah was 600 when the Flood began. Noah's youngest son was Ham (son 3, Gen. 9:24). No time span is specified, but a logical guess is that he was born 2–3 years after Shem. This means that the three sons were probably all born by about 95 years prior to the Flood.

4   510' x 85' x 51' is based on the older and longer 20.35-inch "Nippur" cubit, which is believed to be the most likely cubit length used.

5   It is extremely interesting that when God told King David that his son, Solomon, would build the Temple in Jerusalem, the Spirit placed many details in David's mind, and directed him in creating a written set of instructions. These were passed by David to Solomon. While the Temple was ornate and of immense importance, with the Ark of Noah — which had to withstand the cataclysmic Flood and convey thousands of land animals plus eight people and enough food to sustain them for a year — it seems likely that God provided even more details than he did for the Temple (see 1 Chronicles 28:11–19).

6   Noah was apparently told of the coming Flood when he was 480. In Genesis 6:3, 120 years before the Flood, God declared, to no one in particular, that man only had 120 years before He was going to wipe things away and change the world. The Flood came when he was 600 (Gen. 7:6). Genesis 5:32 says that all three of Noah's sons were born after he turned 500, which means that his oldest son, Japheth, was 100 when the Flood came.

7   One way or another — whether just Noah's family, or with the help of additional laborers — Noah was able to complete the Ark within God's 120-year timeframe. It is likely that it required about 55–75 years for preparation and build-time. See https://answersingenesis.org/bible-timeline/how-long-did-it-take-for-noah-to-build-the-ark/, by Bodie Hodge.

8   See "Did People Like Adam and Noah Really Live Over 900 Years of Age? https://answersingenesis.org/bible-timeline/genealogy/did-adam-and-noah-really-live-over-900-years/ by Drs. Georgia Purdom and David Menton. Consider also "Why Did People Start to Have Shorter Lives After the Flood?" https://answersingenesis.org/bible-questions/why-did-people-have-shorter-lives-after-flood/ by Bodie Hodge.

5. God Sends The Animals!

1   Genesis 6:14.

2   Genesis 6:20, ". . . will come to you to keep them alive."

3   Ark food storage estimate — Regarding weight, it is common for a small adult elephant to eat about 125 pounds of hay per day; 373 days on board x 125 pounds per day x 2 elephants = 93,250 pounds (46.625 tons). However, the average size of an Ark animal is estimated to have been that of an adult sheep, which eats only about 4 pounds of hay per day; 373 days x 4 pounds of hay per animal x 2 animals per pair = 2,984 pounds; 1.492 tons x 3,500 pairs = 5,222 tons of hay. Regarding food volume, at 300 cubic feet per ton for dry chopped hay, a formula for determining how much space 5,222 tons would require is as follows: if 3,500 pairs of animals, then 300 cubic feet per ton x 5,222 tons = 1,566,600 cubic feet. Volume of ark 510 x 85 x 51 = 2,210,850 cubic feet. 1,566,600 / 2,210,850 = .71 or 71% of ark. (Plenty of room for animals, food, humans, and a warehouse of goods.) Alternatively, a grain concentrate, such as corn, would require less than half the volume of hay. Further, animals that are severely restricted in terms of physical activity tend to sleep more and consume less.

4   Two of every unclean land animal, and seven of every clean land animal (of which there were few), and seven of every bird of the air (Gen. 7:2–3 KJV).

5   Somewhere between about 50 and 90 different kinds of dinosaurs have been discovered in the fossil record. Sexually mature juveniles would have been easily facilitated on the Ark. Since dinosaurs were land-dwellers themselves, representatives of each

of the dinosaur kinds clearly were included with the other land animals that God saved during the Flood.

6　Genesis 5:1. ". . . the Hebrew Bible says in Genesis 5:1 that the history of Adam was written! The word for 'book' used here, sefer, always means the account is written." per archaeologist Dr. David Livingston at http://www.answersingenesis.org/articles/am/v3/n2/cave-dwellers.

7　After the animals arrived at the Ark, they may have entered on their own — without the need to be led, carried, or coaxed by humans. See Genesis 7:9 and 7:15. Also see Genesis 6:20 in the ESV and YLT. The more literal English translations indicate that the animals did not simply arrive. At the proper time, they went "in" to the Ark to Noah by themselves to be kept alive by Noah's family. YLT says "two of every [sort] they come in unto thee, to keep them alive," Likewise, the ESV says "two of every kind shall come in to you to keep them alive." Such miraculous choosing, calling, and direction straight from God to the animals would undoubtedly have made loading much easier and faster.

8　Romans 8:29

9　Genesis 6:20 — animals will come to you to keep them alive.

10　"Caring for the Animals on the Ark," by John Woodmorappe, *Answers* magazine vol 2.2 (published by Answers in Genesis), and online at http://www.answersingenesis.org/articles/am/v2/n2/caring-for-the-animals. Many animals have a latent ability to hibernate or for their bodily functions to nearly stop for a time. The Bible does not reference such created capabilities, but if employed by God during the Flood, the daily workload of Noah's family would have been even less.

11　2 Peter 3:7–13, 17; 1 Thessalonians 5:3

6. The Whole Earth Changes

1　Genesis 7:11; Matthew 24:38–39

2　John D. Morris, "The Ice Age: Causes and Consequences," Acts & Facts, 2009, 38 (8): 15 (www.icr.org/article/ice-age-causes-consequences/). Also see "Catastrophic Plate Tectonics: the Geophysical Context of the Genesis Flood" https://answersingenesis.org/geology/plate-tectonics/catastrophic-plate-tectonics-geophysical-context-of-genesis-flood/ by Dr. John Baumgardner, accessed February 2017.

3　Genesis 6:7 ("wipe away" per YLT), 6:17 (destroy). Also note that, "enormous tectonic upheavals on the pre-Flood ocean floor . . . would have caused massive tsunamis. . . . Add to this the fact that earthquakes often trigger volcanoes and we can readily see that the Flood was a world-changing catastrophe of incredible violence and destructive power." Quoted from footnote 19 of Dr. Terry Mortenson's online article, "The Fall and the Problem of Millions of Years of Natural Evil," at https://answersingenesis.org/theory-of-evolution/millions-of-years/the-fall-and-the-problem-of-millions-of-years-of-natural-evil/). Also see or listen to Dr. Andrew Snelling's article, "Five Mass Extinctions or One Cataclysmic Event?" at https://answersingenesis.org/geology/catastrophism/five-mass-extinctions-or-one-cataclysmic-event/.

4　See Dr. Andrew Snelling's excellent article, "Five Mass Extinctions or One Cataclysmic Event?" at https://answersingenesis.org/geology/catastrophism/five-mass-extinctions-or-one-cataclysmic-event/

5　The Bible reveals in Genesis 1:9 that all water was originally together in one place. —logically yielding an original supercontinent as well. This single landmass is commonly called Rodinia by geologists. Computerized Flood modeling that utilizes global catastrophic plate tectonics as the basis for the rapid separation of the continental plates has been done by researchers. An extremely rapid, catastrophic continental breakup is wholly consistent with young earth geological models, but the relatively brief time necessary to accomplish the breakup makes secular geologists unwilling to seriously consider the model. / See also "Noah's Lost World" by Dr. Andrew Snelling at https://answersingenesis.org/geology/plate-tectonics/noahs-lost-world/.

6　Genesis 7:19–22, 24–8:5. Also see "Biblical Overview of the Flood Timeline" by Bodie Hodge at www.answersingenesis.org/articles/2010/08/23/overview-flood-timeline.

7　See "Where Was the Garden of Eden Located?" by Ken Ham, at https://answersingenesis.org/genesis/garden-of-eden/where-was-the-garden-of-eden-located/ as accessed February 2017.

8　Genesis 8:4 says the "mountains of Ararat" (not "Mount Ararat") and 8:5 states "the first day of the tenth month." This was 224 days (about 7.5 months) into the Ark's journey. See www.answersingenesis.org/articles/2010/08/23/overview-flood-timeline by Bodie Hodge.

9　Genesis 8:13. The first day of the first month was 314 days (about 10.5 months) into the journey of Noah's family aboard the Ark.

7. The Rainbow Promise And The New World

1　The Ark ran aground on day 150 of the Flood (also described in Genesis as the 17th day of the 7th month of Noah's 600th year of life). Genesis 7, www.answersingenesis.org/articles/2010/08/23/overview-flood-timeline.

2　Genesis 9:1.

3　Genesis 9:2–4.

4　Genesis 9:6.

5　Genesis 9:15–16.

6　". . . the world appears to have been a pretty balmy place until the Ice Age," Dr. Andrew Snelling and Mike Matthews, *Answers* magazine, Volume 8 Number 2, 2013, page 47. https://answersingenesis.org/environmental-science/ice-age/when-was-the-ice-age-in-biblical-history/.

7　"Geologists have found over a hundred impact craters on earth. On [the table displayed in the article] 39 of the 110 impacts were deposited in the uppermost rock layers, and the rest were spread over the many lower layers. If all these layers were deposited slowly over millions of years, then impacts have been more common in recent times. But if most layers were deposited during the year-long Flood, 71 impacts occurred during only one year. The other 39 were spread over the next 4,500 years." From "Did Meteors Trigger Noah's Flood?" by Andrew Snelling, PhD, in *Answers* magazine online at www.answersingenesis.org/articles/am/v7/n1/meteors-trigger-flood, as accessed February 2017.

8   "For months, seawater covered the continents and then retreated from the land. These processes produced so much heat that the average ocean temperatures climbed to over 100°F (38°C), much warmer than today. This warm ocean set in motion a series of events that would lead to an Ice Age." By professor of atmospheric science Dr. Larry Vardiman at https://answersingenesis.org/environmental-science/ice-age/what-started-the-ice-age/

BONUS – A Rapid Ice Age?

1   For a free, brief video that highlights the basics of "Rapid Speciation," visit http://www.answersingenesis.org/articles/am/v3/n4/rapid-speciation.

2   Fossils laid down during numerous (localized) residual catastrophes in the centuries after the worldwide cataclysm reveal huge numbers of freshwater fish, mammal graveyards, etc. See "Continuing Catastrophes" by Dr. John Whitmore, www.answersingenesis.org/articles/am/v3/n4/continuing-catastrophes. Also of note is recent research that has mapped the migration of mastodons and other species of elephants, plus the people who followed those migrations for food and furs. Data from thousands of archaeologists during the last several decades shows use of former land bridges from Russia to Alaska, and Asia to Australia, thus revealing the routes used to move from the Middle East to virtually all parts of the world. See the *Answers* magazine feature article, "When Was the Ice Age in Biblical History?" by Dr. Andrew Snelling and Mike Matthews, https://answersingenesis.org/environmental-science/ice-age/when-was-the-ice-age-in-biblical-history/).

3   ". . . the biblical creation model recognizes that one kind cannot change into another and that the changes are a result of variation within the created kinds — not descent from a single common ancestor." by Roger Patterson in "Evolution Exposed: Biology" (chapter 3), www.answersingenesis.org/articles/ee/natural-selection-vs-evolution.

4   For example, the antelope kind bore many specialized new species, including gazelles, blackbucks, gerenuks, dibatags, saiga, beira, suni, klipspringer, and others. The camelidae kind bore camels, llamas, vicunas, guanacos, and more. Some animals were born with no hair, some with short hair, some with long. There were thick, dark coats, and thin, light-colored coats. This sort of variation within a kind is often referred to as speciation. It is not the unproven amoeba-to-man idea of evolution popularized by Charles Darwin and others.

5   Genesis 11:2. "And it came to pass, as they journeyed from the east, that they found a plain in the land of Shinar."

6   All of Greenland, Iceland, and Antarctica, nearly all of Canada and New Zealand, and much of modern-day Russia, Europe, the USA, South America, and Australia.

7   Dr. Andrew Snelling and Michael Matthews, "When Was the Ice Age in Biblical History?" *Answers* magazine, vol. 8.2, April–June 2013, p. 46–52.

8   Weather data studied by meteorologist Michael Oard suggests 500 years (rather than 300), plus about 200 years for melt off, (compared to 100). See the technical writings and summaries by Mike Oard, Larry Vardiman, and Jake Hebert on this subject: www.icr.org/article/are-polar-ice-sheets-only-4500-years-old by Michael Oard, M.S., www.icr.org/article/was-there-ice-age/ by Jack Hebert, Ph.D., and www.icr.org/article/7161/ by Larry Vardiman, Ph.D.

9   "It is hard to imagine such extreme changes in weather, landscapes, and vegetation during the rapid Ice Age and the years that followed. Some lush places in the north were stricken by drought, while monsoons filled the Sahara Desert with lakes and grasslands, attracting rhinoceroses, crocodiles, and human settlers. For a time at the end of the Ice Age, the drenched Nile Valley was not even habitable," by geologist Dr. Andrew Snelling in the *Answers* magazine article "When Was the Ice Age in Biblical History," at https://answersingenesis.org/environmental-science/ice-age/when-was-the-ice-age-in-biblical-history/.

8. The Tower Of Babel

1   ". . . it appears that volcanic eruptions and earthquakes were greatest during the Flood and then gradually weakened to today's intensity. These early post-Flood catastrophes had the power to cause enormous geologic change, including massive erosion, altered landscapes, and deposits of sediment layers thousands of feet thick." From *Answers* magazine, "Continuing Catastrophes," by geologist Dr. John Whitmore, accessed February 2017, at https://answersingenesis.org/geology/catastrophism/continuing-catastrophes.

2   Genesis 2:20; Ephesians 5:22–6:4; Colossians 3:18–21. The spiritual principle of male leadership and responsibility clearly began in Genesis 3 when Eve was created as Adam's helpmate, and Adam was the one charged with bringing sin into the world, even though Eve was the first to eat of the forbidden fruit. In addition, Deuteronomy 6:1–9 notes the special responsibility that fathers and grandfathers would be given to communicate the commandments of God to the Israelites.

3   Genesis 4:17–22.

4   Don Landis, *The Genius of Ancient Man* (Green Forest, AR: Master Books, 2012), p. 32. Also see Bodie Hodge, *The New Answers Book 2*, chapter 28, www.answersingenesis.org/articles/nab2/was-babel-dispersion-real-event/, accessed February 2017. A ziggurat is how ancient Greek historian Herodotus described the tower in 440 B.C. after he had the opportunity to climb what he believed to be its ruins.

5   Genesis 11:8 says they ceased building the city. Most conservative Hebrew language scholars are adament that the tower, as well, was not finished when God came down and judged the people. (This includes ancient language specialist/archeologist Dr. Douglas Petrovich, in comments verbalized to hundreds of viewers during a Q&A session after a premiere screening of the documentary *Is Genesis History?* at Answers in Genesis' Petersburg, Kentucky headquarters before its release in February 2017.)

6   See the subsection, "We Don't Speak the Same Language Anymore," at www.answersingenesis.org/articles/nab2/was-babel-dispersion-real-event by Bodie Hodge.

7   See also, "Are There Really Different Races?" by Ken Ham, at www.answersingenesis.org/articles/nab/are-there-diffe ent-races.

9. God's Covenant With Abram

1   "367 years" based on the genealogies of Genesis 11:10–12:4.
2   Joshua 24:2
3   Abram's father was an idolater yet there is no indication that Abram followed in his footsteps. Friction about what to believe could easily have created a less-than-ideal relationship between the two men. Also, the size of the herds of Abram and Lot created conflicts between their herdsmen, and probably between Abram and Lot themselves (Genesis 13:8).
4   Abram allowed, and facilitated that his desirable wife would be taken into the harems of two different national leaders: a king and a pharaoh. Also, he went along with his wife's idea for him to have sex with her servant in order to try to produce a line of offspring, which ended up creating stress in their marriage when the pregnant servant began to take advantage of the fact that she was pregnant but her mistress, Abram's wife, was not.
5   Abram exhibited a less-than-ideal walk. Although he is recognized for great faith in his later years, it was his lack of trust in God and God's promise that resulted in him having sex with Sarai's handmaiden Hagar in order to create offspring on his timeframe rather than trusting in God's. (It is important to note that Abram's extramarital relationship with Hagar was not God's instruction. Ishmael was not Abram's rightful heir, and God didn't count Ishmael as the legitimate son of promise as exhibited in God's command many years later to "Take thy son, thy only son Isaac" to be sacrificed).
6   See Leviticus 18. Marriage of close relatives was not disallowed until c. 1491 B.C. when God gave the Law to the Israelites at Mt. Sinai through Moses, after they were led out of captivity in Egypt. For more than 2,500 years — from creation to the Mosaic law — marriage of close relatives was at first necessary and blessed of God (i.e., Adam and Eve's children at first married one another) and later, common (i.e., Abraham and Sarah were half-siblings, c. 2000 B.C.).
7   Genesis 13:10 describes the land that Lot chose, the Jordan River valley, as being Eden-like. At the time of Abraham, much of the region we now know as Israel was lush and incredibly beautiful with high-quality vegetation.
8   Genesis 13:12–13
9   Genesis 12:10–15 (Sarai taken by the Pharaoh of Egypt).
10 Genesis 20 (Sarai taken by Abimelech king of Gerer).
11 Since Genesis 14:14 says that there were over 300 men in Abram's clan, it is assumed that approximately this number of males were circumcised. Ishmael, Abraham's son by Hagar the servant of Sarah, was among those circumcised that day. He was 13 and Abram 99. See Genesis 17:24–27. Ishmael was not the son of promise, having been born by Sarah's suggested extramarital compromise, not God's covenant promise. Therefore, the yet-to-be-born Isaac was Abraham's only "legitimate" son of the Promise.
12 Hebrews 11:12; Abraham was "as good as dead." Genesis 18:11–12; Sarah was past the age of childbearing. Genesis 17:17; Abraham laughed.

10. Angels Rescue Lot From Sodom And Gomorrah

1   This appearance was likely not more than three months after God's initial declaration (Gen. 17) of the upcoming birth. On that day, Abraham and all the men of his clan were circumcised. Now, enough time had passed that he was healed enough to be able to run to the Lord and the two angels that visited him in Genesis 18:1–2, yet he was still 99 and his son would still be born within a year (Genesis 18:10). The Genesis 18 announcement was apparently new information to Sarah, so she must not have been present at the previous (Genesis 17) announcement. It is also noteworthy that during the interim that separated the two angelic visitations (not more than three months) Abraham subjected Sarah to the nearby King Abimelech (Genesis 20), like he had 24 years earlier when he gave her to a Pharoah in Egypt (Genesis 12).
2   Genesis 19:30–38 reveals Lot was "old" but not too old to father children. The age of his daughters at this time is not known, and though they may have been fairly young they were old enough by the standards of their society to be engaged.
3   Regarding Genesis 19:17 ("do not look behind you") and 19:26 ("his wife looked back behind him, and she became a pillar of salt"), the word "expectingly" is used in Young's Literal Translation ("look not expectingly behind thee") but not in most modern translations. Substitution of a more modern word, such as "longingly" rather than "expectingly" is preferred in order to better understand the situation. Lot's wife was judged for her disobedience and turned into a pillar of salt (possibly actual salt, or possibly encased by the burning sulfur that God was raining down). Her delay indicates a longing to return to the sin-filled cities, rather than obedience and gratefulness at being rescued by God's messengers.
4   Genesis 19:25 — the Lord overthrew (killed) everyone living in those cities; Deuteronomy 29:23 (ESV) says, "the whole land burned out with brimstone and salt, nothing sown and nothing growing, where no plant can sprout…"
5   2 Peter 2:6
6   Genesis 19:30 — Although evolutionary teachers promote the idea that most cave dwellers were not fully human, many normal men and women have for thousands of years taken advantage of the excellent natural protection and ready availability of caves worldwide. The Bible itself refers to numerous people who lived in caves, including Lot and his daughters, David and his warriors, and Israelites at the time of Gideon (Judges 62). "Cavemen" are exactly that; men and women who live in caves for various reasons and lengths of time.

11. Isaac, Nearly Sacrificed!

1   Genesis 16:1–4
2   God created marriage on day 6 of creation week when He brought Adam and Eve together to be the father and mother of all mankind. See the chapter entitled "God Creates Marriage" earlier in this book.
3   Genesis 21:5. Note Isaac's complex family heritage —Beginning with God's dreadful fiery judgment of the Sodomites a year prior to Isaac's birth, fear and doubt led to faithlessness by Abraham and his relatives. The wife of Abraham's nephew Lot was dead

— standing as a pillar of salt — and Lot was afraid to again live in a city (Gen. 19:30). Therefore, Lot and his daughters dwelt in a cave in the hills above the smoldering ashes that had been Sodom and Gomorrah (Gen. 19:30). But because the fiancées of Lot's daughters were both dead and both girls were afraid there would be no men to have children by, they repeatedly got their father thoroughly drunk and became pregnant by him (Gen. 19:31–38). Even Isaac's godly father Abraham was so afraid for his own life that he again allowed Sarah, now 90 years old, to be taken into the harem of a king (Gen. 20), as he had when she was 65 (Gen. 12). It was into this complex, "dysfunctional" family situation that Isaac, the only son of God's promise, was born.

4   Genesis 21:10–11

5   Genesis 22:5 describes Isaac as a "youth" in Young's Literal Translation (YLT).

6   https://answersingenesis.org/contradictions-in-the-bible/unacceptable-offering/.

7   Hebrews 11:17–19

8   Romans 10:9–10 — ". . . if you confess with your mouth the Lord Jesus and believe in your heart that God has raised Him from the dead, you will be saved. For with the head one believes unto righteousness, and with the mouth confession is made unto salvation."

12. Death, Marriage, And The Stairway To Heaven

1   Three years after Sarah died, Isaac was 40 (Gen. 25:20) and Abraham sent his chief servant Eliezer to Haran (in modern-day Turkey) to find a wife for Isaac from among Sarah's relatives. Isaac married his cousin Rebekah, the daughter of Sarah's brother Bethuel, and sister of Laban.

2   Genesis 24:4, 7, 15, 37–38, 40. Abraham was 140 at this time and lived to 175, even marrying again and having more children. Isaac was 40 and lived to 180, so Isaac was just 22% of the way through his life when his father, Abraham, determined it was time for him to get married. As of 2017, a U.S. male has a life expectancy of 76 years and marries when he is 29, which is 38% of the way through life. Since modern U.S. men marry when nearly twice as old as Isaac was (by percent of life lived), the fact that Abraham waited until Isaac was 40 to help him find a bride is not odd. (Note: Modern ages and percentages derived chiefly from the U.S. Census Bureau.)

3   Genesis 24:10–11, The distance to Haran was more than 400 miles. Eliezer took ten camels and other servants.

4   Genesis 24:63–67

5   Genesis 24:15–16. Because Isaac's second cousin Rebekah is described as a "maiden" (ESV) or a "young person" (YLT) it is likely that she was no older than 20 when Isaac was 40 and they married. Genesis 24:67 indicates that Rebekah brought him comfort when they married at that time, about three years after his mother's death. In Genesis 26:6–17, we see that Isaac followed somewhat in his father Abraham's footsteps in that when he was afraid for his life due to his wife's beauty, he deceived the men of Gerar — where Isaac and Rebekah lived for a long time — by telling them that she was his sister. This was a lie. She was his second cousin. Isaac's deception became known to Abimelech, king of the Philistines, when he saw them "frolicking" from his window and chastised Isaac for the lie. Eventually, God blessed Isaac in terms of his wealth and the envious king sent him and his clan away.

6   Genesis 25:20–26 .

7   A "birthright" was a person's future inheritance.

8   Genesis 25:31–34.

9   Per James Ussher's *Annals of the World* (English translation dated 2003 by Larry and Marion Pierce, paragraph 113), Jacob was 77 at this time; 1759 B.C. Though Ussher does not explain his calculation to arrive at the age of 77, following is a complicated, yet clear, biblical calculation that Jacob indeed was 77 when he deceived Isaac.
- Isaac was 40 years old when he married Rebekah, and 60 years old when Rebekah bore Jacob and Esau. Isaac was 180 years old when he died (Genesis 35:28), so his sons Jacob and Esau would have been 120 when Isaac died. Per Genesis 47:9, Jacob was 130 when he went to Egypt during the famine. Genesis 45:11 says Jacob went down while there was 5 years of famine (of the 7 years) left; 130 years minus 2 years of famine already, minus 7 years of good crops, makes Jacob 121 at the start of the good crops. Genesis 41:46 says Joseph was 30 years old when he was assigned to begin overseeing the 7 years of good crops. So Jacob's 121 minus Joseph's 30 makes Jacob 91 when Joseph was born. Jacob served Laban a total of 14 years for Leah and Rachel. Right at the end of the 14 years was when Joseph was born (Gen. 30:25). Now we have to subtract the 14 years from the age of 91, which gives Jacob's age of 77 when he left Canaan for Haran. Per https://answers.yahoo.com/question/index?qid=20090215190920AAYX-Fg9, as accessed April 2017.

10   Hebrews 12:16–17

11   Genesis 25:23. God told Rebekah before the twins were born that "the older shall serve the younger."

12   Genesis 27:18–29. Note also that, "With Jacob, the issue of the blessing and birthright are pretty much one and the same. Esau despised his birthright so much as to sell it to Jacob. Birthright meant Jacob had a right to receive the blessing, and Jacob knew better than to let Esau take it out from under him after he purchased it, and so went along with his mother's scheme. So, although he was not honest with his father (and this was a fault for Jacob), the blessing was his to receive due to the agreement between Esau and Jacob in Genesis 25:31–34. Isaac never repealed the blessing but reaffirmed it afterwards, and even the Lord gave his blessing to Jacob in Genesis 48:3," by Bodie Hodge in the online article "More Righteous Lies?" as viewed February 2017 at https://answersingenesis.org/morality/more-righteous-lies/.

13   Genesis 28:10

14   Genesis 28:11–22

15   John 1:51: ". . . you shall see heaven open, and the angels of God ascending and descending upon the Son of Man."

13. Jacob Wrestles With . . . Jesus?

1   Jacob was now 84. He had been 77 when he deceived his father Isaac and left Beersheba. He was anxious to marry, as evidenced

by the way he approached Laban after his 7-year work commitment was fulfilled; "Give me my wife that I may go in to her, for my time is completed" (Gen. 29:21). Jacob eventually died at age 147 (Gen. 47:28), so at age 84 he was 63% through his life (roughly equivalent to a modern U.S. male getting married for the first time at age 48, based on life expectancy of 76).

2   Jesus' lineage from Jacob went through a son of Leah (Judah), not through his beloved Rachel. Leah was the first of the four women that Jacob had sexual relations with.
3   Genesis 31:3
4   Genesis 30:43
5   Genesis 32:1–2. During Jacob's escape from his brother, on his way to Haran some 20 years earlier, he dreamt of angels. Now on his way back from Haran, angels — literally, messengers of Elohim — "meet" him.
6   Genesis 32:24. The YLT translates the Hebrew as "one" not as "a man."
7   This is called a "Christophany." In the online article "Theophanies in the Old Testament" (see www.answersingenesis.org/articles/2012/01/13/feedback-old-testament-theophanies), apologist Tim Chaffey reminds readers that no one has seen God (the Father) at any time (John 1:18), so Jacob's declaration that he has "seen God face to face, and my life is preserved" must mean that he saw God (the Son), Jesus Christ (Genesis 32:30).

14. Joseph: Imprisoned for Good

1   Genesis 46:34. They were "keepers of livestock" since their youth.
2   Genesis 34:2–3, 19
3   Genesis 35:16–20, 48:7
4   The brothers were near Dothan, which was 10–15 miles northwest of Shechem, a total of about 75 miles from Hebron.
5   Genesis 39:7, 12
6   When Potiphar's wife accused Joseph of trying to make sport of her, it appears that Potiphar simply moved Joseph from a position of responsibility and authority in his household, to a position of responsibility and authority in the prison he controlled. It appears that Joseph was placed by his master Potiphar, the captain of the guard (Gen. 39:1), in the dungeon prison of his own house (Gen. 40:3–4, 7).
7   Genesis 41:45

15. Job Loses Everything

1   "God allows every reader of the Book of Job to witness some extraordinary 'behind-the-scenes' events in heaven, which Job never saw. The Lord had reasons for allowing Job's suffering, but He never told Job these specific reasons, and He demanded that Job not question the decisions of his Maker." (from *Why Is there Death and Suffering?* booklet, edited by Ken Ham and Mark Looy, p. 20). View as PDF at www.answersingenesis.org/assets/pdf/radio/death-and-suffering.pdf.
2   Job 2:3
3   Job 7:3 (nights & months), Job 2:7 (painful boils from head to toe), Job 7:5 (worms, scabs), Job 7:14 (terrifying dreams and visions).
4   Job 29:8–11, 29:25
5   Job 19:18
6   Job 13:3
7   Job 19:20 (skin and bones), 7:5 (putrid), 30:15 (terror/fear), 30:17 (relentless pain).
8   Job 38:31-33 (star systems), Job 38:29-30 (deep frozen waters), Job 36:32 (lightning), Job 38:37 (water in clouds).
9   Job 40:6–9 (". . . can you thunder with a voice like his?").
10 Because the word "dinosaur" was not coined until the 1840s, it was not used in the King James Version or other early translations of the Bible. Instead, words like dragon, elephant, rhinoceros, etc., were used. Later, when Darwin's ideas about evolution quickly began to permeate churches and seminaries, newer translations still did not use "dinosaur" since evolution ideology requires that dinosaurs died out about 70 million years before Job.
11 If either Behemoth or Leviathan had not been active at the time of Job and his friends — to whom God's comments were specifically directed in this passage — use of these two created creatures as examples of God's infinite power would be meaningless (there would be no point of reference). Note also that Leviathan is referenced by the prophet Isaiah hundreds of years later (closer to today) when he tells of "Leviathan the fleeting serpent, Leviathan the coiling serpent . . . the monster of the sea" in Isaiah 27:1. Again, there would be no point of reference for his readers if Leviathan were not living and able to be seen during Isaiah's lifetime, around 700 B.C.
12 Swampy lowlands, grassy plains, and tropic-like mountains were all part of the topography of the presumed region of the Land of Uz when Job lived there — likely east of the Jordan River and south of the Euphrates.
13 See image of the larger but less well-known and more massive *Dreadnoughtus* sauropod dinosaur at http://dinosaurpictures.org/*Dreadnoughtus*-pictures, and elsewhere. *Dreadnoughtus* is projected to have weighed about 65 tons, while the slightly longer *Diplodocus* was much less massive, weighing one-fourth as much, at about 18 tons. (A typical mature African elephant weighs about 5 tons.)
14 Job 41. Leviathan is not precisely known, but may have been similar to the extinct 60-foot-long *Thalattosuchia* or the extinct 40-foot *Sarcosuchus imperator*. Fossils of these massive creatures resemble, to varying degrees, God's descriptions of Leviathan recorded in Job 41 (terrible teeth, tight impenetrable scales, fire breathing from his mouth, and smoke from his nostrils), and in Isaiah 27:1 (a fleeing twisted serpent of the sea).
15 Romans 3:10–12. No one is "good." No one is truly righteous and free of sin. God said in Job 1:8 that his servant Job was the most righteous person of his time. Yet even he was not without sin.
16 Job 19:25–27. Job did not know the Redeemer's name. He was obviously aware, however, that God promised (in Genesis 3:15)

that one day a sent-one would crush the serpent, Satan. This was the Lord Jesus Christ.

17 Job 42:10–17. The Lord blessed Job even more than before.

16. Moses: The Runaway Prince

1 Exodus 1:11–12

2 Exodus 2:3. The Hebrew word used for the basket of Moses (which Moses' mother coated with asphalt and pitch), is *teba*. The same Hebrew word is used for the Ark of Noah in Genesis 6–8. Both were waterproofed vessels of salvation.

3 The adoption of Moses was apparently more of a "taking" by Pharaoh's daughter than a relinquishing by Moses' mother. Moses' mother only gave him up due to his certain death if she kept him. This was not the sweet sort of adoption that most Christians envision today. Rohan McEnor says, "The Bible is a story about a Father. A Father who had children. And these children were stolen from him by the false father — the father of lies. And the Bible is really the story of how our true Heavenly Father pursued us at great cost to Himself, just to buy back His natural children, just so He could make a declaration of the true inheritance He has set aside for us, just to hear us call Him, 'Daddy! Father!' As he truly is." www.originsnsw.com/fathers/id2.html), viewed April 2017.

4 Acts 7:20–23

5 Exodus 2:12; Acts 7:23–24. Acts 7:24 in the YLT identifies this action as justice for the oppressed, not murder.

6 His two sons were named Gershon and Eliezer (1 Chronicles 23:15).

7 At 80 years old, Moses was two-thirds of the way through his life. This would be like a 51-year old male in the U.S. today, since modern U.S. males normally live to about age 76. In this new calling, he would shepherd humans, not sheep.

8 Genesis 12:2. See also "How Long Were the Israelites in Egypt?" at https://answersingenesis.org/bible-questions/how-long-were-the-israelites-in-egypt/: ". . . four hundred years . . . began when Ishmael, son of Hagar the Egyptian, mocked and persecuted Isaac (Gen. 21:9; Gal. 4:29) . . . which fell out 30 years after the promise (Gen. 12:3) which was 430 years before the law (Gal. 3:17) and 430 years after that promise came Israel out of bondage (Exod. 12:41)." The above referenced article quotes British theologian Henry Ainsworth of the early 1600s in his discussion of "Israel's affliction."

9 Exodus 3:19–20

17. Ten Terrible Plagues Devastate Egypt

1 Exodus 18:2-6. Moses sent them back to Jethro, possibly for their safety (or perhaps to heal from their circumcision, Exod. 4:24–26).

2 If the plagues followed immediately on the heels of one another, then the total days add up to slightly more than one month. For an explanation of the various timelines, see, "How Long Did the Ten Plagues of Egypt Last?" at http://jesusalive.cc/ques219.htm, accessed April 2017.

3 Exodus 11:5, 12:30

4 Exodus 5:2; NIV

5 Exodus 10:7

6 Locusts, Exodus 10:13–16

7 Death of the firstborn, Exodus 11:1–12:36.

8 1 Peter 3:18; Galatians 1:4; Genesis 3:15; Colossians 1:20.

18. The Exodus: Crossing The Red Sea

1 Archeologist David Down, in his book *Unveiling the Kings of Israel* (Green Forest, AR: Master Books, 2011), p. 54, affirms the Bible's notation in Exodus 12:37 that there were 600,000 men who departed Egypt. Down says, "Counting wives, children, and old people there would have been some two million people who set out for the Promised Land. Some scholars have questioned this number. They suggest that ELEPH, the Hebrew word for 'thousand' can also be translated 'family.' That is true, though there is only one instance in the Hebrew Bible where it is used in that sense. However, in this instance it must be 'thousands' because when all the able-bodied men were told to bring a half shekel of silver for the building of the sanctuary, it amounted to 301,775 shekels, representing 603,550 able-bodied men (Exod. 38:35–36)."

2 If there were 2,000,000 people total as David Down suggests (above), and if they traveled 120 people abreast with 5 feet total for the person walking and space to the next person in front or behind, the line of Israelites would be nearly 16 miles long; 2,000,000 / 120 abreast = 16,667 rows of people x 5 feet = 83,333 feet / 5280 ft in a mile = a 15.8-mile-long procession of people not including carts, herds, etc. If they traveled at a constant pace of 2.5 miles per hour, it would require 6.3 hours for all the people to walk past a single point.

3 Six days per Ussher note 192; two weeks or so per www.bible.ca/archeology/bible-archeology-exodus-route-travel-times-distances-days.htm.

4 Exodus 14:13

5 Exodus 15:9

6 The parting of the Red Sea was a miracle, not a natural event. This happened when Moses stretched out his hand and lifted his rod over the water (Exod. 14:16). Psalm 78:13 says God caused the waters to part and stand as a heap; Exodus 15:8 notes that the ocean stood upright and congealed; and Exodus 14:16 also documents that the sea floor on which they walked was dry, not muddy.

7 Exodus 14:26–28

8   Exodus 15:1–21. Moses and the men ("sons" in YLT) of Israel sang and spoke praises to Jehovah God. After them, Miriam the prophetess and sister of Aaron and Moses, plus the women, took timbrels (tambourines) and Miriam sang and danced praises to the Lord.

19. Ten Commandments And A Golden Calf

1   Exodus 16:2–5 tells the start of manna. Numbers 11:7–9 describes manna's look and how it was gathered and cooked.
2   Mt. Sinai was the same as Mt. Horeb; Acts 7:30, Exodus 3:1, 12. See also Exodus 19:2.
3   Exodus 19:10–11
4   Deuteronomy 5:22, 10:4–5. God spoke the Ten Commandments to the people the day He spoke to the entire assembly.
5   Exodus 34:28
6   Exodus 31:18, 34:1
7   Exodus 20
8   Exodus 19:8. "Then all the people answered together and said, 'All that the Lord has spoken we will do.'"
9   Exodus 32:27-28. The Levites were instructed to go throughout the camp and kill brother, friend and neighbor. They killed 3,000.

20. Forty Years In The Wilderness

1   Numbers 10:11, 33 (about 10 months since arriving at Sinai).
2   When the Ark was moved, it was to be covered under several layers of sacred fabric plus the skins of animals (Num. 4:5–6). Initially it contained the two stone tablets of the Testimony/Covenant written with the finger of God (Exod. 31:18). Later, Aaron's rod that blossomed leaves and yielded almonds was added (Num. 17:8–10). Also, the golden pot that contained manna (Exod. 16:33; Heb. 9:4).
3   Moses was a prophet (Deut. 34:10–12), and Miriam was a prophetess (Exod. 15:20). But God established an extra special relationship with Moses, as God described when He chastised Miriam in Numbers 12:6–8, and punished her as a leper for a week in verses 9–16.
4   Numbers 13. They were sent from and returned to Kadesh in the Desert of Paran (1490 B.C., Ussher notes 241–245) .
5   Numbers 1:2–3 says 20 years old or older at the time of the first census. Since the first census was about 13 months after the last of the 10 plagues/the first Passover (when the youngest to be excluded from entering the Promised Land were only 18/not yet 19) it appears that those 18 and up at the time of the ten plagues were accountable for what they witnessed of God's mighty power in Egypt.
6   The Korah event was circa 1489 B.C. per Ussher note 250b (documented in Num. 16:1–50).
7   Note 249, *The Annals of the World* by James Ussher.
8   Exodus 16:35 (manna for 40 years).
9   Clothes (Deut. 8:4; Neh. 9:21), sandals (Deut. 29:5), circumcision paused (Josh. 5:2–7), no wine or bread (Deut. 29:5–6).
10   1452 B.C. per Ussher notes 264–265, (Num. 20:1).
11   Nearly four decades earlier, God told Moses to strike a rock for water (Exod. 17:5). However, this time (Num. 20:10–11) God told him to speak to the rock, not to strike it. Though he did speak, he addressed the people not the rock and said "Listen, you rebels, must WE bring you water out of this rock?" WE meant HE was partially responsible. He stole God's glory for himself. Though God loved Moses, He would not allow him to escape the consequence for stealing His glory in front of all Israel. He would die peacefully, one month before the Israelites entered the Promised Land.

21. Greedy Balaam And His Talking Donkey

1   Deuteronomy 3:3–11. The Israelites killed all of King Og's people, plus 60 walled cities, and many rural towns. See also Numbers 21:23–26, 32–35; Amos 2:9–10. For an excellent online article about giants in the Bible, see "Giants in the Old Testament" by Tim Chaffey at answersingenesis.org/bible-characters/giants-in-the-old-testament/, accessed February 2017.
2   In 1967, a significant archeological discovery which included many references to "Balaam son of Beor" exactly as written in the Bible, changed long-held assumptions about where Balaam lived. It is now widely believed that Balaam lived about 25 miles north of Jericho, where the Jabbok and Jordan rivers meet. See article by Dr. Bryant Wood of Associates for Biblical Research at www.christiananswers.net/q-abr/abr-a014.html.
3   Two passages, "Balaam, the son of Beor, who loved the wages of unrighteousness" (2 Pet. 2:15) and "for pay they have rushed headlong into the error of Balaam" (Jude 11), reveal that Balaam's decision to disobey God was due to the love of money.
4   God knows the thoughts and intentions of our hearts. (Heb. 4:12–13; Jer. 17:9–10; 1 Kings 8:39).
5   2 Peter 2:16. The mute donkey spoke in the voice of man.
6   EPILOGUE: Balaam's repentance before the angel was either not genuine, or soon forgotten. Deuteronomy 23:5 reveals that when Balaam arrived for his meeting with the king he still attempted to curse the Israelites. However, God took control of his words and made him speak blessings instead. Later, still wanting the money offered by the king of Moab, Revelation 2:14 says that Balaam "taught Balak [the king] to get God to remove his favor from the Israelites by enticing them to sin through eating food sacrificed to idols and committing sexual immorality." This is confirmed further when Moses speaks of the Midianite women in Numbers 31:15–16: "[The women] were the ones who followed Balaam's advice and were the means of turning the Israelites away from the Lord." Numbers 31:7–8 reveals that Balaam was killed as a Midianite sympathizer when the Israelites went to battle against them. This battle took place less than 6 months after the talking-donkey event — and was one of the last tasks for Moses before he climbed Mt. Nebo, died there (Deut. 32:48–52), and was buried in a secret place in a valley of Moab (Deut. 34:1–8). About a month after that, the Israelites crossed the Jordan into the Promised Land.

22. The Mystery Of The Walls Of Jericho

1   "Man's days are determined. You have decreed the number of his months and have set limits he cannot exceed" (Job 14:5; NIV).
2   Deuteronomy 1:3–4. Moses repeated the whole of the law to the people since they either were too young or had not been born yet when it was originally given approximatley 38 years earlier at Mount Sinai.)
3   Deuteronomy 32:5. He could look but not enter (Num. 20:12, 27:14; Deut. 1:38-39.) Exodus 33:11 says that the Lord spoke with Moses as with a friend.
4   Jude 1:9 reveals that the archangel Michael contended and disputed with the devil over the body of Moses. Bible commentator John MacArthur states, "It would likely be that this confrontation took place as Michael buried Moses to prevent Satan from using Moses' body for some diabolical purpose not stated," in his NASB MacArthur Study Bible notes (Word Publishing/Thomas Nelson, 1997).
5   How tall was the wall? At https://answersingenesis.org/archaeology/the-walls-of-jericho archeologist Dr. Bryant Wood documents that there were two levels; the first/lower wall ranged from 32–41 feet, the second was higher up the hill and reached at least another 12–15 feet.
6   "To understand why Jehovah told Israel to wipe out the Canaanites, one needs to understand Canaanite religion and customs. At the heart of Canaanite religion was sex in all its perversions. The land was polluted with indescribable immorality. They were hopelessly lost and incurable." http://davelivingston.com/mooncity.htm, viewed February 2017. See also Leviticus 18, which is a listing of the sins for which the Canaanites were about to be judged.
7   Joshua 3:4 (a thousand yards).
8   Joshua 4:10 (hurried). Even moving quickly, it would take 2,000,000 people (plus an unknown number of animals and carts) walking 200 abreast at a pace of 3 miles per hour, about 4 hours.
9   Joshua 4:3, 4:18–5:12. The night of the crossing, the people encamped for the first time in the Promised Land. The next day the men were circumcised. Three days after the circumcisions, they celebrated Passover. Then, the day after Passover, manna forever stopped.
10 Joshua 4:13, 6:3–5, 15–17, 20–21

23. Deborah And Barak; The Prophetess And The Warrior

1   Numbers 13:27, 14:8
2   Judges 4:5. Young's Literal Translation, ASV, ERV, Websters, Geneva, and KJV all use the term "dwelling under" or "dwelt under." The significance of the fact that people came to her, rather than her traveling the country indicates something of her domestic/household commitment as she lived with her husband yet offered counsel and judgment to those who came seeking it from her.
3   Judges 4:3. Most Bible translations include the number of Canaanite chariots, 900. However, the ESV leaves that detail out.
4   1 Corinthians 11:8–9; Genesis 2.
5   Judges 5:4, 5:21. Torrential rain swelled the River Kishon, ensnared the chariots in mud, and swept away the enemy.
6   Judges 4:10–17; Hebrews 11:32
7   Judges 4:21. A woman named Jael first hid the general in her tent, then killed him by pounding a tent stake through his temple while he slept. / More about this often misrepresented passage: Barak initially placed more faith in systems; i.e., more soldiers + more powerful implements + more motivation = victory, as many kings typically do (Luke 14:31), but failed to realize that with the Lord on his side he would easily win. Barak compared his armaments and systems to those of the Canaanites, and could only see certain loss and death. Although God promised victory, Barak could not see past the fearsome Canaanites. Deborah, on the other hand, kept her eyes on God. This (perhaps) grandmotherly woman sat beneath her shade tree and people came to her to get proven counsel and hear her good and practical judgments regarding disputes and relationships. She was very sensitive to God's Holy Spirit, yet not bashful about reminding people of God's commands and laws, and when He spoke directly to her as a prophetess, then also His words to those who needed to hear them. The words and context strongly suggest she had a tenacious spirit, winsome and worthy of honor, yet almost biting when necessary. Judges 4 reveals that she was God's messenger to shake the battle-hardened Barak to his core. Barak respected Deborah so much that he felt his recruiting and troop-motivating efforts would be greatly assisted simply by her presence. She loved the families and warriors of Israel, who for 20 years had experienced the harsh treatment of the Canaanites. She yearned so deeply for an end to the oppression of her countrymen that she was willing to accompany the frightened commander, perhaps sensing that his faith in God's promise was not yet mature, and in need of "help" along the way.

24. Gideon's Amazing Shrinking Army

1   Judges 6:11. Gideon was obviously threshing secretly, because he was threshing in a winepress, not out in an open field.
2   Gideon is among the heroes of faith listed in Hebrews 11.
3   Judges 7:5–6 — 300 of the 10,000 men put their hand to their mouth and lapped. This does seem like an odd way to drink and may help explain why there were only 300 who drank in this manner.
4   Three hundred Israelites versus 135,000 Midianites means there was only 1 Israelite for every 450 Midianites!

25. Ruth, Naomi And God's Protection

1   Moabites and Israelites were bitter enemies. Moabites, including Ruth, were descended from the incest of Lot's daughter against her father when she conspired with her sister and each got Lot drunk in order to copulate and have progeny after the destruc-

tion of Sodom and Gomorrah. "To have a Moabite in their midst was often a disgrace. This is also one reason for Ruth to follow Boaz's servants, as other servants from other men might have wanted to harm her and rape her — it was a danger for her," says apologist Bodie Hodge, in communication to the author dated January 2016. For Boaz to marry her was very significant. The other kinsman-redeemer was willing to buy the land until he realized he would have to marry the young Moabitess, too.

26. Samson — Strongman In God's Plan

1   Samson was to be raised as a Nazirite (Judges 13:5). A Nazarite is different than a Nazarene. A "Nazarite" was a person who had taken the Nazarite vow to separate various parts of his/her life to the Lord (see Num. 6:1–21). A "Nazarene" was any person who lived in the town of Nazareth in Galilee. Jesus was a Nazarene, but not a Nazarite.

2   Judges 16:27. An unknown number were under the roof, plus 3,000 men and women on the roof.

27. The Desperate Promise Of A Childless Wife

1   1 Samuel 3

2   *The Genuine Works of Flavius Josephus, the Jewish Historian, vol 1*, chapter 10, p. 345. "When Samuel was twelve years old he began to prophesy, and when he was once asleep, God called to him by name. . . ."

3   1 Samuel 12:2. "I have been your leader from my youth until this day" NIV.

BONUS—The Problem of Polygamy

1   Genesis 4:19 documents that this Lamech had two wives. It is important to note that this was NOT the Lamech who was the father of Noah. The polygamous Lamech was a descendant of Adam's first son Cain (the murderer), whereas Noah's father was a descendant of Adam's third son, Seth.

2   Abraham, Jacob, Elkanah (husband of Hanna and Peninnah), David, Solomon.

28. David & Goliath

1   Saul, who was about a foot taller than any other man in Israel when he was anointed king many years earlier (1 Samuel 9:2), offered David his personal armor to confront Goliath. However, David was not familiar with the armor and knew that the battle would be determined by God's favor, not armor, anyway. Saul, who had lost sight of the need to place his faith in God and seek His will, could not have offered the armor of a shorter soldier if David were much shorter than himself. The Bible clearly states that David turned down Saul's armor because he was not accustomed to wearing it (1 Samuel 17:39). It says nothing about the armor being too big or too heavy. Since both Saul and Goliath saw David as a "boy" in comparison to the giant (1 Samuel 17:33, 17:42), it is probable that Saul's concern was that David was not nearly as experienced as the battle-hardened giant. In the end, Saul could sense David's great faith in God and approved his request to represent God's army against Goliath, without man's armor. See also, "David: Little Guy or Mighty Man of War?" by Tim Chaffey at www.answersingenesis.org/articles/2011/02/01/little-guys-big-things,.

2   Per Ussher's chronologies, David was born in 1085 B.C. Assuming that he was about 18 at the time he fought Goliath (young for a warrior), David's victory over the giant took place around 1067 B.C.

29. Jonathan & David

1   1 Samuel 18:1. Also, it appears likely that Jonathan was at least ten years older than David (see 1 Samuel 14 and 17). This makes Jonathan's respect of David — whose own older brothers had belittled him — even more powerful to consider.

2   1 Samuel 18:10–11. "And it happened on the next day . . . Saul cast the spear (at David)." Per 18:6, this was the day after David was returning from the slaughter of the Philistine.

3   1 Samuel 20

4   I Samuel 22:16–19. At least hundreds of men, women, children, and infants were massacred at Saul's command, including at least 85 priests of the Lord whom Saul accused of being sympathizers of David.

30. King David

1   Examples: 2 Samuel 2:12–17 —12 sets of men battle at the pool of Gibeon and stab each other to death. David's men win. / 2 Samuel 2:23 — Abner the commander of Saul's army spears David's nephew. / 2 Samuel 3:1 — war between the house of Saul and the house of David. / 2 Samuel 3:26–27 — David's nephew Joab and his brother, Abishai, murdered Abner, the head of Saul's army, to avenge the death of their brother Asahel. This was right after David sent Abner away in peace. / 2 Samuel 3:38–39 — David admitted to his men that, although he was king, his nephews Joab and Abishai were too strong for him. He felt weak and inadequate. / 2 Samuel 4:5–8 — Two leaders under Ish-Bosheth, the son of Saul, killed Ish-Bosheth without David's knowledge and then delivered his head to David at Hebron. Angry, David had them killed, cut off their hands and feet, and hanged their bodies in Hebron./ 2 Samuel 8 — David killed Moabites via a cord measurement system, hamstrung chariot horses, struck down tens of thousands of Arameans and Edomites, and the Lord gave him victory everywhere he went.

2   2 Samuel 5:9–11. The king of Tyre sent cedar logs, carpenters, and stonemasons who built a palace for David. (Archeologist Dr. Eilat Mazar describes remains that may be David's palace at Jerusalem. See www.leaderu.com/theology/palacedavid.html from the Jerusalem Christian Review, dated 1998. Also see www.haaretz.com/print-edition/features/a-debate-of-biblical-pro-

portions-1.169365, dated 2005. A 52-minute video with footage of Dr. Eilat Mazar regarding the possible discovery of David's palace is at https://www.youtube.com/watch?v=IXpDpZEViXo&ebc=ANyPxKopZDhyCo2dK4f89OcgkFlAN7KIStk8XuXfhx-s6BnYnhD1PkqJyyzIoO_PNQJAn8CPYLH_JI4bc4_GptjQswuPs1mt0xg&nohtml5=False.

3   2 Samuel 11:2–4. David watches Bathsheba from his palace roof, which undoubtedly included a protective railing/parapet as required in Deuteronomy 22:8. Per Ussher's *Annals of the World,* note 434, this took place in 1035 B.C., 20 years after David became king of Judah in 1055 B.C. (at age 30), and 20 years before his death (at 70). So David was 50 at the time that he impregnated Bathsheba.

4   2 Samuel 11:1–27

5   David wrote Psalm 51 expressing his repentance to God for his adultery with Bathsheba and the murder of her husband, Uriah. 2 Samuel 12:18–19 records David's fasting and prayer for the child after Nathan confronted him. Also, note that the child born of David and Bathsheba's infidelity was apparently never given a name. He is not identified by name anywhere in Scripture.

6   Calamity came to David's family (2 Samuel 12:10–11). The highly successful king was apparently an indulgent parent who had not sufficiently guided his own 19 sons (1 Chronicles 3).

7   David's own son Absalom, whose mother was Maaciah, raped ten of David's concubine-wives in broad daylight on the very palace roof where David first decided to have intercourse with Bathsheba (2 Samuel 16:22, 15:16, 20:3). This was in fulfillment of the judgment "before the eyes of all Israel" delivered to David by the prophet Nathan.

31. The Wisest Man In The World

1   1 Chronicles 21

2   1 Kings 3:5, 15. God appeared to Solomon in a dream at night.

3   2 Chronicles 1:10 (wisdom and knowledge); 1 Kings 3:9 (discernment).

4   1 Kings 3:16–28

5   David gave Solomon the detailed plans/patterns for the Temple, which were put in David's mind by the Spirit. See 1 Chronicles 28:10–12, and especially verse 28:19. David and the leaders gave willingly and wholeheartedly for the Lord's Temple (1 Chronicles 29:1-9). First Chronicles 22:2 and 22:5 state that before he died David had stonecutters prepare dressed stones and gathered materials in great quantity, including great stores of iron, bronze, and cedar timbers. He also commanded the leaders of Israel to help Solomon build the sanctuary of the Lord God. After David's death, in the fourth year of Solomon's reign, the Temple of the Lord began to be built by Solomon on Mount Moriah on the threshing floor of Araunah the Jebusite (2 Chronicles 3:1). Many believe this to be the site where Abraham nearly sacrificed Isaac about 900 years earlier (Genesis 22:2).

6   1 Kings 5:13–15

7   1 Kings 8:10–12 (the Lord's glory in the form of a thick dark cloud).

8   Solomon is widely known as the principal author of Proverbs, plus all of Ecclesiastes and the love poem, Song of Solomon; 1 Kings 4:32 credits him with 3,000 proverbs and over 1,000 songs.

9   1 Kings 11:1–3; Deuteronomy 17:17

10   Solomon added other gods to the one true God, a great sin against The Lord (Exod. 20:23; NKJV).

32. Elijah's Fire From Heaven

1   Those who sacrifice to other gods must be destroyed (Exod. 22:20; Deut. 18:20). The Kishon Valley where the 450 prophets of Baal were slaughtered was the same river valley where Sisera and his Canaanite army were defeated 400 years earlier when Barak's army decimated Sisera's chari[oteers and troops in hand-to-hand battle at the time of Deborah (Judg. 4:7).

2   1 Kings 19:4–7. Note that Elijah did not attempt suicide; he made his request (much like Jesus in the Garden of Gethsemane) but left the decision in God's hands. Rather than removing Elijah from earth at that time, God gave him sleep in the shade, then refreshment and encouragement by an angel before sending him to Mt. Horeb for an extra special meeting.

3   1 Kings 19:8. Horeb the mountain of God was also called Mount Sinai (see http://www.biblearchaeology.org/post/2008/11/What-Do-Mt-Horeb2c-The-Mountain-of-God2c-Mt-Paran-and-Mt-Seir-Have-to-Do-with-Mt-Sinai.aspx#Article, accessed April 2017). Note that God did not call Elijah to the formerly gold-inlaid temple that Solomon built at Jerusalem. The original temple building still stood, but God no longer blessed it with His presence. According to 1 Kings 14:25–26, all its treasures were carried away by Shishak the king of Egypt when he attacked Jerusalem in the 5th year of Solomon's son Rehoboam's reign, with 1,200 chariots, 60,000 horsemen, and innumerable troops (2 Chron. 12:2–4). This was fewer than 35 years after the Temple was completed. God had clearly warned Solomon, "If you or your sons ever turn away from me . . . I will abandon this temple I have consecrated with my presence" (1 Kings 9:6–7; NET). Within only one generation, God's ominous warning was kept and He said through the prophet Shemaiah, "You have abandoned me; therefore, I now abandon you" (2 Chron. 12:5; NET). By the time of Elijah, a century later, the regal stone temple was a shell, a reminder of past glory, and false gods were worshiped there!

33. Jonah And The Great Fish

1   Jonah 1:4

2   The realm of Assyria varied, but Nineveh, Assyria, lay in the region known today as northwest Iraq. The boundaries of the Assyrian realm in Jonah's day included the countries we call Syria, Iraq, and Iran today.

3   The most likely location of Tarshish was "Tartessus" near modern day Gibraltar, a British territory at Spain's southern coast. For a map showing the key cities in the Jonah account, visit; https://visualunit.files.wordpress.com/2011/01/jonah_map.png.

4   Matthew 12:40 records Jesus' reference to the Jonah account as an actual event. The historical reality of Jonah and the fish is linked by Jesus himself to the reality of his own upcoming Resurrection.

34. Isaiah: Living Strong For God

1   Isaiah 20:3. Isaiah walked naked and barefoot for three years. Bible teacher Chuck Smith, founder of the Calvary Chapel church movement of nearly 2,000 churches, observes, "The conquering armies would seek to disgrace the conquered people . . . by making them march naked. Now it is interesting that God would tell his prophet Isaiah to walk around naked for three years. So that it would be the sign to the people. So Assyria is going to embarrass both Ethiopia and Egypt by conquering them and leading away their captives naked. And their confederacy together is not going to stand. And that is why Isaiah is saying, 'Don't make a league with Egypt or look to them for help against Assyria. Look to the Lord. If you look to man, if you look to the arm of flesh, you're going to fall anyhow.'" https://www.blueletterbible.org/Comm/smith_chuck/c2000_Isa/Isa_016.cfm

2   2 Kings 19:35 The NKJV, ESV, NIV, and KJV all say "the angel of the Lord," which infers a Christophany. An excellent article on theophanies and Christophanies is at www.answersingenesis.org/articles/2012/01/13/feedback-old-testament-theophanies. The pre-incarnate Christ (the angel of the Lord) is not an "only-love god" as many prefer to categorize Him today. He executed humans at that time (in this case 185,000), and in His perfect justice will send billions to eternal torment at the end of time (Matthew 25:41, 46).

3   Isaiah 53:4–6

35. Josiah The Boy-King!

1   It appears that the adults in Josiah's life helped him to recognize the wisdom of humbling himself before the Lord and following God's ways. This may have been by his mother, or by one or more godly mentors among the other influencers in his life.

2   2 Chronicles 34:3 / Per Ussher's *Annals of the World* note 456, Bible-based calculations reveal that Josiah was 14 when he had his second son (Jehoiakim, by Zebudah, per 2 Kings 23:36), and 16 when he had his fourth son (Shallum/Jehoahaz, by Hamutal per 2 Kings 23:31). Josiah's four sons are named in 1 Chronicles 3:15 — Johanan, Jehoiakim (aka Eliakim, 2 Chron. 36:4), Zedekiah, and Shallum (aka Jehoahaz, 2 Kings 23:30). Per Ussher note 806, Zedekiah was originally named Mattaniah, but his name was changed by Nebuchadnezzar in 599 B.C. Daughters were likely as well, but are not listed. (The immediate successor to Josiah's throne, his fourth son, is called both Shallum in Jeremiah 22:11 and Jehoahaz in 2 Kings 23:30.)
    *The basis for the understanding that Josiah was only 14 by the time his second son Jehoiakim was born, is as follows: 39 (Josiah's age upon death) -25 (Jehoiakim's age 3 months after Josiah died and Shallum-Jehoahaz began his three-month reign) = 14 (Josiah's age when his 2nd son Eliakim-Jehoiakim was born).

3   2 Chronicles 34:8, 14–18. This was likely Deuteronomy, and may have been Genesis through Deuteronomy.

4   2 Chronicles 34:30; 2 Kings 23:3–4. Josiah evidently took to heart Deuteronomy 31:9–13, which requires that every seven years during a feast where all Israel — men, women, children, even the aliens in the land — was assembled, the law was to be read aloud to them so they could listen and learn to fear the Lord God and follow the law. This evidently had not been happening for hundreds of years (since the book had been lost for that long).

5   2 Kings 23:24–25. "Before him there was no king like him, who turned to the Lord with all his heart and with all his soul and with all his might, according to all the Law of Moses, nor did any like him arise after him."

36. Shadrach, Meshach, And Abed-Nego

1   Shadrach, Meshach, and Abed-Nego were the Babylonian names of the Jewish young men Hananiah, Mishael, and Azariah. Daniel's Babylonian name was Belteshazzar. Jewish historian Josephus records that the four friends were all members of the royal family (*Antiquities of the Jews,* Book 10, chap. 10, sec. 1). This is even more reason to suspect Josiah's godly influence.

2   Daniel 3:1. The image of gold was 60 cubits tall (about 90 feet), by 6 cubits wide (9 feet). It may have been an image of Nebuchadnezzar, or of something else. It is interesting to note that this 10:1 height-to-width ratio is the same as obelisks such as the much larger Washington Monument in Washington, D.C., which is about 555 feet tall by 55.5 feet wide.

3   Daniel 2:37–38 — the most powerful king in the world.

4   "Just like the people in the time of Daniel, Christians (today) are living in exile awaiting the day when we will be taken home. Just like the education systems of the Babylonian empire that Daniel was forced to learn in, the philosophies of our time are being taught to our children in the secular education facilities in state-run institutions in every country. They are designed to rob our children of their knowledge of their true home in Christ's kingdom." Steve Ham, http://blogs.answersingenesis.org/blogs/worldwide/2012/12/17/lessons-from-daniel/#sthash.5YAmM5GB.dpuf

37. Nebuchadnezzar's Animal Insanity

1   Daniel 4:33

38. Daniel In The Lions' Den

1   This punishment was very similar to that called for by Daniel's God in dealing with false witnesses among the Jews — Deuteronomy 19:16–21.

39. Esther, The Orphan Queen

1   As noted by respected Bible teacher Nancy DeMoss Wolgemuth, "We need to recognize that this was not a harmless, 'Miss Persia' beauty contest. These women were conscripted into the king's harem. According to one ancient historian, there were 400

or more of them. This was a horrible, degrading process. These young women were used to satisfy the lust of this lecherous, arrogant, alcoholic, angry king. Once they had been with the king, if he didn't approve of them, if he didn't want them to be his queen, they could never marry again. They would become a concubine and were consigned to be a prisoner in his harem and were destined to spend the rest of their lives in loneliness — never could marry. This was not a happy life. This was not a happy or wholesome thing." For a candid summary of the situation, read or listen to "Esther; God's Woman at God's Time" at www. reviveourhearts.com/radio/revive-our-hearts/no-innocent-beauty-contest-1/.

2   Esther 3:13-14
3   Esther 4:12-16

BONUS—400 Years of Silence

1   "These 'four silent centuries' really are not silent at all. Secular history sheds considerable light on this period — and it is tremendously important. God's providential activity (i.e., his orchestration of human events in a non-miraculous manner) was, in retrospect, both active and effective. This historical period should be considered from several vantage points." From "A Survey of Interbiblical History" by Wayne Jackson, as accessed on August 12, 2015 at www.christiancourier.com/articles/1447-survey-of-interbiblical-history-a).
2   Isaiah 40:3, verified as being about John the Baptist in Matthew 3:3.
3   Galatians 4:4

40. The Announcement And Birth Of Jesus

1   The Greek word tecton (tekton) is traditionally translated "carpenter" when referring to Joseph. It can mean any craftsman (including stone workers) but especially in wood, a carpenter. (Vine's Greek New Testament Dictionary).
2   Did the angels sing, or speak their praises? See "Hark the Herald Angels Said?" by Tim Chaffey at https://answersingenesis.org/holidays/christmas/hark-the-herald-angels-said/.

41. Star-Gazing Wise Men And A Power-Crazed King

1   The magi may have consulted the records of Daniel, the Jew who had been chief magi under Babylon's King Nebuchadnezzar nearly 600 years earlier. The magi informed Herod the Great of the meaning behind the star (Num. 24:17) when they stood before him in Jerusalem some months later. / Matthew 2:9 (ESV) "After listening to the king, they went on their way. And behold, the star that they had seen when it rose went before them until it came to rest over the place where the child was."
2   It seems logical that the magi arrived at Bethlehem 9–18 months after Jesus' birth. Here is why: assembling a caravan of dignitaries and other people, plus animals and supplies, could have been accomplished in a few weeks. Then, since the magi were likely from the area of Babylon, and Ezra 7:9 states that it took Ezra four months to travel from Babylon to Jerusalem, a minimum of at least 5 months total seems necessary. The whole adventure would easily have taken longer if they first had to do significant research to determine the meaning of the star. Due to the expansive influence of Daniel 600 years earlier in the Persian Empire, some scholars believe that his writings referenced the prophecy regarding the star and the Messiah. So, although it seems reasonable that the actual preparation and travel time could have been as little as 5 months, we must remember that Matthew 1 refers to Jesus as a "child," not a baby, when the magi arrived at the "house" where he was living in Bethlehem. This infers a minimum age of at least 8 or 9 months, and due to Herod's tyrannical desire to ensure the death of the announced king of the Jews, Jesus would not have been the full 2 years old (the age up to which Herod murdered). For these reasons, a range of around 9–18 months old seems likely.
3   Micah 5:2
4   "The star may have been a localized object specifically fashioned as a message to the magi. This supernatural object would not be bound by the motions of objects normally found in the sky, and thus its odd behavior, such as appearing over (the house) where Jesus was, is easy to explain. In short, the star of Bethlehem likely was a unique and miraculous local apparition to fulfill God's purpose." From "An Evaluation of the Star of Bethlehem," by astronomer Dr. Danny Faulkner, at www.answersingenesis.org/articles/aid/v5/n1/star-of-bethlehem-dvd.

BONUS—A Synchronized Christmas Reading

1   The Bible does not say the special star was present above the place of Jesus birth, but rather that it appeared to the wise men— who were hundreds of miles east—on that night. Apologist Eric Hovind states, "It would appear from Matthew 2:7 that the star, which the wise men had seen, had appeared at the moment of Jesus' birth. …Because the Shechinah glory was a light that could move, and could point to the presence of God, I would suggest that the star mentioned in Matthew 2 was not an astronomical object, but actually the appearance, after a few hundred years' absence, of the Shechinah glory of God." Noted online as part of a much longer article at http://creationtoday.org/the-wise-men-and-the-star/
2   "If the Holy Spirit did come upon Mary in the sixth month (Elul) or around August/September, as it seems to indicate in Scripture, then Jesus should have been born about nine months later, which would place His birth around May/June." From "The Origin of Christmas" by apologist Bodie Hodge, www.answersingenesis.org/articles/2008/12/19/feedback-the-origin-of-christmas.

42. Jesus — His Boyhood, Baptism, And Early Miracles

1   Luke 2:40–42 — Jesus' "parents" went up to Jerusalem according to the custom of the Feast of the Passover every year.

2 Dr. Ralph F. Wilson provides insights and considerations of the situation faced by Mary, the mother of the Messiah; "Throughout the infancy narratives, Mary has been trying desperately to understand, to make sense of what she is seeing in her son. Gabriel's announcement, Elizabeth's and Zechariah's prophecies, the shepherds' story of an angelic declaration of his birth, Simeon's and Anna's words and blessing in the temple, and this incident in the temple when Jesus is twelve. How do you raise a son whom you believe to be the Messiah? That would be hard enough. But how can she understand that she is raising the Son of God himself? A boy, who, when he calls God his Father, means it literally? Mary cannot take all this in. Perhaps if she had, she would have been completely paralyzed by self-consciousness. But she treasures these moments and ponders them in her heart." www.jesuswalk.com/lessons/2_39-52.htm.

3 Jesus was the first child born to Mary, before Joseph had sexual relations with her (Matt. 1:25). Matthew 13:54–56 clearly reveals that after Jesus' birth, at least six siblings were added to the home (the passage names four brothers and refers to "sisters" — which would be at least two). Other proof texts are sprinkled throughout the New Testament as well: Mark 3:31–35,6:3, 7:3–5; Matthew 12:46–50; Luke 8:19–21; Acts 1:13–14; Galatians 1:18–19; Jude 1.

4 Philippians 2:7 tells us that Jesus "emptied Himself" when He left heaven to take on the form of man, the God-man. He was still deity, but during His years as a man He was subject to hunger, thirst, pain, temptation, etc. Regarding His omniscience, see https://answersingenesis.org/theistic-evolution/jesus-scripture-and-error-an-implication-of-theistic-evolution/

5 Luke 2:52. He grew in wisdom and stature and in favor with God and men. Unlike his relative, John the Baptist, who dressed and lived rough — including living in the wilderness and eating locusts — Jesus gave a more favorable impression and people were attracted to Him. He was probably warm and friendly overall.

6 Malachi 4:6 (NKJV, ESV) says he will turn the hearts of the fathers to the children. Luke 1:17 (NKJV) says he will turn the hearts of the fathers to the children and the disobedient to the wisdom of the just.

7 Mark 1:12-13, Immediately, Jesus was driven by the Holy Spirit into the desert for 40 days. Matthew 4:1–11 says He was led by the Spirit into the wilderness, and Luke 4:1 says that, full of the Holy Spirit, He left the Jordan and was led by the Spirit into the wilderness.

8 Mark 1:32–2:12. Jesus healed, exorcized, traveled, preached, and prayed.

43. Jesus the Submissive Miracle Worker

1 Jesus always had been God (John 8:58, 10:30), but when He was conceived by the Holy Spirit (Luke 1:35) and started growing in Mary's womb (the incarnation) He also became fully human (John 1:14). Two natures, one personality. Also see answersingenesis.org/answers/biblical-authority-devotional/was-jesus-fully-human-and-why-does-it-matter/.

2 Isaiah 53:2. He shall grow up (but) has no stately form or majesty; And when we see Him we observe no beauty that we should desire Him.

3 John 7:10–11 — He went alone to the Feast and although the Jews were watching for Him they did not notice Him. Luke 4:30 — He walked right through the crowd that sought to throw Him off a cliff.

4 This is John 3:16, one of the most famous Scripture verses in the entire Bible (A.D. 30, per Ussher paragraph 6307).

5 John 4:1–42. a.d. 30, per Ussher paragraph 6314.

6 John 6:25–71. On the day that Jesus fed 5,000 with only the lunch of a child (John 6:16), He had to withdraw alone up a mountain to avoid those who wanted to force Him to become king (John 6:15). After the sun had set and His disciples had departed in their boat, He came to them by walking nearly four miles in the darkness atop the stormy waves of the Sea of Galilee (John 6:16–21; Matthew 14:24; Mark 14:13–36. The very next day (John 6:22), in the synagogue at Capernaum (John 6:59) Jesus challenged His many disciples to examine their true motives in following Him (John 6:22–66). Was it for earthly gain, or to gain eternal life? He spoke rigid truth that was offensive to some, and hard to accept (John 6:60–66). John chapter 6 reveals that many deserted Him that day (John 6:60, 64, 66).

BONUS – John the Baptist

1 Matthew 11:10–11

2 "Judea" is the Roman name of Judah, the ancient kingdom of the Jews. It includes Jerusalem, Jericho, Hebron, and Bethlehem. In Old Testament times, the Judean hills near Jerusalem were forested and the ground was good for agriculture and sheep farming.

3 Luke 1:5–25. Mute Zacharias was also unable to hear, per Luke 1:62.

4 Matthew 3:2–3

5 Mark 1:4–6. John baptized in the wilderness and "all the country of Judea and Jerusalem" were going out to him and being baptized.

44. Jesus' Transfiguration; The Turning Point Miracle

1 Mark 1:14–15. Jesus preached the gospel of the kingdom of God and to repent and believe the good news. The good news was that the Kingdom of God had come and they could enter — be saved — by believing on Jesus the Christ, the Messiah, as Lord.

2 Luke 6:19. The crowd sought to touch Him because power was going out from Him and healing all.

3 Peter and other disciples truly believed that Jesus was the Son of the living God, the Creator. Jesus was the Messiah, and they repented of their past sins. At that point, they "entered the kingdom of God" spiritually — they accepted God's authority over their lives. The "kingdom of God" was and is spiritual, not geographical, for living Christians. They accepted Jesus as their King, and became His subjects. Paul said in Colossians 1:13 that living Christians have already entered the kingdom of God. There will also be a physical kingdom of God, the New Jerusalem.

4 Matthew 16:23; Mark 8:33. Jesus turned to the disciples (his back to Peter, who had rebuked Jesus in private) and in the hearing

of the disciples compared Peter to Satan and told him to get behind him/out of the way, because he was an offense to Him (NKJV). In Young's Literal Translation (Matt. 16:23) Jesus told Peter "Get thee behind me, adversary! Thou art a stumbling block to me, for thou dost not mind the things of God, but the things of men."

5   Luke 9:29. As He prayed, the appearance of his face was altered. "The word is metamorphoo from which we get metamorpho-sis, two Greek words, morphe meaning body or form, meta meaning change. His form was changed. . . . This word literally means to transform the morphe, the form, the body, the exterior. It's used four times in the New Testament and always means a radical transformation," at www.gty.org/resources/sermons/41-43/the-unveiled-son, as accessed February 2017. See also https://answersingenesis.org/creepy-crawlies/insects/metamorphosis/.

6   Peter and his two friends were undone by the glory of Jesus' Transfiguration. Peter was probably especially terrified because he knew that he was a foolish sinner in a sinful culture who had been compared to Satan and did not deserve to live. Yet Jesus came to Peter, James, and John and comforted them, assuring them that although they were guilty of sinful and foolish things, they were chosen to tell the people the good news, with Peter as the leader.

45. Jesus' Final Weeks

1   Mark 9:14–15. A multitude surrounded His disciples at the foot of the mountain. They ran to Him amazed/awestruck when they saw Him and greeted Him. Some commentators propose that Jesus may still have glowed after displaying His full glory on the mount. This may better explain why they were "awestruck" upon simply seeing Him.

2   God created a perfect world, but when man chose to disobey His command, sin's curse brought suffering and death. Because we long to be rescued from diseases and the many terrible effects of sin, it was common for throngs to follow Jesus in pursuit of His miracle-working power.

3   Luke 19:9 — salvation for Zacchaeus the tax collector.

4   Fulfillment of Zechariah 9:9 prophesy of triumphal entry on a donkey.

5   Mark 11:1–11

6   Mark 12:13–34

7   Mark 14:29–31 — Peter says he will not stumble and will die with Jesus rather than deny Him. Luke 22:31–34 — Jesus tells Peter that Satan has asked for him specifically and that He (Jesus) has likewise prayed for Peter specifically that he would return to Jesus after disowning Him and that his faith would not fail and he would strengthen his brethren.

8   These three were Peter, James, and John, the same three who witnessed His transfiguration and fell asleep there as well. Matthew 26:36–46, Mark 14:38 — watch and pray.

9   Before that evening, Judas contracted to turn Jesus over for 30 pieces of silver (Mark 14:41–50; Matt. 26:14–15). Now Judas arrived with the unrighteous religious leaders and Peter drew his sword, then brashly slashed off the ear of a servant of the high priest (John 18:10–11; Matt. 26:51), but Jesus spoke of 12 legions of angels at his disposal, and immediately healed the man's ear (Luke 22:49–51).

10 John 13:38; Mark 14:50–72; Matthew 26:59–75, Luke 22:34, 60–62

46. Jesus' Crucifixion

1   Matthew 26:51–53. A disciple cut off a man's ear. Jesus said He could simply pray and the Father would send more than 12 legions of angels to rescue Him. One Roman legion was at least 6,000 soldiers. Twelve legions of at least 6,000 would be at least 72,000 angels. Consider their combined power in that 2 Kings 19:35 reveals that just one angel killed 185,000 Assyrian soldiers encamped outside Jerusalem in a single night.

2   Ephesians 6:11–12 — Our struggle is against unseen principalities, powers, and rulers of the darkness. Matthew 26:50 — When Judas brought the soldiers to Jesus in the Garden, Jesus did not lash out at him. Instead, immediately after Judas betrayed Jesus with a kiss, Jesus called Judas "friend." Even in His darkest human moments, Jesus lived out the reality that His struggle (and ours) was not against men — such as His betrayer or the soldiers and religionists Judas brought — but against the unseen principalities.

3   "Crucifixion was an agonizing, torturous death, but Jesus endured a torture that was nearly as, or perhaps equally, excruciating before he ever got to the cross. This was the pain he suffered when he was scourged. . . . Roman law imposed no limit to the number of lashes inflicted at scourging. Roman law mandated scourging as part of capital sentences, but this probably had the effect of shortening the victim's agony once on the cross. The victim would have been so weak from blood loss and pain that he would die more quickly than if he had not been scourged. This seems to have been the case with Jesus." From "The Scourging of Jesus," by David McClister, accessed April 2017 at http://www.truthmagazine.com/archives/volume44/v440106010.htm.

4   Luke 23:26–30 — a multitude followed and He stopped and told women who mourned Him to pray for themselves and their children because of the coming days of tribulation. Matthew 27:54–56; Mark 15:40–41; Luke 23:49 — Many women who came with Jesus and the disciples from Galilee were there.

5   Psalm 22:16 — pierced my hands and my feet. Luke 24:39–40 — behold my hands and my feet.

6   Luke 23:34. He did not hold them accountable. His perspective continued to be on the bigger picture; Satan and his henchmen, the fallen angels known as demons, were the true focus of the battle.

7   Luke 23:39–43

8   Luke 23:45 — the sun was darkened. 1 Peter 2:24 — Jesus bore our sins on the tree and by His stripes we were healed. 1 John 2:2 — propitiation for the sins of the whole world. Colossians 2:14 — our sin debt was nailed to the Cross. 1 John 1:7–9 — blood of Jesus cleanses us from all sin, if we confess our sin He will forgive us from all unrighteousness.

9   Earthquake struck and rocks split. Matthew 27:51; Luke 23:45; Mark 15:34. In his article "Greatest Earthquakes of the Bible" at

www.icr.org/article/greatest-earthquakes-bible/, accessed April 2017, geologist Steven A. Austin Ph.D. documents a 5.5 magnitude earthquake in the Holy Land in A.D. 33.

10 John 19:38–39. A rich man known as Joseph of Arimathea who was a prominent council member and secret disciple of Jesus asked Pilate for Jesus' body. Joseph came with Pilate's permission and took Jesus' body. He had with him the Pharisee Nicodemus who visited Jesus at night about three years earlier. Nicodemus brought a burial mixture and the two of them wrapped the body in a linen cloth and laid it in Joseph's new tomb. They rolled a large stone against the door and left. Two of the women, Mary of Magdala (Mary Magdalene) and Mary the mother of Joses, were sitting in front of the tomb, watching (Matt 27:57–61; Mark 15:43–47; Luke 23:51; John 19:38–42).

11 "The demons may have been celebrating their seeming victory in the wake of Christ's death and burial — but only to soon be profoundly and permanently disappointed when the living Christ Himself arrived." from "Where Did Jesus Go Between His Death and Resurrection," by John MacArthur at http://www.gty.org/resources/bible-qna/BQ080612/where-did-jesus-go-between-his-death-and-resurrection.

47. Alive Again! Resurrection to Ascension

1 This account synchronizes and summarizes the numerous Bible passages that document what took place beginning the morning of Christ's Resurrection and continuing until His ascension to heaven 40 days later. It is compiled from all four gospels (Matthew, Mark, Luke, John), plus Acts, 1 Corinthians, and Isaiah. Also see the excellent article by Dr. Elizabeth Mitchell entitled, "The Sequence of Christ's Post-Resurrection Appearances," at https://answersingenesis.org/jesus-christ/resurrection/the-sequence-of-christs-post-resurrection-appearances/, accessed February 2017.

2 Luke 24:2 (rolled away by an angel); John 20:1; Mark 16:4; Matthew 28:2.

3 Matthew 28:2–4 references the earthquake, a lightning bright angel in white who rolled back the stone, and the guards who shook and fainted ("became like dead men"). Mark 16:4 documents that the stone was extremely large.

4 Luke 24:4 — in dazzling apparel; Matthew 28:2 — apparel as white as snow; John 20:11–12 — both angels there that morning wore white clothes.

5 Mark 16:5–7 says an angel, inside on the right, calmed them and told them what had happened. Jesus had risen from the dead and they should go and tell His disciples.

6 Matthew 28:8–9 (fear and great joy); Luke 24:3–11; Mark 16:8; John 20:1–3. Two nights earlier, Peter and John initially fled the Garden of Gethsemane with the other nine disciples when Jesus was arrested. However, they remained in the city and witnessed parts of His trial and crucifixion. By Sunday morning, they were evidently staying at the same house (since both came to the door when Mary Magdalene arrived). It is likely that the other disciples were in Bethany, since the women who were running away from the garden tomb to tell them what the angels had said did not encounter Peter, John, and Mary, who were simultaneously running toward the garden tomb.

7 Matthew 27:52–53 says that the dead saints came out of the graves after His Resurrection and went in to the holy city where they appeared to many people.

8 John 20:19–24 — that same day at evening, Luke 24:33. Bible commentator/pastor John MacArthur says, "Now get the picture of the disciples. 'When the doors were shut,' and the Greek is they were locked and barred. Now they're afraid. 'The disciples were assembled for fear of the Jews.' They were in there shivering in terror, expecting at any minute the temple police would knock on the door and get them. And this is so good. 'Came Jesus and stood in the midst and said unto them, Peace be unto you.' O man, this must have been something. I would love to have loved to have (sic) been there. . . . The Bible says He came. You say, 'How did He come?' He walked through the wall. You say, 'Do you believe that?' I believe that. Listen, if He could ascend out of His grave clothes, what's a wall? If Jesus Christ even in His physical form prior to His resurrection could walk on water, don't you think He could rearrange the molecules to walk through a wall?" per sermon transcript at www.gty.org/resources/print/sermons/1577, viewed online April 2017.

9 Luke 24:37 — spirit.

10 Luke 24:36–43, John 20:19-20

11 John 20:24–29 Jesus appeared to "doubting" Thomas eight days after Resurrection. The Bible does not say 'Thomas touched Jesus' wounds,' or "Thomas did not touch Jesus." Here is what Jesus actually said: "Thomas, because you have seen Me, you have believed. Blessed are those who have not seen and yet have believed" (John 20:29).

12 Matthew 28:18–20. — Jesus gave the eleven the Great Commission to go to all nations and make disciples, baptize, and teach them to obey (context is Matthew 28:16–20). Mark 16:15 — Jesus told the eleven to go into all the world and preach the gospel (context is Mark 16:14–16). Acts 1:8 — Jesus told the apostles they would receive power from the Holy Spirit to witness from Jerusalem to the end of the earth, then He ascended into a cloud and into heaven (context is Acts 1:1-11). Multiple scriptures appear to indicate that before the end of the first century A.D., the "go to all the world" mission was complete (see Col. 1:23; Rom. 10:18). However, the commission to make disciples, baptize, and teach is never complete.

13 Acts 1:9–11 — "While they looked steadfastly toward heaven as He went up, behold, two men stood by them in white apparel, who also said, 'Men of Galilee, why do you stand gazing up into heaven? This same Jesus, who was taken up from you into heaven, will so come in like manner as you saw Him go into heaven.' " Mark 16:19 — He was taken up into heaven and He sat at the right hand of God. Hebrews 1:3 says Jesus is the radiance and exact representation of God's glory and He now sits at God's right hand in heaven.

48. Pentecost Power

1 John 16:13 — Jesus said the Spirit of truth would guide into all truth those He was speaking to in the upper room. Luke 24:49 — they would receive power from on high. Acts 1:4 — the gift of God is promised. John 14:26 — the Holy Spirit will teach them all things. Galatians 5:22–23 — by the indwelling of the Holy Spirit and our obedience we can live a life that produces the fruits of

the Spirit.

2   Matthew 27:5 and Acts 1:16–18 combine to reveal that Judas hanged himself in a field, and his body fell headlong, was split open, and his entrails gushed out.

3   In personal correspondence to the author during August 2016, apologist Bodie Hodge included the following note regarding Matthias and other Apostles and disciples: "He would be counted as one of the twelve apostles, but there were other apostles too like Paul (e.g., 1 Timothy 1:1) and Barnabas (Acts 14:14) and even James was counted as an apostle (Galatians 1:19). . . . Jesus had many disciples (not elevated to apostles) that we often overlook — 72 were sent out in Luke 10:1 and a great number were with Jesus at Luke 6:17 and Luke 19:37. Joseph of Arimathea was a disciple (John 19:38)."

4   Acts 2:1–3

5   In his online article, "Babel," theologian Dr. John Whitcomb writes, ". . . a great linguistic miracle occurred: 'There were Jews living in Jerusalem, devout men, from every nation under heaven. And . . . they were each one hearing [the Apostles] speak in their own language' (Acts 2:5–6). Not just Greek, but over a dozen other languages are listed (vs. Acts 2:9–11)! Here was Babel in reverse in one sense: in the days of Peleg the Earth was divided; but in the days of the Apostles thousands of people from many lands were united for many months, 'continuing with one mind . . . and continually devoting themselves to the apostles' teaching' (Acts 2:42-46)." Accessed February 2017 at https://answersingenesis.org/tower-of-babel/babel/.

6   Acts 3:1–16 — Peter healed a crippled beggar. Acts 5:14–16 — they brought the sick out into the streets and all were healed as were the sick and demonized brought from nearby cities.

7   Acts 5:1–11. Ananias and Sapphira lied and tested the Spirit of the Lord by trying to make others think they gave more to the brethren than they actually did. After Peter's confrontation of each, they were killed and buried.

BONUS — Who Were the 12 Disciples?

1   A good discussion of the idea that most of the 12 disciples were only teenagers when originally called is David Paul Kirkpatrick's "Jesus' Bachelors — The Disciples Were Most Likely Under the Age of 18," which can be found at www.davidpaulkirkpatrick.com/2013/03/25/jesus-bachelors-the-disciples-were-most-likely-under-the-age-of-18/.

49. The Stoning of Stephen

1   Acts 6:7 — "the number of disciples multiplied greatly in Jerusalem, and a great many of the priests were obedient to the faith."

2   Acts 6:9–10 — opposers of the gospel of Jesus arose among the non-believing Jews from the regions we now call Egypt, Libya, Turkey, and elsewhere, and they argued with Stephen.

3   Acts 7

4   Acts 7:55–60

50. The Conversion of Saul

1   Acts 9:1, 22:4, 26:10–11. Saul (Paul) was involved in threats, arrests, executions, and murders of the disciples of Jesus, In his *Annals of the World,* section 6525, James Ussher states, "Saul, in an exceedingly great rage, made havoc of the church. He received authority from the chief priests and testified against the saints who were killed. He also entered into every house and took men and women captive. He bound and put them in prison and often beat them in every synagogue. He compelled some to deny Christ and to blaspheme, while others, who kept the faith, he persecuted to death."

2   The first instance in the Bible of calling the followers of Jesus Christ "the Way" is at Jerusalem in Acts 9:1-2. Roman guards are credited with first calling them "Christians" over ten years after Christ's resurrection, at Antioch (Acts 11:19–26).

3   Acts 8:27–30. The Holy Spirit told Philip to catch up to the chariot. He ran to it. The eunuch who had just been to Jerusalem to worship was reading from a scroll. He was likely very different from Phillip in other ways as well, including his skin color. Nevertheless, Phillip immediately obeyed and offered to tell the meaning of the scroll.

4   Acts 8:26–40 — Philip and the Ethiopian eunuch.

5   Acts 26:10–11 Paul tells King Agrippa that before his conversion he was authorized by the chief priests to imprison believers in the gospel of Jesus, and that he voted for the death of many of them.

6   In Acts 9:3, the writer (Luke) only reports that Saul fell to the ground, but in Acts 26:13–14 he quotes Paul himself in more detail when he says "at midday . . . I saw a light from heaven, brighter than the sun, shining around me and those who journeyed with me. And when we had all fallen to the ground, I heard a voice speaking to me in the Hebrew language." Acts 22:6–7 — "As I journeyed and came near Damascus at about noon, suddenly a great light from heaven shone around me. And I fell to the ground and heard a voice saying to me, 'Saul, Saul, why are you persecuting Me?' "

51. The Secret That Could Not Be Kept

1   Acts 22:6–7 — "As I journeyed and came near Damascus at about noon, suddenly a great light from heaven shone around me. And I fell to the ground and heard a voice." Acts 22:11 — Saul could not see for the glory of the light and was led by the hand into Damascus. Acts 9:8 — led by the hand.

2   Acts 9:8-22 — Paul was blind and ate nothing for three days as he stayed and prayed in Damascus at the house of a man named Judas. He was healed through Ananias, a disciple sent by Jesus. Placing his hands on Saul, Ananias said, "'Brother Saul, the Lord Jesus, who appeared to you on the road as you came, has sent me so that you may receive your sight, and be filled with the Holy Spirt.' Immediately there fell from his eyes something like scales, and he received his sight at once; and he arose and was baptized. So when he had received food, he was strengthened. Then Saul spent some days with the disciples at Damascus."

3   Acts 9:18–22 — Something like scales fell from Saul's eyes and he was baptized, ate and was strengthened, then immediately preached in the synagogues that Jesus is the Christ, the Son of God. 1 Timothy 1:13 says Saul was formerly an insolent blasphemer and violent persecutor. Acts 18:28 — Paul "vigorously refuted the Jews publicly, showing from the Scriptures that Jesus is the Christ."

4   Acts 9:22–25; 2 Corinthians 11:32–33. Unbelieving Jews conspired to kill Saul and had a garrison of men guarding Damascus to arrest him, so his followers lowered Saul through the city wall at night to escape the Jews who wanted to kill him. He then went to Jerusalem.

5   Acts 9:31 says there was a time of peace, edification, and multiplication after Saul left.

6   Acts 10:1–11:18 — Peter's vision and the immediate aftermath.

7   Acts 17:16–34 — "I even found an altar with this inscription: TO THE UNKNOWN GOD" (vs. 23). The missions/evangelism strategy known as "Creation Evangelism" is based on Paul's example in Acts 17 and has been widely utilized by such groups as New Tribes Mission (www.ntm.org/about), www.AnswersinGenesis.org, and others for decades. As with the Athenians, modern cultures have little knowledge of Christianity and are steeped in the belief that evolution is responsible for the universe and mankind. Therefore, they need to know the full extent of the gospel of Jesus, which begins in Genesis and explains the Fall, the origin of sin, the origin of suffering and death, and the need for a Savior and restoration. See https://answersingenesis.org/gospel/evangelism/evangelism-for-the-new-millennium/..

8   1 Peter 1:23–25 — ". . . the word of God which lives and abides forever . . . the grass withers, and its flower falls away, but the word of the Lord endures forever. Now this is the word which by the gospel was preached to you."

9   People began to have access to the Bible in their own birth-language, rather than Latin, which had dominated since the early days of the Church (e.g., Vetus Latina and the Latin Vulgate).

52. The Hope Of Heaven

1   Powerful telescopes continually scan distant star systems in search of evolved, extraterrestrial life. However, the written record provided by the only eyewitness account of the origin of life, the Holy Bible, clearly documents that the universe and life were designed and placed into operation by God the Creator. We did not magically come into being from a primordial soup or stardust.

2   Living in the limitations of our terribly broken world affects what we expect of eternity. If heaven sounds boring, as it does at first to many people, we will not look forward to the incredible endlessness that begins when the effects of Adam's Fall cease. See Isaiah 65:17-25 and Revelation 21-22 for hints at heaven's greatness.

3   John 3:16 — eternal life. John 11:25–26 — believe in Jesus for eternal life. 2 Timothy 2:10 — chosen. Matthew 25:46 — eternal punishment vs eternal life.

4   We will recognize and be reunited with redeemed loved ones in heaven. Furthermore, we will apparently be able to recognize people we have never seen before, as Peter, James, and John did when they recognized Moses and Elijah at Jesus' transfiguration (Matthew 17:3).

5   1 Corinthians 2:9 states, ". . . it is written: Eye has not seen, nor ear heard, nor have entered into the heart of man the things which God has prepared for those who love Him." Conversely, Isaiah 65:17 reveals that once we are in the new heavens and new earth, ". . . the former things will not be remembered or come to mind." As the composer Helen Howarth Lemmel wrote in her worship song "Turn Your Eyes Upon Jesus," the things of life on the present earth will grow strangely dim in the light of His glory and grace. https://www.hymnal.net/en/hymn/h/645.

6   The Old Testament Hebrew word for grave is queber. The body goes to the grave (queber), but the soul goes to Sheol. "In the Old Testament, Sheol is the place of the souls of the dead, both the righteous (like Jacob, Genesis 37:35, and Samuel, 1 Samuel 28:13–14) and the wicked (Psalm 31:17)." Accessed February 2017 at www.desiringgod.org/articles/he-descended-into-hell.

7   The place called "Sheol" in Old Testament Hebrew, is "Hades" in New Testament Greek. "In the New Testament, the Hebrew word Sheol is translated as hades." Accessed February 2017 at www.desiringgod.org/articles/he-descended-into-hell.

8   Matthew 7:13–14. Jesus said that many go to destruction but few go to life. Luke 13:23–24 says many seek to enter the narrow gate but will not be able.

9   No one is in the eternal Lake of Fire, yet. That is future. For the final reckoning (the Great White Throne judgment), the current temporary place of punishment known as the hell, part of Sheol-Hades will be emptied and its occupants will be judged, then sent to the eternal Lake of Fire (Rev. 19:20, 20:13–15, Matt. 18:8), which is a place described as being of burning sulfur and unrelenting agony. Fallen angels and all of the unsaved humans will both go there (Matt. 25:31–41, everlasting fire prepared for the human "goats" and the devil and his [fallen] angels, Mark 9:45–46).

10 Isaiah 57:1–2; Revelation 14:13; Matthew 11:28. It is not likely that loved ones in heaven are watching what is happening on earth. The "great cloud of witnesses" of Hebrews 12:1 refers to the previous chapter, Hebrews 11 (see the "therefore"), which is about the saints/martyrs of earlier days. (NOTE: See the digital version of this book, where significantly more space is able to be given with hundreds of additional endnotes and references.)

11 1 Thessalonians 4:14, 16 — The Lord will descend from heaven and bring with Him those who "sleep."

12 1 Corinthians 15:51–53 — the dead in Christ will be raised, changed in the twinkling of an eye and "clothed" with the imperishable. 1 Thessalonians 4:13–17 — the dead in Christ will rise at the shout, trumpet blast, and coming of the Lord. John 5:28-29 — at "His voice" the dead will be resurrected for heaven and hell.

13 1 Thessalonians 4:14–18. (NOTE: The purpose of this chapter is to provide basic facts about heaven, hell, and eternity, not to endorse a particular end times view. However, as a service to the reader, the most common end times (eschatology) interpretations of events described in The Revelation and other books of the Bible are summarized in the digitial edition of this book.)

14 Revelation 20:10 — the devil and the beast and the false prophet will be thrown into the lake of fire where they are tormented forever. Revelation 20:15 — those not found written in the Book of Life are cast into the Lake of Fire. Revelation 21:8 — unrighteous people will burn in the lake of fire.

15 2 Peter 3:10–12 and Revelation 21:1 both state that the present earth will burn up, melt, and pass away. An alternative view, "earth renewal," espoused by others but popularized by evangelical theologian Wayne Grudem and bestselling author Randy Alcorn, proposes that earth will not be consumed by fire, but rather that the surface things — much of the ground and the things on the ground — will be renewed. In his book *Heaven* (Tyndale House, 2004), Alcorn credits Grudem with the view, and in chapter 57 of *Systematic Theology* (InterVarsity Press, 1994, p. 1160–1161), Grudem explains his basis by saying it "seems preferable" because "it is difficult to think that God would entirely annihilate his original creation." Grudem provides no scriptural support. This opinion-based theology seems to fly in the face of his own statement on page 835 of the same work, that "we should realize that our inability to understand or explain something should never be a reason for rejecting it if it is clearly taught in Scripture."

16 The separation of people into tribes and nations began at the Tower of Babel when God sent scores of languages, due to the people's refusal to fill the earth. It seems likely, therefore, that everyone in heaven will either speak the same language, or will effortlessly understand one another. For God is not a God of disorder (confusion), but of peace (1 Cor. 14:33, 14:40).

17 Revelation 21:1–4

18 The throne of God in heaven emphasizes the glory of God in the Book of Revelation 4:2–11 as well as 22:1–3. Also see Jonathan MacKinney, *Revelation Plain and Simple* (Xulon Press, 2006), p. 119–131.

19 What biblical justification is there for the idea that Adam and Eve will be in heaven? "Eve displayed her hope in God's promised Seed through the naming of her sons. She was looking forward to Christ and the destruction of sin and despair that Adam's sin had brought upon the world. Just as Eve did nearly 6,000 years ago, we too have a choice concerning our own legacies. Will we choose to be like Eve at the Fall and not obey God's Word, which leads to a legacy of sin and despair? Or will we choose to be like Eve when she named her sons and evidenced hope in the Savior, Jesus Christ, who came to save us?" Dr. Georgia Purdom, "Eve's Legacy: Hope Amid Despair," originally published in *Answers* magazine, vol. 6.2 (April–June 2011), online at www.answersingenesis.org/bible-characters/adam-and-eve/eves-legacy-hope-amid-despair/. See also Ken Ham's "Did Adam and Eve Go to Heaven" at https://answersingenesis.org/kids/adam-and-eve/did-adam-and-eve-go-to-heaven/.

20 1 Peter 1:8

21 www.answersingenesis.org/about/good-news/. See also Romans 10:9 and John 14:6.